Raymond Elliott

Daybreak With the Master

by

B. Raymond Elliott

DEDICATION

I dedicate this book to Virginia Ruth Slaughter Elliott who has been my loving wife for 58 years. She has been my constant companion, confidant, encourager and truly the "wind beneath my wings." As a preacher's wife, she has experienced the joys and challenges during the 55 years of our work with various congregations of Christ. I am so thankful that God brought us together while we were students at Alabama Christian College in Montgomery, Alabama.

FOREWORD

Raymond Elliott and I met indirectly many years ago when I preached in Michigan and he in Alabama. A young military officer who was a helicopter aviator attended the church in Alabama where Raymond preached. This officer later married his fiancé who lived in Michigan. The husband went to war in Vietnam where his helicopter was shot down. Raymond came to Michigan to preach his funeral. That occurred a time before we moved to work with that congregation. The widow always seemed cheerful and we became close friends.

It was from her that I first heard the name "Raymond Elliott." Incidentally, my wife and I introduced the widow to a widower whom I had baptized and had preached his wife's funeral. They married shortly afterward. So, when we arrived in Alabama in 1982 and met Raymond it was like we had known each other for ages and became fast friends.

In some of my darkest days it was Raymond who was my greatest comforter, urging me to believe that God had better things for us—and he turned out to be wonderfully right. In return, I have tried to encourage Raymond while a lingering illness pestered him, but I lack his warmth of character to succeed as well as him.

I was delighted when he asked me to write the Foreword to this book. It is good to see him get into bound print since he has written so many articles on a multiplicity of topics, many of which appeared in our journals and on his blogs on computer. He never wavers in his conviction that God is supreme over His Word, the Bible, and that it is entirely from the Almighty hand of Jehovah (Yahweh). He believes that every church problem has a biblical solution and the answer can be understood by all honest folk. His writings are clear, concise and with a compassion for the persons or topics with which he deals. He has an underlying and true hope that everyone will come to the knowledge of Word of God I have told him that I want him to preach my funeral since he's a few months younger than me, but he insists that I be a pallbearer at his (he has a droll wit). His real glory may not come in this life, but it will in the next; for I see in him great traces of the "meek and lowly" Jesus, yet with a fire in his bones when endeavoring to keep the church pure.

My great wish is for this book to go far and wide testifying for the Lord and pleading for a full restoration of New Testament Christianity. He deserves the reward of a great defender of the faith in this life. He is beloved by all who know him.

— Martel Pace, Faulkner University

Table of Contents

PREFACE

It was about the year 2000 that I began e-mailing my religious articles to various individuals and congregations. They were often used in church bulletins and some in our brotherhood publications. A Christian friend, Nancy Hood, suggested that I should broaden my 'readership' by permitting her to work up a 'blog' for me so people could read my articles on the internet. We chose Early Morning Meditations to be its heading. Dave Laton, a deacon in the Prattville, Alabama church of Christ began using my articles in a link to the church's website and gave it the title of Raymond's Writings. While sitting and working in my office, I observed many activities occurring as I looked out the window so I wrote a series of articles under the heading of Scenes from My Window. On various occasions friends would ask me what I had seen on a particular day so I knew they were reading my articles. The articles contained in this volume are from those 'blogs'. I am indebted to Dr. Michael Turner and Dr. Don Shackelford for encouraging me to compile these articles in the making of this book. It is my desire that my writings will strengthen the faith of the readers in God and in His Word.

B. Raymond Elliott

Section 1

CHRISTIAN LIVING, RESPONSIBILITIES AND BLESSINGS

ADVERSITIES, AFFLICTIONS AND ATTITUDES

We are often overwhelmed with the adversities in life that are very difficult to accept and hard to understand. At the moment, it seems that all is loss, that life is not worth living and that our sorrow is too much to bear. No doubt, Job felt this way when he experienced the tragedies in his life. The problem is with our perception of matters. We deal more with the immediate and not the overall view of life. That which is seemingly against us at the present may, in fact, work out for our good. The Psalmist declared, "Before I was afflicted I went astray; But now I keep Your word." Again he writes, "It is good for me that I have been afflicted, That I may learn Your statutes" (Psalms 119:67, 71). The Psalmist had lived long enough beyond his traumatic experiences to grasp the significance of his sorrows.

Not all men are able to perceive the silver lining amidst the clouds of despair. As finite beings, we are so limited in our knowledge and we often fail to grasp the ultimate reasons for our conflicts and sorrows in life. In contrast, the Heavenly Father, Almighty God, who is from everlasting to everlasting, is able to see the panoramic scene; and, in His great providence, He is powerful enough to ultimately work out everything for our eternal welfare (Romans 8:28). It is a real challenge to our faith in God to seek the lessons to be learned from our failures, injuries and our losses in life. It isn't necessary that we fully comprehend nor is it even possible that we always understand the tragedies that we may experience; but, it is important that we trust in God, knowing that He cares for us and that He can overcome evil with good. In all his grief, Job expressed himself in this manner, "Though he slay me, yet will I trust him..." (Job 13:15 KJV).

Let us remember that afflictions, sicknesses, tragedies and death come to all men, saints and sinners. It is important therefore that the children of God understand that it is our acceptance of these experiences and our attitude toward them that distinguishes us from the people of the world who manifest no faith or trust in the providence of God. The unbeliever's heart is often hardened when calamities come his way. In contrast, the believer's heart is made more sensitive and responsive to God's design and purpose in the perplexities of life. We are like small children in our understanding and we should place our trust in our Heavenly Father even as David when he wrote in Psalms 131:1, 2: "Lord, my heart is not haughty, Nor my eyes lofty. Neither do I concern myself with great matters, Nor with things too profound for me. Surely I have calmed and quieted my soul, Like a weaned child with his mother; Like a weaned child is my soul within me."

We all have no doubt heard the expression, "The same sun that melts ice, hardens clay." Adversities, sorrows and heartaches in life will have different effects on various people. It depends largely on the recipient. In John 6: 66-69, after some hard sayings of Jesus we read, "From that time many of his disciples went back and walked with him no more. Then Jesus said to the twelve, do you also want to go away? But Simon Peter answered Him, Lord, to whom shall we go? You have the words of eternal life. Also we have come to believe and know that You are the Christ, the Son of the living God." Disciples of Jesus who really trust in Him have no one else in whom they can find refuge and strength in the times of trouble in this life. So, whatever sorrows and afflictions may occur in life, it is to Jesus that we must go. He is the great physician and there is healing in His wings.

FLEXIBILITY

There are times when an individual has to be steadfast, not giving ground but remaining unmovable in doctrine and in morality (I Corinthians 15:58). The writer James (1:6-8) condemned the double minded man, unstable in all his ways and compared him to the surge of the sea, driven by the wind and tossed. Jesus, in praising John the Baptist asked the question, "What did you go out into the wilderness to see? A reed shaken by the wind?" (Matthew 11:7). The apostle Paul encouraged spiritual maturity and that Christians should longer be tossed to and fro and carried about with every wind of doctrine (Ephesians 4:11- 16). There is a great need for stability among saints in this present age.

However, there are times when an individual needs to bend with certain winds of circumstances. If he doesn't, he is liable to break. Some people are so set on being stern, no matter what, that they have become miserable in life. Confucius wrote, "The grass must bend when the wind blows across it." We have to learn to be flexible concerning things that we cannot control or change. There are disappointments that we must accept in life. Most of us have planned a trip at one time or the other and something happened that prevented us from doing so. There is the example of an individual who seemingly was in perfect health but contracted a crippling disease that prevented him from participating in sports. He either learns to bend or he will eventually break. There are events that occur in our lives that truly test our adaptability.

The Old Testament character, Joseph, stands out as an example of one who learned to lean and bend with the winds of bitter trials. If we can truly believe that God is able to make all things work out for the eternal welfare of His children (Romans 8:28), we will indeed enjoy life better and more fully. Adversaries come and go. No one is immune from disease and disappointments. How you accept them and learn to live with them is the true test of how strong and flexible you really are in life. "O God, give us serenity to accept what cannot be changed, courage to change what should be changed, and wisdom to distinguish the one from the other." (Reinhold Neibuhr, The Wikipedia Encyclopedia)

11

GOD USES PLIABLE PEOPLE

In one understanding, Christians are to be people of conviction much like John the Baptist who was not a reed shaken by the wind. Disciples of Christ are not to be unstable and double-minded; but they are to have their minds set on following the Lord, regardless of the cost.

Yet, there is a real sense in which stubbornness, rebellion, arrogance, human pride and intellectual haughtiness cannot have any part in serving the Lord. The spirit of Christ demands that we deny ourselves if we desire to follow the Lord (Matthew 16:24). That which pleases God is a broken spirit, a broken and contrite heart (Psalms 51:17). Haughty eyes are actually an abomination to God (Proverbs 6:17). Only the person who is pliable can please the Heavenly Potter. Webster defines 'pliable' as that which is "easily bent; flexible, easily influenced or persuaded, adaptable." The prophet Jeremiah was instructed by God to go down to the potter's house in order to fully understand the words, which Jehovah was to give him (Jeremiah 18). Israel, because of stubbornness, often was marred in the potter's hand. It was only when the nation of Israel became pliable that the Heavenly Potter was able to mold the people into a useful and beautiful vessel of honor.

It is not accurate to state that God can use everyone in His kingdom today. There are people who are unwilling to submit their wills to the Lord. There are individuals who consider themselves as deity; others would consider themselves too intellectual to humble themselves to follow the lowly Nazarene. Many are indeed called but few are chosen (Matthew 22:14). Often, the wise and understanding of the world willfully reject the call of the gospel. The world in its secular wisdom does not know nor appreciates God. The cross of Christ to them is mere foolishness (I Corinthians 1:18-25). The Holy Scriptures to a segment of our society is considered to be antiquated and irrelevant to our enlightened age. The spirit of the Laodiceans exists in the church today (Revelation 3:14-16). Many members feel no need of the Lord because their wealth, education, position and social prestige have filled their hearts with complete satisfaction.

Only the lowly spirits can be exalted and used in the Master's kingdom today. The Heavenly Potter can mold and make us into vessels of honor. Complete submission to His will is a prerequisite to entering the kingdom of our Lord. Our stubborn wills must yield to His touch. We must permit God to mold us after His will, not ours. When we progress from "all of self and none of Thee" to "none of self and all of Thee" can we really be what the Lord wants us to become in His service.

Disobedience to God is predicated upon such attitudes as stubbornness and rebellion. Because of such sins of mental dispositions, Saul was rejected as the king of Israel (1 Samuel 15:22, 23). Those same attitudes will prevent us from serving faithfully the Lord today in His church. If we are not submissive in this life, there is coming a time when every knee will bend and every tongue will confess the precious name of Jesus (Philippians 2:9-11). The warfare continues for the Christian soldier; that is of "casting down arguments and every high thing that exalts itself against the knowledge of God, bringing every thought into captivity to the obedience of Christ" (II Corinthians 10:5).

"My Jesus, as thou wilt! O may thy will be mine;
Into thy hand of love I would my all resign;
Thro' sorrow and thro' joy, conduct me as thine own,
and help me still to say, 'My Lord, thy will be done.'"

— Benjamin Schmolck, 1704, Translated by Jane Borthwick, 1854. 1[1]Eckert, Paul, Steve Green's MIDI Hymnal, (Oak Harbor, WA: Logos Research Systems, Inc.) 1998. Or, Hymnary.org

"I NEVER GIVE UP"

"So, because I hold a place in this ministry and that because I have had God's mercy shown me, I never give up" (2 Corinthians 4:1; Charles B. Williams Translation). I use various translations in my daily Bible reading and as I was reading this passage from Williams translation, I was moved to write an article to encourage Christians never to give up on the Lord but to remain loyal and faithful while we live on this earth. The expression, "I never give up" is also found in verse 16 of 2 Corinthians 4. Other translations render these two verses that involve the other apostles in this manner: "We do not lose heart" (NASB & NKJV); "We faint not" (ASV); and, "That's why we never give up" (CEV). The apostle Paul wrote in Galatians 6:9, "And let us not grow weary while doing good, for in due season we shall reap if we do not lose heart" (NKJV). Steadfastness and perseverance is woefully lacking among many members of the church today. Seemingly it takes but a small amount of discouragement to cause a brother or sister to leave the Lord and His church. I am reminded of what the wise man wrote in Proverbs 24:10, "If you faint in the day of adversity, Your strength is small." The fact is you never know the strength of a man until you know what it takes to discourage him. When Paul stated that "I never give up" or "We do not lose heart", he truly meant it because he had been tested and tried and had been proven to be faithful to his Lord.

Please ponder carefully his description of how his faith had been tested. "We are hard-pressed on every side, yet not crushed; we are perplexed, but not in despair; persecuted, but not forsaken; struck down, but not destroyed—always carrying about in the body the dying of the Lord Jesus, that the life of Jesus also may be manifested in our body. For we who live are always delivered to death for Jesus' sake, that the life of Jesus also may be manifested in our mortal flesh. So then death is working in us, but life in you" (2 Corinthians 4:8-12). Later in this epistle he wrote, "Are they ministers of Christ?—I speak as a fool—I am more: in labors more abundant, in stripes above measure, in prisons more frequently, in deaths often. From the Jews five times I received forty stripes minus one. Three times I was beaten with rods; once I was stoned; three times I was shipwrecked; a night and day I have been in deep; in journeys often, in perils of waters, in perils of robbers, in perils of my own countrymen, in perils of the Gentiles, in perils in the city, in perils in the wilderness, perils in the sea, in perils among false brethren; in weariness and toil, in sleeplessness often, in hunger and thirst, in fasting often, in cold and nakedness—besides the other things, what comes upon me daily: my deep concern for all the churches" (2 Corinthians 11:23-28).

In spite of all the adversities that he had to endure, he remained strong in his convictions, knowing that the time was coming when he would be with the Lord Jesus Christ whom he had served faithfully in this life. "Therefore we do not lose heart. Even though our outward man is perishing, yet the inward man is being renewed days by day. For our light affliction, which but for a moment, is working for us a far more exceeding and eternal weight of glory, while we do not look at the things which are seen, but at the things which are not seen. For the things which are seen are temporary, but the things which are not seen are eternal. For we know that if our earthly house, this tent, is destroyed, we have a building from God, a house not made with hands, eternal in the heavens" (2 Corinthians 4:16-5:1). We should imitate this great man of faith and never despair to the extent that we would forsake our Lord (I Corinthians 11:1). If we keep our eyes on Jesus we will never falter along life's uneasy pathway (Hebrews 12:1-4).

"IN EVERYTHING GIVE THANKS"

In I Thessalonians 5:18 the apostle Paul wrote, "In everything give thanks; for this is the will of God in Christ Jesus for you." A preacher by the name of Martin Rinkhard wrote the lyrics of the song, "Now Thank We All Our God" to be used as an expression of gratitude by his family at meal time. The unusual background of this song of praise was that it was written during the "Thirty Year's War" when the preacher was conducting as many as forty funerals a day, including that of his own wife. Yet in spite of war and plagues, he was able to give thanks to God for his blessings. The lyrics of the first stanza of his song is as follows: "Now thank we all our God, With heart, and hands, and voices, Who wondrous things hath done, in whom His world rejoices; Who from our mother's arms Hath blessed us on our way With countless gifts of love, And still is ours today." This true story amazes me but it does not surprise me. It seems that in times of extreme and difficult circumstances, people who believe in God can find in their heart expressions of gratitude.

In contrast when a nation is greatly blessed with a bounty of material and physical substances there is a tendency of man to forget the source of such blessings. Someone has suggested that our lack of expressing our gratefulness to God for the blessings we receive would be like animals eating the acorns that have fallen to the earth without ever realizing the source of their food. The lesson is obvious and clear. Most of God's children are more apt to make requests, petitions and supplications rather than the giving of thanks. The nation that is greatly blessed with a bounty of material and physical substance is most likely to forget the source of such blessings. The writer James declared that "Every good gift and every perfect gift is from above, and comes down from the Father of lights, with whom there is no variation or shadow of turning" (James 1:17). The psalmist encourages us by his response from being a recipient of God's blessings in this manner, "What shall I render to the Lord for all His benefits toward me? I will take up the cup of salvation, And call upon the name of the Lord. I will pay my vows to the Lord now in the presence of all His people." "I will offer to You the sacrifice of thanksgiving, And I will call upon the name of the Lord" (Psalm 116:12, 13, 14, 17).

16

The children of the Heavenly Father should remember daily the blessings that flow from His bountiful hand of grace. Especially there should be an awareness of "every spiritual blessing in the heavenly places in Christ" (Ephesians 1:3). Everyday is Thanksgiving for the redeemed. However it is good that families and friends can be together on the national day of Thanksgiving. Let us never forget the sacrifices made by our forefathers and loved ones to ensure us of the liberties and freedoms we now enjoy and experience. "O that men would give thanks to the Lord for His goodness, And for His wonderful works to the children of men!" (Psalm 107:8). "Let us come before His presence with thanksgiving; Let us shout joyfully to Him with psalms" (Psalm 95:2).

"Praise God, from whom all blessings flow;
Praise Him, all creatures here below;
Praise Him above, ye heav'nly host;
Praise Father, Son, and Holy Ghost!"

— Thomas Ken, 1674, Wikipedia, the free encyclopedia, Or, hymnstudiesblog

'JESUS KNOWS ME THIS I LOVE'

Most believers in the Lord have sung or have heard the song "Jesus loves me this I know, for the Bible tells me so..." But the expression 'Jesus (God) knows me' is equally as scriptural and we all should love this great truth and the One who knows us. In II Timothy 2:19 we read, "Nevertheless the solid foundation of God stands, having this seal: "The Lord knows those who are His," and, "Let everyone who names the name of Christ depart from iniquity." The church of our Lord has a sure foundation and the gates of hades cannot successful prevail against it (Matthew 16:16-18; I Corinthians 3:11). In the New Jerusalem the wall "had twelve foundations, and on these were the names of the twelve apostles of the Lamb" (Revelation 21:14). The house of God (the church) has this seal, "The Lord knows those who are His..." In Nahum 1:7 the prophet wrote these comforting words, "The Lord is good, A stronghold in the day of trouble; And He knows those who trust in Him."

God is all knowing. The Psalmist declared this in Psalm 139:1-6, "O Lord, you have searched me and known me. You know my sitting down and my rising up; You understand my thought afar off. You comprehend my path and my lying down, And are acquainted with all my ways. For there is not a word on my tongue, But behold, O Lord, You know it altogether. You have hedged me behind and before, And laid Your hand upon me. Such knowledge is too wonderful for me; It is high, I cannot attain it." Rather than being a frightening thing to me, as His child I should be so thankful that the Almighty God, the creator and sustainer of life, knows my heart's intentions, my weaknesses, my heartaches, my cares, my trials and tribulations, my desires, my needs and yes, even the number of hairs on my head. He knows my name. He knows more about me than my wife, my children, my friends, my brethren and even the federal government. The mere thought is overwhelming. To know that He cares for me moves me emotionally. And I love it so.

Among the teeming millions who live on this earth, He hears me when I pray to Him. How can this be? There is not a place I can go but that He is there (Psalm 139:7-12). And I love it so. He knew me when I was in my mother's womb and He knows the way I shall go (Psalm 139:13-16). The Psalmist closes the chapter with these words, "Search me, O God, and know my heart; Try me, and know my anxieties; And see if there is any wicked way in me, And lead me in the way everlasting" (Psalm 139:23, 24).

THE PROVIDENCE OF GOD

"The mighty God, Omniscient One! His ways we cannot trace.
He reckons every good begun And crowns it with His grace.
Lo! I can see Him in His word—I will not doubt or fear;
My steps are ordered of the Lord, His guiding hand is near.
No trial can my spirit break, For God will not forsake;
He will with each temptation make A way for my escape.
The future beckons and I bow –My God removes the care! Behold, He goes before me now, And will my way prepare.
He's here, and there, and everywhere in all the ways I've trod.
I've never passed beyond the sphere of the providence of God."

"KEEP YOURSELF PURE"

The apostle Paul, in writing to Timothy, gave this young man some timely advice which is sorely needed in this 21st century. In I Timothy 5:22, we read, "Do not lay hands on anyone hastily, nor share in other people's sins; keep yourself pure." It is the last statement of that verse that I want to emphasize presently. Jesus taught, "Blessed are the pure in heart: for they shall see God" (Matthew 5:8). Christians are exhorted in Hebrews 12:14 to "Pursue peace with all people, and holiness, without which no one will see the Lord." It is implied from these latter two passages that a pure heart and a pure life are essential in order for one to see God. A pure life is the outgrowth of a pure heart. Solomon declared, "For as he thinks in his heart, so is he" (Proverbs 23:7). It is impossible to think evil continuously and live a good life; likewise, it is impossible to think pure continuously and live an evil life.

It is important that we all understand that our thought process controls our actions. That is why Paul instructed the Philippian brethren to think on things that are true, noble, just, pure, lovely of good report and things that would be worthy of praise (Philippians 4:8). To do such would prevent evil thoughts and evil deeds. Jesus taught, "But those things which proceed out of the mouth come for the heart, and they defile a man. "For out of the heart proceed evil thought, murders, adulteries, fornications, thefts, false witness, blasphemies. "These are the things which defile a man, but to eat with unwashed hands does not defile a man" (Matthew 15:18-20).

Our thoughts are influenced by what we see, what we hear, what we read and by our association with other people. Scenes on television, movies, and computers which portray nudity, sexual acts, etc. cause one to think impure thoughts. This is also true with pornographic literature. Even scantily attired women can contribute to a man thinking lustful thoughts. Jesus mentioned this as recorded in Matthew 5::27, 28, "You have hard that it was said to those of old, 'You shall not commit adultery.' "But I say to you that whoever looks at a woman to lust for her has already committed adultery with her in his heart." Some men, of course, have "eyes full of adultery and that cannot cease from sin..." (2 Peter 2:14). However, women professing godliness should be very careful in their actions and dress so as to not encourage evil thoughts in the hearts of men. Christian ladies are instructed by Paul to "adorn themselves in modest apparel, with propriety and moderation..." (I Timothy 2:9). When women wear apparel that reveal eighty percent of their bodies, such could hardly be called "modest". And what is said in regards to the women should also apply to the men.

Christian young people should avoid places and people which would encourage impure thoughts. Movies, television and the internet programs that are filled with illicit sex, suggestive remarks and dirty jokes will eventually pollute the mind. Heavy petting on dates often contributes to the sin of fornication. It is difficult for one to keep pure in this sexually oriented society in which we live but the requirement is still to be heeded that was given nearly two thousand years ago, and that is "Keep yourself pure."

"LITTLE IS MUCH WHEN GOD IS IN IT"

The subject of this article is the title of a beautiful and meaningful religious song. The lyrics are as follows:

"In the harvest field now ripened,
There's a work for all to do.
Hark, the voice of God is calling,
To the harvest calling you.
Does the place you're called to labor
Seem so small and little known?
It is great if God is in it,
And He'll not forget His own.
When the conflict here is ended
And our race on earth is run,
He will say, if we are faithful,
"Welcome home, my child, well done."
Chorus
Little is much when God is in it.
Labor not for wealth or fame.
There's a crown and you can win it,
If you go in Jesus' name.

— Kittie J. Suffield

In Matthew 13:31, 32, we read the words of Jesus about small beginnings: "Another parable he put forth to them, saying: "The kingdom of heaven is like a mustard seed, which a man took and sowed in his field, "which indeed is the least of all the seeds; but when it is grown it is greater than the herbs and becomes a tree, so that the birds of the air come and nest in its branches." The church of Jesus Christ began small, comparatively speaking, with 3,000 souls being saved on Pentecost (Acts 2). The early church not only added members but "multiplied greatly" (Acts 6:7; 2:47; 5:14; 6:1). It is estimated by the time of the death of Stephen there were some 20,000 members in the city of Jerusalem. Rapid numerical growth among religious groups does not necessarily mean that God is pleased with their teaching and practices. There are 'mega' churches today that simply teach what is pleasing to the hearers and provide instrumental music during their assemblies that would arouse more emotionalism than true spiritual strength.

However, there are devout Christian men and women who will travel thousands of miles to begin a work in a Christ-less country and live for years in the preaching and teaching of the gospel of Christ. Such sacrifices are deserving of our financial support and prayers. There are Christian families who have moved to areas in our own country where there was not a congregation and they began worshiping in their homes and inviting friends and neighbors to visit with them. These dedicated Christians are to be commended for their faithfulness. There are several strong churches existing today because of such commitment to our Lord Jesus Christ.

And then there are churches in small cities and rural areas that are suffering the loss of members due to deaths and the moving of their young adults to large cities in order to find work. Of course there are some who become unfaithful and that contributes to the lessening of the number present for the various assemblies. The fact is that in many areas we are not converting others to Christ as in years past. The field may or may not be as fertile as it once was when people would allow you to have Bible studies in their homes and when our neighbors would attend our gospel meetings. Also there are 'inner city churches' that have suffered the loss of members who have chosen to identify with larger congregations in suburban areas where their children can be with other children of the same age group and where more activities are planned for the youth. Nevertheless, the small groups of Christians who remain faithful year after year are worthy of our encouragement for their steadfastness.

It is not recorded in Revelation 3:7-13 the size of the church in Philadelphia and that is not the important thing to remember about these saints. It was their faithfulness that mattered with the Lord. He said, "I know your works. See, I have set before you an open door, and no one can shut it; for you have little strength, have kept My word, and have not denied My name" (Vs.8). It is implied in this verse that the church in that city was few in number but strong in faith because the Lord did not find fault with them. The Christians had kept His word and had not denied His name. The Lord expressed His love for them (vs.9); they had persevered and He exhorted them to permit no one to "take your crown" (Vs. 11). Finally He makes this promise to them: "He who overcomes, I will make him a pillar in the temple of My God, and he shall go out no more. I will write on him the name of My God and the name of the city of My God, the New Jerusalem, which comes down out of heaven from My God. And I will write on him My new name" (Vs. 12).

Always remember it is not the size but the faithfulness of a congregation that is important in the sight of our Lord Jesus Christ. Read again the words found in the second stanza of the song, "Little Is Much If God Is In It":

"Does the place you're called to labor
Seem so small and little known?
It is great if God is in it,
And He'll not forget His own."

In conclusion, may these inspired words of the apostle Paul be inscribed in your heart when you become discouraged: "And let us not grow weary while doing good, for in due season we shall reap if we do not lose heart" (Galatians 6:9)

LOVE DOES NOT REJOICE IN INIQUITY

God is love and love is of God. God is more than love but one of the great attributes of God is that He loves mankind and He desires that all men and women be saved (I John 4: 9-11; 2 Peter 3:9). And if the love of God dwells within us, we love one another (I John 4:12). While love has many positive characteristics, there are some negative characteristics of this God-like love and one is that love does not rejoice in the wrong doing of others. In I Corinthians 13:4, 6 we read that "Love ... does not rejoice in iniquity". Other translations are now presented that will enable us to understand more fully this statement. The Revised Standard Version, "it does not rejoice at wrong". McCord's New Testament Translation, "does not rejoice in wrongdoing". The New International Version, "Love does not delight in evil but rejoices with the truth." Berry's Interlinear Greek English New Testament translates I Corinthian 13:6 in this manner, "rejoices not at unrighteousness."

The church of God at Corinth needed this lesson concerning the characteristics of love. In chapter five we read of a brother who was living with his father's wife (step-mother) and the church was not doing anything about it. Rather, some were puffed up about the matter and seemed to enjoy the situation existing in the congregation. The apostle Paul wrote them a rather stern rebuke and instructed them to deal with the problem in a scriptural manner. This they did and the brother was restored to fellowship with God and the church (2 Corinthians 2). The love of God in the hearts of the Corinthian disciples would have prevented their attitudes being what they were toward this brother and all the family involved.

Permit me to present an example of what I writing about concerning the Christian's attitude toward a brother or sister who may be guilty of a public sin in their lives. Several years ago while working with a congregation, a brother in Christ became involved in an illicit relationship with a woman. This brother was married and had a family of his own. This ungodly relationship went on for sometime before members of the local church learned about it. When this adulterous relationship became known to the brothers and sisters of the local church, hearts were broken because all the members loved this brother. It was a very personal matter with me because he was one of my closest friends and a dear brother in Christ and I loved him very much. Do you think that any of us rejoiced in this brother's sin? Of course we did not delight in his wrongdoing. Rather we wept openly and begged this brother to repent of his sins which he eventually did and was restored to full fellowship with the Lord and the church.

I have intentionally reserved until now mentioning two translations of I Corinthians 13:5, 6. Phillips translation is as follows, "It does not keep account of evil or gloat over the wickedness of other people." The New English Bible, "does not gloat over other men's sins." For example, a denominational preacher in a nearby city has been accused by law officials of sexually molesting children. Should we gloat over his sins simply because we may differ with him and his denomination over some biblical subjects? It is a proven fact that scores of Catholic priests are pedophiles. Should we gloat over this immoral situation because we cannot accept the organization of this religious entity as being acceptable to God? How are we to deal with the terrible news that a sister in Christ has killed her husband for whatever reason? Shall we weep with those who weep (Romans 12:15) or shall we delight in this horrible tragedy? Shall we accuse the church collectively for her action? The difference in how you treat this unfortunate tragedy will depend on whether or not the love of God dwells within your heart. William Barclay in his commentary on the letters to the Corinthians writes the following concerning the passage of scripture in I Corinthians 13, "Love finds no pleasure in evil-doing. It might be better to translate this that love finds no pleasure in anything that is wrong. It is not so much delight in doing the wrong thing that is meant, "as the malicious pleasure which comes to most of us when we hear something derogatory about someone else. It is one of the queer traits of human nature that very often we prefer to hear of the misfortunate of others rather than of their good fortune. It is much easier to weep with them that weep than to rejoice with those who rejoice. Christian love has none of that human malice which finds pleasure in ill reports."

Individuals who gloat over the mistakes and sins of other people because of religious prejudice or for any other reason are not truly disciples of the Lord. To be a Christian is to be Christ-like and to be Christ-like is to have the love of God in one's heart. And that measure of love in one's heart prevents him from rejoicing in iniquity; delighting in evil and from gloating over another's sins.

MORE IS BETTER?

The television commercial portrayed a young family looking wistfully at a pleasure boat. The problem was that enough money to purchase the boat was not available. It was at this point that a particular bank was put forth as the institution that would provide the needed money to the family through a generous loan. The next scene depicted the happy family driving off in their car pulling the newly purchased pleasure boat. Then the statement was made that "more is better" and for one to come and borrow the money from this bank in order to buy whatever one desired. But is more better?

In his effort to fight inflation the former president Jimmy Carter made a statement in a speech that "we have learned that more is not better." Have we in fact learned that more is not better? The evidence is to the contrary. It seems that we all have been adversely affected with the disease of materialism. Webster defines materialism as being "the doctrine that comfort, pleasure, and wealth are the only or highest goals or values." The philosophy that "more is better" permeates our society today. However it is not peculiar to the twenty-first century. It seems that in every age there are those who equate happiness with material possessions. Yet Jesus warned against this idea when he said, "Take heed and beware of covetousness, for one's life does not consist in the abundance of the things he possesses" (Luke 12:15). In the parable of the sower, Jesus explained that which fell among the thorns were those who heard but were "choked with cares, riches, and pleasures of life, and bring no fruit to maturity" (Luke 8:14). The church in Laodicea was condemned because of lukewarmness. These brethren gave too much emphasis in possessing wealth. "Because you say, 'I am rich, have become wealthy, and have need of nothing' – and do not know that you are wretched, miserable, poor, blind, and naked" (Revelation 3:17). These brethren were rich in the world's goods but poor toward God. They were 'poor rich men'.

We all need to learn that material wealth can never bring satisfaction even if we had enough money to purchase everything that our hearts desired. Consider Solomon for an example of this truth. In Ecclesiastes 2:8-11 we read,

"I also gathered for myself silver and gold and the special treasures of kings and of the provinces, I acquired male and female singers, the delight of the sons of men, and musical instruments of all kinds. So I became great and excelled more than all who were before me in Jerusalem. Also my wisdom remained with me. Whatever my eyes desired I did not keep from them. I did not withhold my heart from any pleasure, For my heart rejoiced in all my labor; And this was my reward from all my labor. Then I looked on all the works that my hands had done And on the labor in which I had toiled; And indeed all was vanity and grasping for the wind. There was no profit under the sun" (Ecclesiastes 2:8-11). Later he wrote the following by inspiration and from experience, "He who loves silver will not be satisfied with silver; Nor he who loves abundance, with increase. This also is vanity. When goods increase, They increase who eat them; So what profit have the owners Except to see them with their eyes" (Ecclesiastes 5:10, 11)?

The possession of material things does not insure peace of mind, contentment, and happiness. Such qualities of the heart come about because of one's right relationship with God and one's fellowman. This was taught by Jesus as seen in the Sermon on the Mount (Matthew, chapters 5, 6, 7). Paul wrote that "Now godliness with contentment is great gain. For we brought nothing into this world, and it is certain we can carry nothing out. And having food and clothing, with these we shall be content" (I Timothy 6:6-8). The wise man of Proverbs wrote in chapter 15:16, 17, "Better is a little with the fear of the Lord, Than great treasure with trouble. Better is a dinner of herbs where love is, than a fatted calf with hatred." Psalm 37:16-17, "A little that a righteous man has is better than the riches of many wicked. For the arms of the wicked shall be broken, But the Lord upholds the righteous." Again in Proverbs 13:7, "There is one who makes himself rich, yet has nothing; And one who makes himself poor, yet has great riches."

More is not better with reference to the heaping up of material things. A person can be "rich in faith and heirs of the kingdom" if he seeks "first the kingdom of God and His righteousness" (James 2:5; Matthew 6:33). All can be happier in this life if this great lesson is learned at a young age. Individuals should seek salvation in the Lord Jesus Christ and "lay up treasures for yourselves treasures in heaven, where neither moth nor rust destroys and where thieves do not break in and steal. "For where your treasure is, there your heart will be also" (Matthew 6:18, 19).

"ARE YOU OVERWORKED AND 'UNDERPRAYED'?"

This question placed on a sign in front of a church building really caught my attention. There are some observations I wish to make about this relevant question. First of all, scores of individuals are so busy in their secular pursuits that they are spiritually drained. Honest toil is required and is needful; but, some people have become workaholics. Others have need of more money and thus they pursue multiple careers. They are never at home with their families. They never have time to meet with brethren in the various assemblies of worship.

Then, there are Christians who are always on the go. They move about in their daily activities helping others and they participate in all the programs of the local congregation. They equate Christianity with motion. Such endeavors are essential ingredients if we are to meet the needs of others; however, an individual can be involved in various activities and at the same time be deficient in real spiritual strength. The problem is a common one. A person can be overworked and 'underprayed'.

There should be times when a child of God can stop all his/her busy activities and meditate on the grace, love and mercy of God. Some people call it 'quiet time.' We all need moments of meditation and prayer. The Heavenly Father has said, "Be still, and know that I am God" (Psalms 46:10). Also, He tells us to "Meditate within your heart on your bed, and be still (Psalms 4:4). In our relationship with God, we should allow Him to lead us "beside the still waters" (Psalms 23:3). Prayer will keep us near to God. Communication with the Lord will calm a troubled soul. There is power in prayer. An automobile will eventually run out of gas if it is not filled up from time to time. The life that is void of prayer and meditation will become empty and meaningless.

Take time to be holy, Speak oft with thy Lord;
Abide in Him always, And feed on His Word.
Make friends of God's children; Help those who are weak,
Forgetting in nothing, His blessings to seek.

Take time to be holy, The world rushes on;
Spend much time in secret with Jesus alone.
Abiding in Jesus, Like Him thou shalt be;
Thy friends in thy conduct His likeness shall see.

Take time to be holy, Be calm in thy soul;
Each thought and each motive, Beneath His control.
Thus led by His Spirit to fountains of love,
Thou soon shall be fitted for service above.

— George C. Stebbins, Copyright, 1918,
Renewal, by Geo. C. Stebbins,
Hope Pub, Co., owner

THE ESSENTIALITY OF ASSEMBLING TOGETHER

An indispensable ingredient of the Christian life is to assemble with those of like precious faith for the purpose of worshiping God and to edify and exhort one another. God, in His infinite wisdom, created man to be a social being, that is, in need of fellowship with other men. It is a misunderstanding and a disregard of the intent of God when men abstain from the assemblies of the Lord's people. The corporate worship of the body of believers is not the whole of Christianity; nevertheless, assembling together is necessary for the spiritual growth and welfare of the individual disciple. It has never been the design and purpose of God for His followers to isolate themselves from other children of God. One can readily read of the various assemblies under the Mosaic economy and to learn the necessity of such gatherings (Exodus 5:1, 3; 12:6; Deuteronomy 16:8).

A proper investigation of the disciples of Christ will determine that various assemblies were in evidence in the first century. At the beginning of the church in Jerusalem you can read in Acts 2:44: "Now all who believed were together..."

Following the first persecution, saints "assembled together" (Acts 4:31). It is recorded in Acts 11:26, that Barnabas and Saul assembled themselves with the church for a year in order to teach the brethren. After the first missionary journey, Paul and Barnabas returned to Antioch and "gathered the church together; they reported all that God had done with them (Acts 14:27). All Bible students are aware that the early Christians met upon "the first day of the week" "to break bread", that is, to partake of the Lord's Supper (Acts 20:7). In fact, when Paul wrote to the brethren in Corinth, he admonished them to give as God had prospered them "on the first day of the week" (I Corinthians 16:1, 2). He knew that they were already meeting on the first day of the week to partake of the Lord's Supper because he mentioned this fact earlier in chapter 11. Notice in I Corinthians 11:18: "For first of all, when you come together as a church..." Again in 11:20: "Therefore when you come together in one place..." In chapter 14:23: "Therefore if the whole church comes together..."

The fact was, one sure way to denote a Christian who was becoming unfaithful to Christ was in their habitual absence from the assemblies of the saints. Please study carefully the context in which you find Hebrews 10:24, 25. In our assemblies, we can exhort one another in the matter of love, good works, and, in short, faithful Christian living. Even in our songs we can teach and admonish one another (Colossians 3:16). Redeemed people find joy, strength and security in coming together to praise God the Father and the Lamb, Jesus Christ. Expressions of gratitude, honor, homage and devotion are natural for one whose heart is filled with love for God because of our salvation and the hope of eternal life. It is God's desire that we worship Him "in spirit and in truth" (John 4:23, 24).

THE GOODNESS AND SEVERITY OF GOD

"Therefore consider the goodness and severity of God: on those who fell, severity; but toward you, goodness, if you continue in His goodness. Otherwise you also will be cut off" (Romans 11:22). One of the first truths that small children learn about God is that He is good. A prayer of thanksgiving offered by boys and girls is: "God is great, God is good; let us thank Him for our food..." The Bible speaks often of the goodness of God. "The earth is full of the goodness of the Lord" (Psalms 33:5). "For the Lord is good; His mercy is everlasting, And His truth endures to all generations" (Psalms 100:5). "Oh, give thanks to the Lord, for He is good! For His truth endures to all generations" (Psalms 118:29). It was said of the seed of Abraham, God's chosen people, in ages past: "Truly God is good to Israel, To such as are pure in heart" (Psalms 73:1). Yes, God blessed Israel abundantly as long as the people were faithful to Him.

Likewise, God's goodness and mercy have been manifested toward all men in the giving of Jesus to die for the sins of mankind (Romans 5:8; John 3:16, 17). James declared in his epistle "Every good gift and every perfect gift is from above, and comes down from the Father of lights, with whom there is no variation or shadow of turning" (James 1:17). In order to enjoy the blessings of a spiritual nature in Christ, man has to turn to God in trust and in obedience. These blessings are "in the heavenly places in Christ" (Ephesians 1:3). And, the way a penitent believer gets into Christ through the act of baptism (Galatians 3:26, 27). However, all men, both good and evil, enjoy the temporal and physical blessings (Matthew 5:45). The apostle Paul wrote in Romans 2:4: "Or do you despise the riches of His goodness, forbearance, and longsuffering, not knowing that the goodness of God leads you to repentance?"

On the other hand, God is also a just God, exacting severity upon all those who disobey Him. Both the Old and New Testaments are replete with examples of God punishing the disobedient. Adam and Eve brought suffering and death to the human family through their sin (Genesis 2:16, 17; 3:1-2). God also drove them from the Garden of Eden and from the tree of life

(Genesis 3:22-24). The Lord placed a curse on Cain for murdering his bother Abel (Genesis 4:9-15). The people of Noah's day were destroyed by water because of the greatness of their corruption and sin (Genesis 6:5-7). Nadab and Abihu, priests of God and sons of Aaron were consumed with fire because they dared to violated God's law regarding the fire that should have been used in the offering of animal sacrifices (Leviticus 10:1-3; 6:8-13). The Lord even scattered Israel from off the land of Canaan because of their sins (Leviticus 26:33: Nehemiah 1:8). God is indeed one of severity.

Today, warnings can be found in the testament of Jesus Christ concerning punishment for those who live in sin. The Lord taught that they who enter the wide gate and travel the broad way will eventually suffer destruction (Matthew 7:13, 14). Jesus frequently spoke of a place called hell (Greek, Gehenna, see Matthew 5:22, 29, 30). The wicked will enter this place of eternal punishment when the Lord comes again (Matthew 25:46). Paul declared that "the wages of sin is death" (Romans 6:23), that is, everlasting separation from God. The apostle John mentioned that "the smoke of their torment ascends forever and ever..." (Revelation 14:11).

Yes, God is a God of love, goodness, mercy and grace, but He is also a God of justice and severity. Every sin not covered by the blood of His Son must be dealt with and justice must be exacted. We all should desire to place our faith in Jesus Christ as being the Son of God and give our lives in humble submission to the will of the Heavenly Father (Mark 16:15,16; Matthew 7:21; Hebrews 5:8,9; Revelation 2:10).

'THE MENTALIST' AND SUICIDE

One of my wife's favorite television programs is 'The Mentalist' that comes on every Sunday night. In fact, I enjoy the program myself, even though from time to time, the writers endeavor to influence society with some moral (?) characteristics that are questionable to say the least. The week of March 31, 2011, in the closing scene, Patrick Jane visited a doctor who helped somewhat in solving the case of a 'missing body'. The man asked Patrick to witness his suicide so that his body would not undergo an autopsy. Patrick starts to leave but then he has a change of mind and asked that he might make a cup of tea for the two of them. The doctor understands that Patrick will now stay while he commits suicide. They both sit down and begin drinking their tea while the doctor, who has taken an overdose of pills, is slowing dying. If I remember correctly, Patrick Jane, after the doctor's demise, picks up his cup of tea and takes another sip. He then looks at the doctor sorrowfully. The program soon ends.

Why did the producers inject this scene in an otherwise enjoyable program? What purpose did it serve? What are the viewers to understand about the suicide scene and the main character being a witness to a person's suicide? In October of 1991, I purchased the book Final Exit that was written by Derek Humphry. He was the author also of Jean's Way and Let Me Die Before I Wake. On the front cover of the book 'Final Exit', were these words "The Practicalities of Self-Deliverance and Assisted Suicide for the Dying". I was appalled first of all that this book could legally be sold to the public. It is a manual on the best method of committing suicide. The states of Oregon, Washington and Montana in our nation have legalized assisted suicide, along with several countries. I honestly believe that the writers and producers of 'The Mentalist' injected the scene wherein the man committed suicide was to influence our thinking to the point that we will soften our stance on this matter of self-murder. One reviewer of this particular program wrote the following: "I appreciated the way Jane balked at first at the request to witness this man end his life. This wasn't something to be taken lightly and the normally glib Jane was obviously taken aback. When he decided to stay, I found it moving that he used his own rituals of comfort to assuage the man's distress. Jane sharing a cup of tea and his magic tricks was heartbreakingly beautiful." Television programs not only reflect our moral/immoral standards in society but they also indoctrinate the viewers with the beliefs and convictions of the writers and producers.

Human life is so precious to God that He stated in Genesis 9:6: "Whoever sheds man's blood, By man his blood shall be shed, For in the image of God He made man." When God gave Moses the Ten Commandments He included this command: "Thou shalt not kill" (KJV). The New King James Version records this directive in this manner: "You shall not murder" and that is exactly what this verse means. Not all killing is murder but all murder is killing. Jesus relates as to the source of sins that a person commits as recorded in Matthew 15:19, 20: "But those things which proceed out of the mouth come from the heart, and they defile a man. For out of the heart proceed evil thoughts, murders, adulteries, fornications, thefts, false witness, and blasphemies. These are the things which defile a man, but to eat with unwashed hands does not defile a man." In Matthew 19:16-18, an individual came to Jesus and asked Him, "Good Teacher, what good thing shall I do that I may have eternal life?" Jesus replied that he should "keep the commandments." The Lord then mentioned among others, "You shall not murder". Therefore it is a sin to murder another person or oneself. There is no difference. The circumstance may vary with individuals committing suicide. One might not have complete control of his mental faculties at the time when he takes his own life. Only God will know that and will judge the person accordingly. But the person who deliberately and knowingly commits suicide is guilty of self- murder. Also the individual who murders himself does not have the opportunity to repent of this sin and he must face Jesus Christ on the judgment day and give account of this evil deed (2 Corinthians 5:10).

THINGS THAT DRAW US
NEARER TOGETHER

Several years ago as I was leaving a place of business a friend engaged me in a conversation regarding the difficulties that were facing our nation at that time. He mentioned that during the depression years people were closer together as friends and neighbors. He emphasized the need existing in the hearts of people for one another. There seemed to have been a closeness prevailing among the citizens of our nation during those trying years.

This brought to my mind a lesson relative to those things that tend to bring people nearer together. First of all, it might be good to mention those things that do not necessarily contribute to a closer relationship with others. Whenever money, material and physical blessings exist in abundance people are apt to feel self-sufficient, self-reliant and become very selfish. A person who has everything feels no need of leaning on others for assistance. The tendency is not to be close to neighbors, friends and even family at times. Even in a marriage relationship, husbands and wives who both have professions may feel so independent that there is not the need of inter-dependence. Many are often prone to stay ahead of neighbors regarding the obtaining of the material and physical. Such blessings can become a curse if an individual feels no need of God and others.

Much to the surprise of many, it is during periods of trials, tribulations, sorrows and adversities that we are drawn nearer to one another. Consider the early years of marriage when the abundance of money was indeed a rare commodity. It may have been during those college years or while in the military but the memories linger concerning those lean years. But, you would not trade those years for anything. Why? It is because such difficulties brought you nearer to one another as husband and wife. Think of the times when a baby was sick or a mate was confined to bed for a lengthy period of time. It was then that the family felt the need of one another. It is when a loved one dies that the family leans heavily on one another for strength. Even during a national crisis like the destruction of the Trade Center Buildings on September 11, 2001, there was good to be found. There was the tendency for people to feel the need of others for strength and comfort.

The Lord has taught in the Holy Scriptures that members of the church should feel the need of one another. Paul wrote in I Corinthians 12:26, "And if one member suffers, all the members suffer with it..." He also stated "that there should be no schism in the body, but that the members should have the same care for one another" (I Corinthians 12:25). The Hebrew writer spoke of a time when Christians "endured a great struggle with sufferings" and others "had compassion on them that were in bonds" (Hebrews 10:32-34). The Jerusalem church suffered persecution but such adversity caused the members to be "of one heart and soul" (Acts 4:32). We are taught to "Bear one another's burdens, and so fulfill the law of Christ" (Galatians 6:2). It is when the odds are terribly against us that we should be strengthened and stand together.

Finally, the admonition is given in James 4:8, "Draw near to God and He will draw near to you." This involves all of a person's relationship with God. When we trust in God and obey Him He will surely be with us. He will never fail us nor forsake us (Hebrews 13:5).

"TILL THE STORM PASSES BY"

On Friday, March 2, 2012, our country was ravaged by an outburst of terrible tornadoes that brought death and destruction in at least 13 states. One tornado in the state of Kentucky stayed on the ground for 95 miles! Two others stayed on the ground for some 40 miles. At least one town was completely destroyed. Some forty plus persons lost their lives in a moment of time when their houses and other buildings fell on them. One infant was found critically injured in a field and later we learned that she, as well as the rest of her family, died. Hearts were broken and heads were bowed down with grief and sorrow as people saw the destruction of properties and learned of the loss of lives. You are made to feel so small and insignificant when you consider the onslaught of nature's forces. My wife and I prepared the best we could by getting into closets when the warning came for our county but even then we did not feel secure. It is only when the clear signal was given did we feel relieved.

In life we all experience storms of various kinds. Sometimes like the tornadoes, they come upon us so suddenly that we are overwhelmed. Please excuse the personal experience but one of the greatest encounters with the storms of life was the death of my 'baby brother' who was only 35 years of age when he was killed while walking across a four lane highway in the state of Pennsylvania. I received the news by telephone at 1:00 A.M. the following morning. The next day I had the responsibility of identifying his body. I sought refuge under the sheltering wings of my Heavenly Father.

I have been with families who have lost loved ones and have witnessed the tremendous grief they suffered; especially do I remember when close friends lost their teenage daughter in an automobile accident. Then there is a friend who has been greatly affected with the 'Lou Gehrig' disease. In but a short time she has become almost completely helpless. Individuals as 'wage earners' for their families have lost their jobs because of the economical situation in our nation. People like widows who are on a limited income have to make decisions as to whether to fill their much needed medicine prescriptions or to buy groceries. Almost daily we learn of families who have lost their loved ones in a foreign county as they serve in the military. There is the constant threat of war between Israel and Iran that would involve our nation, along with others. Even our schools are not safe because of the real threat of some students bent on killing their classmates. Evil is ever present in our society. Slowly, but surely some of religious rights are being threatened, by leaders on different levels of our government. We will all experience 'storms of life', especially If we live long enough we will experience some kind of 'storms' that will bring us much sorrow and try our faith.

One of the basic reasons why I am thankful for the book of Psalm is that David suffered so much because of the 'storms of life'. And that brings me to Psalm 57:1 which may have been written in a cave while he was hiding from King Saul who sought to kill him. Read carefully his words: "Be merciful to me, O God, be merciful to me, for in you my soul take refuge; in the shadow of your wings I will take refuge, till the storms of destruction pass by" (English Standard Version).

As Christians many of our hymns bring comfort and solace to our troubled hearts in the time of storms that we experience. In 1958, Mosie Lister wrote both the lyrics and music to this beautiful song. May you fine strength in it.

"TILL THE STORM PASSES BY"
In the dark of the midnight,
Have I oft hid my face;
While the storm howls above me,
And there's no hiding place;
'Mid the crash of the thunder,
Precious Lord, hear my cry;
"Keep me safe 'til the storm passes by."
Many times Satan whispers,
"There is no need to try;
For there's no end of sorrow,
There's no hope by and by";
But I know Thou art with me,
And tomorrow I'll rise;
Where the storms never darken the skies.
When the long night has ended,
And the storms come no more,
Let me stand in Thy presence.
On that bright, peaceful shore.
In that land where the tempest

Never comes, Lord may I
Dwell with Thee when the storm passes by.
(Chorus)
'Til the storm passes over,
'Til the thunder sounds no more;
'Til the clouds roll forever from the sky,
Hold me fast, let me stand,
In the hollow of Thy hand;
Keep me safe 'til the storm passes by.
Hold me fast, Let me stand,
In the hollow of Thy hand;
Keep me safe 'til the storm passes by.
'Till the storm passes by.

Words and Music by Mosie Lister, Copyright 1958

TOGETHER WE HAVE STRENGTH

A friend of mine related to me how that during World War II a squadron of B-17s was nearly indivisible while flying bombing raids over enemy targets. He mentioned that the enemy fighter planes were in the air constantly but would not attack the squadron because of its firepower. Only when a plane in the squadron became disabled in any manner and fell out of the formation did it become vulnerable to the enemy. Together, the squadron of B-1 7s protected each other. But when one aircraft lagged behind it was usually destroyed immediately.

There is somewhat an analogy contained in this story. When Christians have the moral support of one another it is very difficult for a member to be lost to Satan. However, the Christian who falls behind through indifference and negligence soon becomes easy prey for "the fiery darts of the wicked one", who "walks about like a roaring lion, seeking whom he may devour" (Ephesians 6:16; I Peter 5:8).

Our Heavenly Father, in His infinite wisdom, and knowing that man was a social being, provided in His scheme of redemption the bringing together of His people in public assemblies for worship and edification. This is clearly set forth in Hebrews 10:24,25: "And let us consider one another in order to stir up love and good works, not forsaking the assembling of ourselves together, as is the manner of some, but exhorting one another, and so much the more as you see the Day approaching." In the light of this context and that is to "consider one another in order to stir up love and good works", the exhortation is given, "not forsaking the assembling of ourselves together." In addition to rendering praise and adoration to God, the next important reason given for our assemblies is to exhort one another. It is encouraging and strengthening to the Christian when one is faithful in attendance to the various gatherings of the local church. It is very unlikely that one would ever become unfaithful to God if he were present for these assemblies. It isn't that he couldn't, it is that he will not want to leave his Lord and His body, the church.

But, one of the first signs of a brother or sister becoming unfaithful is the steady decline in the attendance of the various periods of Bible study and worship. When a Christian 'falls out of the formation' and begins to lag behind, separating himself from the other members, you can just about know that he is going to be 'shot down' by the "fiery darts of the wicked one."

While assembling to worship God and to build one another up in the most holy faith is not the sum total of Christianity, it is an essential ingredient in the Christian's harmonious relationship with His Lord and Savior Jesus Christ.

WHAT CAN I DO?

Have you ever felt over-whelmed with a feeling of inadequacy when you observe some of the situations in life? There are scenes on television that depict wars being fought on foreign soils in which not only the soldiers but innocent civilians are killed. News reports fill our minds with the facts that thousands of people are actually starving to death because of an acute shortage of food. You learn of embittered conflicts being waged between citizens of the same country and even of the same city wherein people of all ages are murdered or maimed for life. Practically every day stories are brought to our attention of injustices abounding in our own land. Because of the greed of some, the poor and illiterate are taken advantage of and are caused to suffer in various ways.

Then there are the aged who are lonely. Because of inflation, they are deprived of proper food and other necessities of life. The nursing homes are filled with the old and infirmed. All know those who are very sick, some with terminal diseases. Others are plagued with emotional problems. There are individuals whose hearts are broken due to the untimely death of a child, the passing of a parent or one's mate. It seems that on every hand, we find the downtrodden, the bereaved, the oppressed and the broken-hearted.

Thus, we ask ourselves the question, 'What can I do'? The problems of this world are so complex and vast and I am but one person with limited ability and resources, we declare. Many rush to assist in good works that are needful in our society that deal with benevolent and humanitarian deeds. But, is this enough? Is there something I can do as an individual for my fellowman that will enrich his life beyond all physical and material aid? The answer is a simple 'yes'. As a child of God, I can teach them of God and His love and of Jesus and His vicarious death for all of mankind. With the Bible in my hand and love in my heart, I can lead them to salvation in Christ by relating the facts to believe, the commands to be obeyed and the assurances and promises given to all who would obey the Christ (I Corinthians 15:1-3; Mark l6:15,16; Acts 2:38). There is no greater gift in this world that I could inform them of than the redemption that is in Jesus Christ.

My brethren, we cannot afford to deprive dying humanity of this knowledge. Every sinner led to Christ is one less person who will be serving Satan. I urge you to begin right now, where you are, while you can, to teach others of Jesus Christ.

WHENEVER I AM AFRAID

A few years ago, I heard the late beloved Franklin Camp deliver a moving sermon as one of the speakers on the Faulkner University Lectureship in Montgomery, Alabama. I believe the theme of the lectureship that year was, "Blessed Assurance". Brother Camp was referring to various passages of scriptures that had sustained him over the years. He also related that in the month of May, 1981, he learned that he had to have open-heart surgery. He said that he had to wait twelve days before he could have surgery. While lying on a hospital bed for that length of time, he thought of the great seriousness of this type of surgery. He admitted that he was afraid, realizing the seriousness of the kind of surgery. He then thought of Psalm 56 that was written by David during a very trying time in his life. David had to flee from the presence of Saul who sought to kill him and he also had to deal with the Philistines who wanted him dead. In this particular psalm, David is seeking the help of God to deliver him from those who sought his life. In verses 3 and 4, David writes, "Whenever I am afraid, I will trust in You. In God (I will praise His word), In God I have put my trust; I will not fear. What can flesh do to me?" Again, in verses 10 and 11, "In God (I will praise His word), In the Lord (I will praise His word), In God I have put my trust; I will not be afraid. What can man do to me?" Brother Camp noted that David was a strong man, having killed a lion and a bear while protecting his sheep and had killed Goliath the giant (I Samuel 17). Yet, David said that he was afraid. Brother Camp said that if David could be afraid, so could he. But, the encouragement is to be found in the statement, "In God I have put my trust; I will not be afraid." Please note that there seemed to have been a progression from verse 3 when David said "I will trust in You" to verse 11 when he declared "In God I have put my trust". As I listened to this great man of God confess his fear along with David's, I thought to myself, if David and brother Camp could be afraid at times, surely I could also be afraid in certain circumstances.

But, David said that he trusted in God when he was afraid. And, that trust in the Lord will calm the troubled soul. The word trust is mentioned 74 times in the book of Psalm and carries the idea of leaning on and trusting in some-one; to have implicit faith and full confidence in another. In Psalm 46:1 we have these beautiful words, "God is our refuge and strength, A very present help in trouble..." Again David exclaimed, "Be merciful to me, O God, be merciful to me! For my soul trusts in You; And in the shadow of Your wings I will make my refuge, Until these calamities have passed by" (Psalm 57:1). Recently, two of our dear Christian lady friends were diagnosed with breast cancer. The 'C' word does not need defining. It is one word that brings fear to our very souls. This passage in Psalm is one that I encouraged these ladies and others to read and meditate on and do as David did: "In God (I will praise His word), In the Lord (I will praise His word)" (Psalm 56:4, 10). Our Father has promised, "I will never leave you nor forsake you" (Hebrews 13:5). Go to Him in prayer and leave there your every care and He will uphold you with His everlasting arms.

> "The Lord is my strength and my shield;
> My heart trusted in him, and I am helped;
> Therefore my heart greatly rejoices;
> And with my song will I praise Him."

> Psalms 28:7

WHO AM I?

I customarily read the obituaries in the local newspaper and one morning I observed something unusual. In the obituary of a lady who had recently died it was mentioned that she was a descendant of one of our earliest presidents of our country. It was evident that her family members wanted this fact of her ancestry known.

It seems that a basic need we have is to know who we are and where we came from. Alex Haley's deep desire to know his family's ancestry led him over an extended period of time to do much research and travel. He then wrote the book, "Roots". We have known individuals who were adopted as children who made every effort to know the identity of their biological parents. While these people loved and appreciated their adopted parents, there was a real longing in their hearts to learn of their family background.

Even in biblical times we learn of the Jews' great pride in being the offspring of Abraham. They would proudly exclaim that "Abraham is our father" (John 8:39). They seemed always to be involved in tracing their lineage back to the great patriarch. Paul warned Timothy not to give heed to "endless genealogies" (I Timothy 1:4).

The most important family relationship however is not the physical but the spiritual. Most of us cannot gloat in a 'blue blood' ancestry. By faith, having been baptized into Christ, we are the children of God (Galatians 3:26, 27). "And if you are Christ's, then you are Abraham's seed, and heirs according to promise" (Galatians 3:29). Jesus is our elder brother and we are "joint-heirs" with him (Romans 8:17). It is more important also to know where we are going than to know where we came from. This earthly pilgrimage will soon end and eternity will be before us. The question might be asked, "Where will you be a million years from now?" The child of God possesses confidence through faith that he will be with his Father. However the person who has not been born of "water and the Spirit" cannot manifest that hope (John 3:5). Only eternal darkness, despair and destruction await that individual (Matthew 25:41). We must understand that the end is better than the beginning.

If one dies in Christ he will live with the Lord throughout the ceaseless ages of eternity (Revelation 14:13; Matthew 25:34).

The person who is only a pauper in this life but who is rich in faith in the Lord Jesus Christ will have laid up treasures in heaven and will inherit the crown of righteousness that is promised to all who have fought the good fight, finished the course and kept the faith (Matthew 6:20; II Timothy 4:6-8).

The blood of Jesus Christ that washes away our sins is much more important to us than the blood that might be found in our ancestry (Revelation 1:5). The apostle Peter states this truth in I Peter 1:17-19, "And if you call on the Father, who without partiality judges according to each one's work, conduct yourselves throughout the time of your stay here in fear; knowing that you were not redeemed with corruptible things, like silver or gold, from your aimless conduct received from your fathers, but with the precious blood of Christ, as of a lamb without blemish and without spot." The question is, have you been washed in the blood of Jesus Christ for the remission of your sins (Acts 2:38; Ephesians 1:7; Revelation 1:5)?

Section 2

FAITH, DOCTRINE, CHURCH

A CANDLE BURNING
(A satire of a sort)

As time to begin our Sunday morning worship was nearing and the members had grown quiet and were waiting for the brother to get up and make some announcements, I happened to look to the right of the pulpit area and saw something that I had never noticed before. It was a candle burning and the flames presented such an aesthetic scene. It is amazing how a candle burning can cause you to become meditative and calm in your soul. But wait, why was this candle burning in the place where we were worshiping God and the Lamb? Had some brother placed it there to enhance our worship? No, you see there was this moldy, musky scent in the auditorium and the candle was burning and releasing a sweet fragrance to help overcome the offensive scent to our nostrils.

There was not any degree of a religious overtone in the burning of the candle. But then I thought if the candle had been lit for the purpose of enhancing our worship to God, where could I find any prohibition to do so. I am acquainted enough with the teachings of the New Testament to know that there is not one verse that states "Thou shalt not have a candle burning in the worship." In fact, the New Testament is completely silent about this matter. Now that is a thought. Could this be the authority that I could use to justify having a candle burning in the worship? After all there was the candlestick in the tabernacle as mentioned in Exodus 25:31-37; 37:17-24. And then I thought about the burning of incense as a sweet fragrance to the Lord. This was customarily done in the Old Testament times as we notice Zacharias doing as recorded in Luke 1:8-10. Again there is no mentioning of the early church participating in this practice. In Revelation 8:1- 4, with the opening cf the seventh seal, a golden censer, a golden alter as well as the offering of incense is mentioned. It is understood that this is symbolic language represented the prayers of the saints. But if the burning of incense is in heaven, surely we can have the same in our worship in the church here on earth. Besides that, the New Testament is silent about this matter as a part of the worship; therefore, we should be permitted to include such in our worship, right? Then my thoughts turned to having a holy dance to interpret a biblical story as a part of worship and praise to God. Sometimes an interpretive dance can be more meaningful than the singing of a song. Perhaps this would be the "time to dance" (Ecclesiastes 3:4) as Miriam and the ladies did when the Israelites had crossed the Red Sea (Exodus 15:20). Undoubtedly the women of Shiloh were dancing as a part of a religious festivity (Judges 21:19-23). Furthermore, the New Testament is completely silent about having religious dancing in our worship assemblies.

Then my mind was really active as I thought about robes for the preachers, perhaps the use of bells and how about some nice instruments of music like a piano or a harp. After all John said he heard a sound like "harperists playing their harps in heaven" (Revelation 14:2). If they are in heaven why should they not be in the worship assembly today? Did not David mention instruments of music in Psalms 150? Furthermore, the New Testament does not say anything about the use of instruments in the worship. Doesn't such silence grant me the right to have all the aforementioned items in our worship? What, the congregation has just finished singing the first hymn and I must concentrate on worshiping God myself and stop this type of musing. And besides, I really don't miss the candles burning, the burning of incense, the holy dance, the wearing of a robe, the ringing of bells or the sound of any kind of musical instrument as we endeavor to worship God in spirit and truth (John 4:24). The fact is, the New Testament does not authorize the use of any of those things previously mentioned and that is the very reason we do not use them in our worship to God.

A GATED CHURCH?

No doubt, we all have of heard of a 'gated residential community'. But a 'gated church'? Well, the church is not really 'gated' but the property is sometimes 'gated' to keep unwanted people off of the premise who might break into the building or to enter the grounds for immoral purposes. I have heard of some churches having fences around their parking lot in order to keep would be thieves from breaking into the automobiles while the members were worshiping. For the first time to my knowledge there is a church of Christ in the city where I live that has installed a gate to keep cars and trucks from entering their property except during their worship assemblies. The famous city of Jerusalem, the center of the Jewish worship, was indeed a literal 'gated' city as mentioned in the Bible.

In the New Testament we find several references to 'gates' being mentioned. The first one I desire to observe is the "narrow gate" that is found in the words of Jesus as recorded in Matthew 7:13, 14. In most instances, you will have to be invited into a 'gated community' before receiving permission to enter the premise if you do not live there. The "narrow gate" that Jesus mentioned is open to all who will accept His invitation that he extended as found in Matthew 11:28: 30: "Come unto Me all you who labor and are heavy laden, and I will give you rest. "Take My yoke upon you and learn from Me, for I am gentle and lowly in heart, and you will find rest for your souls. "For My yoke is easy and My burden is light" (NKJV). But a person cannot accidently enter the "narrow gate"; rather every effort will be required as is plainly taught in Luke 13:24: "Strive to enter through the narrow gate, for many, I say to you, will seek to enter and will not be able." Those who enter the "narrow gate" and walk the "straitened" way will eventually enjoy eternal life with God. In contrast, there is the "broad gate".

There is much sadness in the Lord's statement, "many are they that enter in thereby" (ASV). Those who enter the "broad way" simply fail to make proper preparation or they rebel against the Lord and His word. This is the easy way to travel but the end leads to "destruction".

55

In Matthew 16:18, Jesus made this precious promise before He died on the cross: "And I also say to you that you are Peter, and on this rock I will build My church, and the gates of Hades shall not prevail against it." One understanding of the latter part of this verse is that though Jesus would die on Calvary's cross and His soul would go to Hades (the unseen world of departed spirits), He would not remain there (See Acts 2:27). No power could prevent Him from coming forth from the grave and fulfilling His promise to establish His church. This He did on the first Pentecost Day following His resurrection when He sent the Holy Spirit upon His twelve apostles (Acts 2). It was then that the gospel of Christ was preached and some 3,000 penitent believers responded and were immersed and the Lord added them to the church (Acts 2:36-38, 41, 47). The church of Jesus Christ has an 'open door' policy. No one is to be excluded or prevented from entering the church which is the body of Christ (Ephesians 1:22, 23). The church is where both Jew and Gentile can be reconciled to God and be "fellow heirs, of the same body" (Ephesians 2:11-18; 3:3-6).2

There is a 'gate' found in Hebrews 13:12 that is of great importance, especially to all who have had their sins forgiven by the blood of Jesus Christ (Ephesians 1:7; Revelation 1:5): "Therefore Jesus also, that He might sanctify the people with His own blood, suffered outside the gate." In his commentary on the book of Hebrews, Martel Pace makes this observation regarding verses 12 and 13: "The idea of the animals being incinerated outside the camp on the Day of Atonement is introduced. The bull offered for sin was carried outside the camp (see Lev. 16:27). The idea of Jesus' being crucified outside the gate (v. 12, Emphasis, mine, RE); see Jn.19:20) fulfilled that symbol. By accepting the stigma of guilt (a probable meaning of "outside the gate"), Jesus could bear our sins. Leaving the camp (v.13) suggest a total break from the synagogue and the temple."

In contrast to the church, heaven is a 'gated community'! Jesus has gone to prepare a place for all who prepare to go there when this life on earth is finished (John 14:1-3). Jesus Himself is "the way, the truth and the life. No one comes to the Father except through Me" (John 14:6). It is only when we give our lives to God that we will be permitted to enter into "the everlasting kingdom of our Lord and Savior Jesus Christ" (2 Peter 1:10, 11). In Revelation chapters 21 and 22, the gates in heaven are mentioned six times. They are described as follows: "Also she had a great and high wall with twelve gates, and twelve angels at the gates and names written on them, which are the names of the twelve tribes of the children of Israel: three gates on the east, three gates on the north, three gates on the south, and three gates on the west"

(21:12, 13) "The twelve gates were twelve pearls: each individual gate was of one pearl" (21:21). "Its gates shall not be shut at all by day (there shall be no night there)" (21:25). Now, please note who will be able to enter the eternal city of God: "But there shall by no means enter it anything that defiles, or causes an abomination or a lie, but only those who are written in the Lamb's Book of Life" (21:27). "Blessed are those who do His commandments that they may have the right to the tree of life, and may enter through the gates into the city" (22:14). This is the final invitation our Lord will extend to the redeemed: "Then the King will say to those on His right hand, 'Come, you blessed of My Father, inherit the kingdom prepared for you from the foundation of the world" (Matthew 25:34).

Individuals who will not be permitted to enter the gates of heaven are described as follows: "But outside are dogs and sorcerers and sexually immoral and murders, and idolaters, and whoever loves and practices a lie" (22:15). "But the cowardly, unbelieving, abominable, murderers, sexually immoral, sorcerers, idolaters, and all liars shall have their part in the lake which burns with fire and brimstone, which is the second death" (21:8).Gates can be used to keep someone in or out. Often gates function in both directions for people to enter and/or leave. In heaven, the gates open only one way and that is to permit saved people to enter for eternity. "Dad," said Charles H. Gabriel, Jr., from the embrace of his father, "if I never see you again here, I'll meet you where the gates never swing outward." His father, the beloved song writer, had gone to New York to bid his son God-speed as he departed for France during the First World War. It was while clasped in that last good-bye, his eyes turned toward the gates through which he must pass to go on shipboard. Those gates of entrance to war and death swung both ways; it gave him apt figure of speech to phrase his parting from his father. "I'll meet you where the gates never swing outward!" The words sketched a picture in the mind of his father, who, while the train journeyed westward toward his Chicago home, held in his heart his son's heart-warming good-bye of love and... affection. From his meditation came this tender song: "Where the gates swing outward never!" (From Forty Gospel Hymn Stories by George W. Sanville, 1943, p. 80.

WHERE THE GATES SWING OUTWARD NEVER

Just a few more days to be filled with praise, And to tell the
Old, old story: Then, when twilight falls, and my Savior calls,
I shall go to Him in glory.

Just a few more years with their toil and tears, And the journey
Will be ended; Then I'll be with Him, where the tide of time
With eternity is blended.

What a joy t'will be when I wake to see Him for whom my
Heart is burning! Nevermore to sigh, never more to die –
For that day my heart is yearning.

Chorus
I'll exchange my cross for a starry crown,
Where the gates swing outward never;
At His feet I'll lay every burden down,
And with Jesus reign for ever.

— *Charles H. Gabriel*

CALLING ON THE NAME OF THE LORD

"And here he has authority from the chief priests to bind all that call Your name" (Acts 9:14). These words were spoken by the disciple Ananias to the Lord in reference to Saul, the former persecutor of the church of Jesus Christ. Saul had authority to cast into prison "all that call Your name," that is, the name of the Lord. But what was it and what is it to "call on Your name"? We can believe with confidence that it is not a mere repeating of the name of the Lord. On one occasion Jesus stated, "Not everyone who says to Me, Lord, Lord, shall enter the kingdom of heaven, but he who does he will of My Father in heaven (Matthew 7:21). In Luke 6:46, we read, "And why do you call me, 'Lord, Lord', and do not the things which I say?" One can readily see that whatever calling on the name of the Lord is, such is more than saying his precious name. The two passages noted previously greatly emphasize the need of obedience to the commands of the Lord.

The first instance wherein we find an inspired man using the prophecy from Joel 2:32 was Peter on the day of Pentecost (Acts 2:21). That prophecy was, "And it shall come to pass that whosoever shall call on the name of the Lord shall be saved." Peter continued preaching to his audience that Christ had died and had been resurrected by the power of the Father (Acts 2:23, 24, 32). Those Jews who believed Peter's preaching concerning Jesus Christ inquired of the apostles, "Men and brethren, what shall we do?" "Then Peter said to them to "Repent and let every one of you be baptized in the name of Jesus Christ for the remission of sins; and you shall receive the gift of the Holy Spirit" (Acts 2:36-38). Some three souls "gladly received his word" and "were baptized" (Acts 2:41). Thus, the people on Pentecost understood clearly that calling on the name of the Lord was not merely an utterance of his name but it included actions on their part motivated by their faith. In Romans 10:13 we find the expression used again with reference to calling on the name of the Lord. But, one needs to read carefully the context in verses 10 through 15 to understand what is mean by this expression. If we begin with verse 15 and revert back to verse 13, we will understand all that is involved in such a promise and that when one calls on the name of the Lord, salvation will be given. There is the preaching of the gospel of Christ, the hearing of that message and then the believing of the gospel. The calling on the Lord is subsequent to these foregoing requirements and embodies the same.

The biblical example that really clarifies this matter is found in the conversion of Saul. Ananias was sent by the Lord to give further instructions to Saul the sinner concerning what to do in order to complete his obedience. In Acts 22:16 we read what was said to this penitent believer, "And now why are you waiting? Arise and be baptized, and wash away your sins, calling on the name of the Lord" We must come to the inevitable conclusion that cannot be denied and that is, "calling on the name of the Lord" in order to be saved involves God's scheme of redemption for the alien sinner, namely, faith in Christ, repentance of sins and baptism in the name of Jesus Christ for the remission of sins." "What can wash my sins? Nothing but the blood of Jesus". The apostle John wrote in Revelation 1:5, "...To Him who loved us and washed us from our sins in His own blood." Paul expressed the same in Ephesians 1:7, "In Him we have redemption through His blood, the forgiveness of sins, according to the riches of His grace." Paul also stated in Romans 6:3, "Or do you not know that as many of us as were baptized into Christ Jesus were baptized into His death?" And so it is, when we are immersed into Jesus Christ as the Lord has directed in Mark 16:16, our sins are washed away by the blood of the Lamb. Have you called on the name of the Lord?

CHRISTIAN LIVING

Holiness is an important factor in matters pertaining to church growth. Holiness is a way of life, that is, the character of all those people who are pure in heart (Matthew 5:8; Hebrews 12:14). How we think, talk and live before our fellowman is important. A light that flickers and salt that loses it preserving power contribute to the stagnation of a local congregation. Christians who are living godly and involving themselves in the care of others will influence sinners in the way of the Lord. Hypocrites, who deceive, negligent members who are filled with apathy and brethren who stray, injure the cause of the Lord more than they realize. Preaching without practicing prevents many from obeying the gospel.

A congregation may possess the greatest orator for a preacher but no one will come to hear him if the church is not respected in the local community. The fact is, neighbors and friends visit mainly because of their respect for you, the life you live before them, and the example you are. They may disagree doctrinally but they will respect your convictions. A 'holier-than-thou' attitude turns people away; however, a true sense of concern and compassion for others will entice them to listen to what you say.

It is not necessary to wear certain kinds of apparel or to carry a placard advertising that you are member of some religious group. Your friends and neighbors already know what you are. They notice your enthusiasm or your indifference. They observe your faithfulness or your ungodliness. You are preaching and practicing before them every day.

Our peers are listening to our speech, watching what we are wearing, observing our habits, noticing our recreational activities, learning of our dealings with others and they are even concerned with out loyalty to the Lord and the local church. Your family relationships also are observed and impress them. In fact, someone is scrutinizing every aspect of your daily life. You may, in fact, be the reason a person decides to become a Christian or to remain in sin. Never underestimate the power of your influence for good or bad!

The sentiments expressed by the apostle Paul as found in Philippians 2:12-16 should be considered and obeyed by the children of God: "Therefore, my beloved, as you have always obeyed, not as in my presence only, but now much more in my absence, work out your own salvation with fear and trembling; for it is God who works in you both to will and to do for His great pleasure. Do all things without complaining and disputing, that you may become blameless and harmless, children of God without fault in the midst of a crooked and perverse generation, among which you shine as lights in the world, holding fast the word of life, so that I may rejoice in the day of Christ that I have not run in vain or labored in vain."

One of the greatest sources of church growth is the individual Christian who is living faithfully to the Lord before his fellowman. What kind would your congregation be if all the members lived just like you?

DECISIONS, DIRECTIONS AND DESTINIES

"Enter by the narrow gate" (Matthew 7:13). Man is a creature of choice. God made him that way. Even in Eden, Adam had the power to choose between obeying God's commands and disobeying them. The very fact that God had placed the tree of the knowledge of good and evil in the midst of the garden implies that man possessed the power to make moral decisions. God's foreknowledge does not preclude the free moral agency of man. If it did, man would be no more than a mere robot. Nor would he be responsible for his actions, good or bad.

In the context of Matthew 7:13, 14, the Lord admonishes and encourages us all to "enter by the narrow gate; for wide is the gate and broad is the way that leads to destruction, and there are many who go in by it. Because narrow is the gate and difficult is the way which leads to life, and there are few who find it." The mere fact that Jesus presented two choices strengthens the premise that men possess the power to make decisions in regards to spiritual matters. If not, why urge men to enter by the narrow gate.

The decision made determines the direction one will travel in life, and, the direction one travels will eventually determine a person's eternal destiny. There are two masters, the Savior and Satan; two gates, one narrow and one wide; two ways, one difficult (strait), the other broad; and, two destinies, one is eternal life and the other is eternal destruction. A person's eternal destiny actually depends largely on the decisions made in this life.

The infinite grace of God does not nullify man's responsibility in this matter. Indecision is making a choice not to follow the Lord. Jesus said, "He who is not with Me is against Me, and he who does not gather with Me scatters abroad" (Matthew 12:30). There is no neutral ground where a person who is accountable might linger, free of responsibility in decision making. If it could be heard, the voice of Felix crying from the grave would shout that one should make that positive decision before it is eternally too late (Acts 24:24,25) Almost is not good enough either. A person may know the truth,

63

understand the facts to be believed and the commands to be obeyed, and yet, if obedience to the gospel is not completed, salvation will not be received and enjoyed. King Agrippa bears mute evidence these many years of the awful fate that awaits the procrastinator (See Acts 26:27 - 28).

One of the saddest statements ever uttered by the Savior was, "and there are many who go in by it" in reference to the broad way that leads to everlasting destruction. The percentage has not changed with the passing of the centuries. How sad that the majority of people choose to live separate and apart from God in this life and then in eternity to "be punished with everlasting destruction from the presence of the Lord and from the glory of His power" (II Thessalonians 1:7-9).

We all should choose now the narrow gate and the difficult (strait) way that leads upward to life everlasting. It is not easy but demanding in that it requires our complete submission to His will. One must give the very best. Wherein we have failed, God's grace is extended. This is the way of Christ, the cross and the church. The burdens of life are made easier to bear because of the Lord's help. The abundant life can be enjoyed now and in the world to come, eternal life. Our decision will either bring us doom and despair or blessings and heavenly bliss. All are encouraged to choose the narrow gate while the mercy of God lingers.

"DON'T FOLLOW ME, I'M LOST"

One day while driving my automobile, I came near enough to the car in front of me to be able to read the sticker on the back bumper. It read, "Don't follow me, I'm lost." I was reminded of a personal experience of mine that occurred a few years ago.

I was endeavoring to find a particular building located near a lake and I began following some people I thought were going to the same gathering of brethren where I was supposed to be making a speech; and, that they would be able to lead me safely to my destination. I was wrong. After traveling some distance on a dirt road, we came to a dead end. The car in front of me stopped and the driver got out and came to my side of the car and started to ask if I knew where the building we both were looking for was located. I answered quickly that I did not know and that I had been following them, thinking that they knew the directions. Eventually, we all arrived at our desired destinations.

In religious matters, we must not assume that others know the way of salvation. This would include preachers, teachers, parents, loved ones and friends. There is the probability that a blind leader could cause you to be lost (Matthew 15:14). Just because a certain way seems right does not insure that it is a safe path to travel (Proverbs 14:12). The sad fact is that the majority of people are traveling the wrong highway in this life (Matthew 7:13, 14). Individually, we have the responsibility to search the scriptures for ourselves (2 Timothy 2:15; Acts 17:11). The Bible is the only road map that can safely direct us from this life to eternal bliss (Psalms 119:105; Acts 20:32).

Another point that I want to emphasize is that people who are lost spiritually and know it, would do a tremendous service to others by wearing a sign that reads, "Don't follow me, I'm lost." A father who refuses to obey the gospel could lessen his influence with his children by making it clear that he was lost and that he did not want them to follow his example of disobedience. An unbelieving marriage partner, by wearing this sign would greatly encourage the other mate not to listen to his/her excuses for not obeying Christ. The moralist would no doubt keep innocent people from believing that he was saved and they could also be saved separate and apart from the blood of Jesus Christ. The hypocrites and backsliders could really help in this matter by wearing this sign, thus informing all people that Christ was not living in them and that they were lost and doomed to eternal perdition (Matthew 13:41,42; 2 Peter 2:20-22). This might prevent others from following their ungodly examples.

The only sure and safe way to travel in this life is to follow Jesus who is "the way" (John 14:6). And, He is the one who says to us, "Follow me" (Matthew 16:24).

"I'M DRINKING FROM MY SAUCER 'CAUSE MY CUP HAS OVERFLOWED"

When I was a lad I often saw men pour coffee from their cups into their saucers. The reason being was to permit the coffee to cool because it was boiling hot. I can almost hear them slurping the coffee from their saucers. But the title of this article is based on a religious song that emphasizes the goodness of God. I feel sure that the thought for the song was found in Psalm 23:5 when David wrote, "My cup runs over." There is an outstanding statement made by the apostle Paul as found in I Corinthians 3:21, "Whether Paul or Apollos or Cephas, or the world or life or death, or things present or things to come--all are yours." The fact is you have been made richer than you have ever imagined. I am not necessarily thinking about the physical or material blessings of life, even though we are recipients of multitude of blessings from our Heavenly Father (James 1:17). But if you have given your life in full submission to the will of God and the Lord Jesus Christ as a penitent baptized believer, you are rich toward God. A child of God is "rich in faith and heirs of the kingdom" (James 2:5). Jesus said "I have come that they may have life, and that they may have it more abundantly" (John 10:10). We have been made "alive together with Christ" (Ephesians 2:5). We are a "holy priesthood" and a "royal priesthood" (I Peter 2:5, 9). Jesus Christ has made us to be "a kingdom" (Revelation 1:5). No wonder we are "drinking from my saucer 'cause my cup has overflowed." The apostle Paul wrote in Ephesians 1:3, "Blessed be the God and Father of our Lord Jesus Christ, who has blessed us with every spiritual blessing in the heavenly places in Christ." Listed below are just a few of the spiritual blessings we possess and enjoy in Christ.

1. We have been saved by the grace of God through the blood of His Son Jesus Christ. Ephesians 2:5, "by grace you have been saved". Ephesians 1:7, "In Him we have redemption through His blood, the forgiveness of sins, according to the riches of His grace."

2. The blood of Christ continues to cleanse the faithful children of God. I John 1:7, "But if we walk in the light as He is in the light, we have fellowship with one another, and the blood of Jesus Christ His Son cleanses us from all sin."

3. We are children of God by faith in Jesus Christ. Galatians 3:26, 27, "For you are all sons of God through faith in Christ Jesus. For as many of you as were baptized into Christ have put on Christ."

4. We are members of the body of Christ which is His church. Colossians 1:18, "And He is the head of the body, the church, who is the beginning, the firstborn from the dead, that in all thing He may have the preeminence." I Corinthians 12:13, "For by one Spirit we were all baptized into one body – whether Jews or Greeks, whether slaves or free – and have all been made to drink into one Spirit."

5. We have a peace of mind that surpasses understanding. Philippians 4:7, "And the peace of God, which surpasses all understanding, will guard your hearts and minds through Christ Jesus."

6. We have the promise that God will be our provider and protector. Matthew 6:33, "But seek first the kingdom of God and His righteousness, and all these things shall be added to you." Hebrews 13:5, 6, "Let your conduct be without covetousness; be content with such things as you have. For He Himself has said, "I will never leave you nor forsake you." So we may boldly say: "The Lord is my helper; I will not fear. What can man do to me?"

7. We have the hope of eternal life. Romans 8:24, 25, "For we were saved in this hope, but hope that is seen is not hope; for why does one still hope for what he sees? But if we hope for what we do not see, we eagerly wait for it with perseverance." I John 5:11, 12, 13, "And this is the testimony: that God has given us eternal life, and this life is in His Son. He who has the Son has life; he who does not have the Son of God does not have life. These things I have written to you who believe in the name of the Son of God, that you may know that you have eternal life."

8. We have the promise that God will hear and answer our prayers. I John 5:14, 15, "Now this is the confidence that we have in Him, that if we ask anything according to His will, He hears us. And if we know that He hears us, whatever we ask, we know that we have the petitions that we have asked of Him."

9. He will grant us strength to face the many trials, tribulations and temptations in this life. Romans 5:3, "And not only that, but we also glory in tribulations, knowing that tribulation produces perseverance; and perseverance, character; and character, hope" Afflictions in life can actually contribute to our spiritual growth in Christ. Psalms 119:67, "Before I was afflicted I went astray, But now I keep Your word." Psalms 119:71, "It is good for me that I have been afflicted, That I may learn Your statutes." I Corinthians 10:13, "No temptation has overtaken you except such as is common to man; but God is faithful, who will not allow you to be tempted beyond what you are able, but with the temptation will also make the way of escape, that you may be able to bear it."

10. For Christians, death is our passage way from this world to life everlasting. To the unsaved death is the beginning of eternal suffering but the child of God knows that it is the beginning of eternal bliss with God, Jesus Christ and the redeemed of all the ages. Philippians 1:21, 23, "For to me, to live is Christ, and to die is gain." "For I am hard-pressed between the two, having a desire to depart and be with Christ, which is far better." Revelation 14:13, "Then I heard a voice from heaven saying to me, "Write: 'Blessed are the dead who die in the Lord from now.'" "Yes," says the Spirit, "that they may rest from their labors, and their works follow them."

It is because the Lord Jesus Christ gave His life on Calvary that we have become rich in Him and possess the manifold spiritual blessings that God has given to us. "For you know the grace of our Lord Jesus Christ, that though He was rich, yet for your sakes He became poor. that you through His poverty might become rich." My, my cup is really running over and I indeed have to drink from my saucer!!

FAITH AND FEELINGS

Many religionists trust solely on their feelings in deciding the right or wrong of a matter. One can be heard to say, "I had rather have this feeling in my heart than a stack of Bibles", or, "I know I am right because I feel it in my heart." Certainly a person should be conscientious in whatever one believes. The Lord requires a man to be honest of heart; however, sincerity alone does not guarantee that which is believed is the truth. The heart can be deceived and be deceptive. Jeremiah declared in chapter 17:9, "The heart is deceitful above all things, And desperately wicked: who can know it?"

There are some things that a person may believe and be wrong without jeopardizing his salvation. A businessman may place his trust in some financial investor and yet lose his savings due to the dishonesty of the person in whom in believed. You could have all faith in the man selling you an automobile, believing the mileage on the odometer yet learn later that you had been deceived. In both cases, there would have been the loss of money and/or the value of the product purchased but one's eternal salvation would not have been adversely affected.

There are biblical examples wherein feelings felt in one's heart were deceptive and even fatal. In I Kings 13 we learn of a man of God from Judah being sent by God to cry out against the altar erected by Jeroboam, King of Israel. He was faithful in discharging his duties. The Lord had instructed this man of God not to eat food nor drink water while in Samaria and not to return home the way he came. But an old prophet lied to him, saying that God had told him that the man from Judah could stop at his house to eat bread and drink water. The man of God believed this lie and was later killed by a lion. No doubt the man of God felt in his heart that the old prophet was telling him the truth; however, he paid dearly for his trust in the false prophet.

Saul of Tarsus, prior to his conversion, truly believed that he was doing God's will by persecuting Christians. After he became of a believer in Christ he made this statement regarding the feelings he had in heart, "Men and brethren,, I have lived before God in all good conscience until this day" (Acts 23:1). Again, "Indeed, I myself thought I must do many things contrary to the name of Jesus of Nazareth. This I also did in Jerusalem, and many of the saints I shut up in prison, having received authority from the chief priests; and when they were put to death, I cast my vote against them"(Acts 26:9, 10). There was not a person more sincere than Saul of Tarsus but he was wrong even though he felt in his heart that he was right.

Jesus spoke of the blind leading the blind and both falling into a pit (Matthew 15:14). The blind followers are to be pitied, not only because of the error of their way; they undoubtedly felt in their hearts that the direction given to them by their leaders was accurate.

In contrast, faith is not produced by floundering feelings. Faith is based on reliable evidence. John wrote of the reason of the miracles performed by the Jesus: "And truly Jesus did many other signs in the presence of His disciples, which are not written in this book; but these are written that you may believe that Jesus is the Christ, the Son of God, and that believing you may have life in His name" (John 20:30, 31). Faith therefore is not a 'leap in the dark'. The apostle Paul stated it in this fashion, "For I know whom I have believed, and am persuaded that He is able to keep what I have committed Him until that day" (II Timothy 1:12). He possessed this great faith because of the proper evidence that Jesus was the Son of God. This kind of faith produces a victorious life. John wrote these encouraging words, "For whatever is born of God overcomes the world. And this is the victory that has overcome the world - our faith" (I John 5:4). There is to be found no wavering in the affirmation of faith by these men. They believed because their faith was founded, not upon mere feelings but upon solid evidence.

Today, we can possess the same quality of faith. How is that possible? In Romans 10:17 we read that the word of God produces faith in the hearts of all honest seekers of truth. Our faith is in proportion to our knowledge and acceptance of the divine word of God. Thomas confessed, "My Lord and my God!" because he had seen the resurrected Christ. Jesus told him, "Thomas, because you have seen Me, you have believed, Blessed are those who have not seen and yet have believed" (John 20:28, 29). Presently, our faith is based upon the testimonies of faithful witnesses who saw the Lord and wrote His word down in order for us to read and come to believe in Him as being the divine Son of God. The Holy Spirit instructed the writers of the Bible into all the truth (II Timothy 3:16, 17; II Peter 1:20, 21). While conscience is a guide, it is only a safe guide if it is directed by the word of God. The apostle Paul wrote in II Corinthians 5:7, "For we walk by faith, not by sight." Feelings alone are not good enough in matters pertaining to salvation, we must be guided by the only acceptable guide in religious matters and that is the 'God breathed' Holy Scriptures.

"FAITH PLUS OBEDIENCE EQUAL SALVATION"

While preaching for a congregation recently I noticed this sign on the door of a classroom in the brethren's building. This is such a familiar statement among us. It is similar to "He who believes and is baptized shall be saved" (Mark 16:16) or "Repent and be baptized everyone of you in name of Jesus Christ unto the remission of sins" (Acts 2:38). We know that Jesus Christ is the Savior of all who obey Him (Hebrews 5:8, 9). We often sing the lyrics "Trust and obey for there is no other way." We know from scripture that "without faith it is impossible to please Him, for he who come to God must believe that He is, and that He is a rewarder of those who diligently seek Him" (Hebrews 11:6). The faith that saves is one that obeys. We have no problem with this understanding; however there is something lacking in the statement "Faith Plus Obedience Equals Salvation." This statement is true as far as it goes but it is not the sum of what is revealed in the Bible regarding our salvation from our sins. What then is the most important ingredient that is not found in this formula?

It is the grace and love of God as revealed in the sacrificial death of His beloved Son Jesus Christ (John 3:16. The apostle Paul emphasized this in Ephesians 2:5 when he wrote that we are saved by grace. He also stated in Titus 2:11, "For the grace of God that brings salvation has appeared to all men."

It is only through an obedient faith that we have access to His saving grace. This is clearly taught in Romans 5:1, 2, "Therefore, having been justified by faith, we have peace with God through our Lord Jesus Christ, through whom also we have access by faith into this grace in which we stand, and rejoice in hope of the glory of God". In Ephesians 2:8, Paul wrote, "For by grace have you been saved through faith, and that not of yourselves; it is the gift of God". In the vernacular it might be stated this way, 'we must not put the cart before the horse'. The commands to believe and obey should not be given before one hears of the unmerited grace and love of God manifested in the death of Jesus on Calvary's cross (John 3:16; Hebrews 2:9).

GOD ALLOWS U-TURNS

While traveling in another city, I noticed a sign in front of a church building with this message: "Traveling down the Wrong Road? – God Allow U-Turns" I suppose that many of us have found ourselves traveling in the wrong direction and needed to turn around. However, when we needed to make the turn, a sign that read, "No U-Turns", warned us. On our Interstate highways, it is not possible to make a U-Turn without violating the law.

In contrast, if a person is traveling down the wrong road in life, God does allow U-Turns; in fact, He not only allows a U-Turn, He requires that we make a U-Turn if we want to travel the way that leads to eternal life (Acts 17:30). That way is in Jesus Christ (John 14:6). Though God demands a U-Turn, man has the power of choice to decide whether he will or will not avail himself of this privilege.

Repentance is that pivotal position in life that enables a person to change directions. God desires that all men come to repentance (II Peter 3:9). His goodness should lead men to repentance (Romans 2:4). To repent simply means to change one's mind; that is, to resolve to stop living in sin and determining to give one's life to the Lord, to submit oneself to the Lordship of Jesus Christ. Godly sorrow produces repentance unto salvation (II Corinthians 7:10). And, true repentance brings forth a reformation in the life of the penitent person (Matthew 3:8).

The prodigal son in Luke 15 is an example of a person who was traveling down the wrong road in life. Eventually, he came to himself, realized his plight and made a complete U-Turn. He came back home, confessing his wrongs and was received warmly by a forgiving father. This story depicts the mercy and forgiveness of our Heavenly Father. There is no sin but that God will forgive and forget if we will repent and obey His Son.

GPS — God's Plan of Salvation

I had thought that I might enjoy having one but I never dreamed that some-one would give me a GPS! Much to my surprise, some of my children gave me a GPS for a Christmas present. A son took charge of getting the thing ready for me to use in my car. He put the address of a local business into the GPS and this lady's voice instructed me when and where to turn in order to get to my destination as I looked at a map where I was to travel. In case you might not be familiar with this gadget, here is a brief definition: "The Global Positioning System (GPS) is a satellite-based navigation system made up of a network of 24 satellites placed into orbit by the U.S. Department of Defense. GPS was originally intended for military applications, but in the 1980s, the government made the system available for civilian use. GPS works in any weather condi-tions, anywhere in the world, 24 hours a day" (Wikipedia Free Encyclopedia). Theoretically I should never get lost while traveling using my GPS.

In the beginning of man's existence on earth he was in a safe place and in a perfect relationship with God. In a sense man was not saved because he had never been in a lost condition. But he became estranged from his God and in a lost condition because of his disobedience to the commands given to him from God (Genesis 2:15-17; Isaiah 59:1, 2; Romans 5:12). However, in the darkest day of man's existence in the beautiful Garden of Eden, God's plan for man's salvation is found in Genesis 3:15 when the "seed of woman" was mentioned. The "seed" is also referred to as being the "seed" of Abraham. The apostle Paul defined that "seed" as being Jesus Christ (Galatians 3:19, 16). The fact is, Jesus Christ, the Lamb of God was referred to by John in Revela-tion 13:8 as being "slain from the foundation of the world." The Lord God, in His infinite wisdom, foreknowledge and marvelous grace and love, planned aforetime to provide salvation for mankind through the death of His beloved Son (Hebrews 2:9; Ephesians 2:5, 8; John 3:16).

Throughout the Old Testament there is the theme that 'someone is coming' and that being the promised Messiah who would bring salvation to the hu-man race. Isaiah, the messianic prophet, prophesied hundreds of years before the coming of the Savior: "Therefore the Lord Himself will give you a sign: Behold, the virgin shall conceive and bear a Son, and shall call His name Immanuel" (Isaiah 7:14); and His name was to be called Jesus "for He will save His people from their sins" (Matthew 1:21). Jesus, in answering Thomas who asked Him, "Lord, we do not know where You are going, and how can we know the way?" said, "I am the way, the truth, and the life. No one comes to the Father except through Me" (John 14:5, 6). The road map that leads to salvation and to the Father is found in the person of Jesus Christ. He is the only way (Acts 4:12)! So He says to all who would be His disciples, "If anyone desires to come after Me, let him deny himself and take up his cross and follow me" (Matthew 16:24). The way that Jesus leads us is "narrow" and "difficult" but the reward is eternal life (NKJV, Matthew 7:13, 14). God has given us the perfect and complete directions in His Holy Word that will lead us to Jesus Christ and salvation (Psalms 119:105; John 6:44, 45; 2 Timothy 3:16, 17; 2 Peter 1:2-4). God's plan of salvation certainly involves man's response.

A person must believe that Jesus Christ is the Son of God (John 8:24); repent of sins (Acts 17:30) and based upon a confession of faith in Christ, be immersed in His name for the remission of sins (Romans 10:9, 10; Mark 16:16; Acts 2:38). Following in the steps of the Savior we will never stray from the way that is infallibly safe and secure and that leads to "the everlasting kingdom of our Lord and Savior Jesus Christ" (2 Peter 1:10, 11). May our attitude always be as found in the song, "Where He Leads Me I Will Follow".

HEARING BUT NOT BELIEVING

One of the frustrations experienced by preachers is to know that the gospel has been taught, yet there have been no responses by the hearers to obedience. This may occur when sinners refuse to obey the gospel of Christ and/or when members of the church fail to comply with the teaching of Christ to mature in the faith. There can also be puzzlement in the teacher's heart when one family obeys and another family rejects the same teaching while being instructed privately in their homes. The same gospel is being taught but is bringing different responses. It is easy to become discouraged, blaming oneself for the failure to convert all the people being taught the way of salvation.

We must understand and come to realize that all who hear will not believe and obey the gospel. The hearer has a responsibility in the process of conversion. This principle is clearly taught in the parable of the soils presented by the Lord and recorded in Matthew 13:1-23. In the usage of the words of Isaiah, Jesus mentioned that there were those who would hear but not understand. The apostle Paul referred to this prophecy of Isaiah on various occasions in his work when the Jews would not respond to the teaching of this inspired man (Acts 28:25-29; Romans 10:16-21).

While it is true that faith is produced by the hearing of the word of God (Romans 10:17), there are times when the gospel is heard but obedience to Christ is not the end result. Why? The answer can be found in the example of so many Israelites who failed to enter the promised land. The writer of the book of Hebrews informs us that the glad tidings had been preached to the children of Israel "But the word which they heard did not profit them, not being mixed with faith in those who heard it." (Hebrews 4:1-3). Earlier we learned that the reason why some did not enter into that rest was because of unbelief (disobedience) (Hebrews 3:18, 19). Had they not heard? Yes, but the word of God had not been united or mixed with faith on the part of the hearers. And without faith a person cannot please God (Hebrews 11:6).

The hearer of the gospel indeed has a great responsibility. If the heart is not receptive, there cannot be any faith. As food eaten cannot benefit the body if

76

it is not digested, neither can the gospel of Christ save the individual unless it is united with faith. We are exhorted to "receive with meekness the implanted word which is able to save your souls" (James 1:21). It is only then that the desired results will occur.

"IS THERE LIFE BEFORE DEATH?"

Several years ago while viewing the 'Today Show' on television I became quite interested in an interview that the host was having with a noted author who had written a book about the civil strife in Northern Ireland. The author's wife who was a professional photographer had taken many pictures in the city of Belfast and the surrounding areas which depicted the physical destruction caused by the bombings. One scene was of a building that had only one wall standing. I could not help but be over-whelmed with a sign painted on the wall. It was painted in large letters and asked the question, "Is There Life Before Death? Such a question reflected the remorse of a person's heavy heart. It is difficult to imagine circumstances being so deplorable that one could not enjoy life, at least to some degree. But here was a person asking if a one could live before one dies. How sad! This so different from the usual question asked by the masses of people and that is, "Is there life after death?" This is the all consuming inquiry of persons seeking hope beyond this earthly pilgrimage. But the question remains in our minds, "Is There Life Before Death?"

First, one must understand that all people outside of the spiritual relationship with Christ are dead (lost) presently. The basic meaning of death is the absence of life. Physically, death occurs when the spirit of a man departs from his body (James 2:26). And in the moral and spiritual realm a person is dead (lost) when he is living in sin. Jesus Christ is life (John 1:4). Therefore, when a person is outside of Christ, he is dead, spiritually speaking. Often the statement is made that a sinner is going to be lost unless he obeys the gospel. That is only partially true. The fact of the matter is the disobedient person is dead (lost) presently. Please observe the following passage: "And you He made alive, who were dead in trespasses and sins" (Ephesians 2:1). The sinner is "dead" outside of Christ. Paul declared that the widow who gave herself to pleasure is dead while she lives" (I Timothy 5:6). How can a person be dead while living? We must understand that Paul was speaking of the spiritual condition of the widow who gave herself over to the lust of the flesh. Please note also the description given in Ephesians 2:11, 12 of the Gentile brethren prior to their conversion to Christ: "Therefore remember that you, once Gentiles in the flesh-who are called Uncircumcision by what is called the Circumcision made in the flesh by hand-that at that time you were without Christ, being aliens from the commonwealth of Israel and strangers from the covenants of promise, having no hope and without God in the world." Therefore there is the absence of spiritual life in all persons who have never been redeemed by the blood of Jesus Christ (Ephesians 1:7). A person can be 'dead' while he lives and before he experiences a physical death. One might appear to be healthy and possess all the vital signs but as far as salvation and spiritual life is concerned be dead (lost). Second, those persons in Christ are really living, spiritually speaking. Notice again these two passages of scripture in Ephesians 2:1, 5: "And you He make alive..." Paul emphasized this point again when he said that God "made us alive together with Christ..." Those obedient believers who have been buried with their Lord in baptism have been raised to "walk in newness of life" and being "dead indeed to sin, but alive to God in Christ Jesus our Lord (Romans 6:4, 11). Jesus spoke of this abundant life for His followers (John 10:10). The apostle Peter refers to Christians as being a "holy priesthood" and a "royal priesthood" (I Peter 2:5, 9). John wrote that Christ has "Made us kings and priests to His God and Father" (Revelation 1:6). All these expressions denote the spiritual wealth and position of the children of God. This is truly living but not according to the world's standard.

Third, let us observe the various aspects of this rich and abundant life in Christ. All spiritual blessings are to be in Jesus Christ (Ephesians 1:3). This implies that none are to be enjoyed by those people outside of a spiritual relation with the Lord. It is wonderful to know that our God "is able to do exceeding abundantly above all that we ask or think..." (Ephesians 3:20). We now mention several of those blessings bestowed upon all followers of Jesus Christ.

1. Forgiveness of sins through the blood of the Lamb (Ephesians 1:7). This fact alone should cause us to greatly rejoice (Acts 8:36-39; 16:34).

2. By faith in Christ Jesus we become children of God. He is our Father. This stresses the family relation we sustain with God (Galatians 3:26, 27).

3. We become members of the great spiritual body of Jesus Christ which is His church (I Corinthians 12:13, 27; Colossians 1:18).

4. We have a clearness of conscience and peace of mind in Christ Jesus (I Peter 3:21; Philippians 4:7).

5. God is truly our provider and protector. He has promised to be with us always and never to forsake us (Matthew 6:33; 28:20; Hebrews 13:6).

6. In Christ we have the hope of eternal life (Romans 8:24, 25; John 3:36; I John 5:11).

In Matthew 25:31-46 we are given a glimpse of the coming judgment. On that day there will be some who will be granted by God's grace a 'deathless life'. Jesus has promised, "He that believes on Me, though he may die, he shall live" (John 11:25, 26). In heaven, "there shall be no more death (Revelation 21:4). However those on the "left hand" shall depart into a place of a 'lifeless death'. This will be the final "wages of sin" for the disobedient (Romans 6:23). All those who have lived according to the flesh must die and experience eternal corruption (Romans 8:12, 13; Galatians 6:7, 8).

Several years ago a prominent religious cult predicted that Christ was soon returning to the earth. The date was even set by this group. A slogan was coined that claimed that "Millions Now Living Shall Never Die." But Jesus did not come as they had promised. The sad fact is that 'Millions Now Dying Shall Never Live" — eternally.

A person can enjoy true living now in Christ Jesus and in the world to come, eternal life (Mark 10:29, 30). The penitent believer who will confess His name and be immersed for the remission of sins will become a new creature in Christ (Acts 2:36-38; Romans 10:9, 10; II Corinthians 5:11). A "crown of life" will be given to all Christians who live faithfully to God (Revelation 2:10; II Timothy 4:6- 8).

"IS THIS THE CHURCH OF GOD?"

Several years ago while I was in my office one day the telephone rang. When I answered, a lady inquired if a certain person was there. I replied in the negative. She asked, "Is this the Church of God?" I answered, "This is the church of Christ." She replied, "Oh, I have the wrong number." I then said, "I want to assure you that this is the church of God."

This short conversation made me realize once again how denomination-alism has really confused matters regarding biblical terms applicable to the church of the Lord. In fact, it made me feel uncomfortable to answer the lady in the manner I did. While I did not deny that this was the Church of God, realizing the confusion this would cause, I answered by saying this was a church of Christ. I knew if I answered in the affirmative to her question, she would not understand as to why the party she was asking for did not work here. What would you say if someone asked you if you were a member of the church of God? Now, think before you answer. And, why would you answer in the way that you would. Could it be that you would not want to be associated with another religious group? Would you be truthful and unashamed by answering in the positive? Several years ago, I preached a sermon relative to the undenominational nature of the church of Jesus Christ. I emphasized the scripturalness of using all the biblical terms for the body of Christ. Of course, I mentioned that the term "church of God" was scriptural (See I Corinthians 1:2; Acts 20:28 KJV). After the assembly that evening, one very fine Christian lady was heard to say, "I will never call us the church of God." Herein lies a deep-seated problem among many brethren.

There has evolved within our brotherhood the notion that the term "church of Christ" is the name to be worn to the exclusion of all other terms found in the Bible. Please understand the term "church of Christ" is scriptural (the singular of "churches of Christ", Romans 16:16). But, the Lord never intended for us to make this the official name of the church. Actually, the term "church of Christ" is not a name but a biblical term that denotes ownership. Jesus said in Matthew 16:18, "I will build my church". That is possessive in nature. The church belongs to Christ. We often speak of the Lutheran Church, the Presbyterian Church, and the Church of Christ in the same manner. Of course, our religious friends consider us to be just another denomination. The sad fact is, by our attitude and the improper usage of biblical terms, we may contribute to the confusion. Brethren are often heard to say, "The church of Christ teaches", "he is a church of Christ preacher", "he is a church of Christ person", "church of Christ church", "church of Christ college", "church of Christ literature" and even a "church of Christ ball team".

The fact is we should not use one term to the exclusion of other biblical terms regarding the church. If we do, we have denominationalized a scriptural expression. Study the Bible and observe the other terms that can be used in regards to the body of Christ. It is right to refer to the Lord's church as being the "church of God" (I Corinthians 1:2), "church of the First-born" (Hebrews 12:23), "church of the Lord" (Acts 20:28 ASV), etc. The term used the most in the New Testament; especially in the book of Acts is "the church" Let us become more aware that the expression "church of Christ" is not a proper name per se but a term denoting ownership; and that by using other scriptural terms regarding the body of Christ, such would help in clarifying the undenominational nature of the New Testament church of our Lord in the thinking of others.

LOOKING UNTO JESUS

One of the fundamental lessons to be learned in playing golf is to keep your eye on the ball. This is easier said than done. In years past, I played this game each week. I received most of my instructions from a dear friend when I lived in the city of Ozark, Alabama. When I would look down the fairway just before I was about to take a swing with my club, he would say, "Keep your eye on the ball." Practically every time I would top the ball or hit it in the wrong direction, the problem usually could be traced back to my breaking that basic rule, that is, of not keeping my eye on the ball.

In his exhortation to those early Christians to "run with endurance the race that is set before us", the inspired writer gave them a basic and necessary rule to follow in the game of life when he wrote, "looking unto Jesus, the author and finisher of our faith" (Hebrews 12:1, 2). In other words, 'keep your eyes on Jesus.' He knew that there were many temptations in life which would cause them to turn their attention elsewhere. To them, the urge to return to the tenets of the old law with its rituals and ordinances was very real and enticing. To others, it may be the lusts of the flesh or the call of the world.

Among the body of believers today there are distractions that cause us to turn our eyes away from Jesus. It may be that some brother or sister has disappointed us. It could be that someone has spoken words against us. Perhaps family members have been unfaithful or a child has become involved in sinful living. Satan is a very strong and wise adversary. If he could get our parents to sin in the garden of Eden, don't you know that he is a having a field day with Christians while we live in this world permeated with sin?

The answer to our problems can be found in the encouragement to look unto Jesus. He walked among mortal men, suffered the agony connected with the rejection of His people and the crucifixion on the Roman cross. Now, he says, "Follow me" (Matthew 8:22). However, we cannot really follow Jesus unless we look at Him. It was when Peter took his eyes off of Jesus and became concerned about the wind, that he began to sink into the sea (Matthew 14:30). So, when you become discouraged and feel like quitting, remember this fundamental rule of life, 'Keep your eyes on Jesus'.

"MAKES YOU THINK OF YOUR OWN MORTALITY, DOESN'T IT?"

These were the very words spoken by my doctor during a visit to his office following my having a stent placed in a main artery leading from my heart on Friday, May 4, 2001. My cardiologist had been successful in the procedure to insert the stent. I know this personally because seven years later here I am writing this article. There was a ninety-five percent blockage in the artery but I had not suffered any pain which made me completely unaware of the impending danger. What I had was what doctors call 'a widow maker.' For extending my life to this moment of time I am very grateful to my Heavenly Father who has added seven years to my life (As in the case of Hezekiah, 15 years, Isaiah 38:4).

But this is not the only time that I have considered my own mortality. Just recently Virginia and I made new wills. Our older ones were out of date and needed revising. These were more complex since we have added 'stuff' to our possessions over the intervening years. When you make wills you realize more and more that you are going to leave all of your material blessings behind because you can't take anything with you. It is important that you "lay up treasures in heaven, where neither moth nor rust destroys and where thieves do not break in and steal" (Matthew 6:19, 20). The apostle Paul said it in this manner: "Then you were raised with Christ, seek those things which are above, where Christ is, sitting at the right of God. Set your mind on things above, not on things on the earth" (Colossians 3:1, 2).

The older a person becomes the more he thinks of the hereafter. In addition to the Word of God, I have read scores of articles and books on what awaits us after this earthly life has ended. Now the authors of the various articles and books have never experienced what it is like in the 'great beyond'. They will either base their findings on the inspired scriptures and/or the various philosophies of mortal men. The fact is, the individuals raised from the dead as mentioned in the Old and New Testament (including Lazarus who was dead for four days, (John 11) never mentioned anything about what lies beyond the grave. Even the one (I believe Paul) who was caught up to the third heaven and into Paradise was not permitted to write what he saw and heard (2 Corinthians 12:1- 7). The unbeliever would desire that when a man dies he is like the 'dog Rover and is dead all over'. Others might concede that the wicked will be punished but not for eternity. But what if these teachers are wrong? It will be too late to make changes in my belief and in my manner of life. I will not be able return to this life and prepare to meet my Lord in eternity. There is to be no second chance.

Another thought came to my mind and that is, am I to believe that when I die I cease to exist in both body and spirit. This might be better than being in torment for eternity but it does not satisfy my longing to continue to be when this life is over. There is so much I don't understand about afterlife but I do have an unwavering trust in my Lord Jesus Christ who said, "I am the resurrection and the life. He who believes in Me, though he may die, he shall live. And whoever lives and believes in Me shall never die, Do you believe this" (John 11:25, 26)? The apostle Paul wrote that "to die is Gain" "and to be with Christ, which is far better."

(Philippians 1:21, 23). It was my Lord Jesus Christ who said, "I am He who lives, and was dead, and behold, I am alive forevermore. Amen. And I have the keys of Hades and Death" (Revelation 1:18).

Because He Lives

God sent His son, they called Him, Jesus;
He came to love, heal and forgive;
He lived and died to buy my pardon,
An empty grave is there to prove my Savior lives!
How sweet to hold a newborn baby,
And feel the pride and joy he gives;
But greater still the calm assurance:
This child can face uncertain days because He Lives!
And then one day, I'll cross the river,
I'll fight life's final war with pain;
And then, as death gives way to vict'ry,
I'll see the lights of glory and I'll know He lives

Chorus

Because He lives, I can face tomorrow,
Because He lives, all fear is gone;
Because I know He holds the future,
And life is worth the living,
Just because He lives!

Words and music by William J. Gaither © 1971

MORALITY ALONE CANNOT AND WILL NOT SAVE!

There is the tendency among many people to equate morality with being a Christian. While it is true that every devout Christian is a good moral person, it does not follow that every good moral person is a Christian. The moralist, separate and apart from Christ is a sinner. The apostle Paul, quoting an Old Testament passage, stated that "There is none righteous, no not one." He further declared, "for all have sinned, and fall short of the glory of God" (Romans 3:10, 23). It isn't that a man is born a sinner; he simply becomes one through violating the commands of God (I John 3:4).

The moralist may be known for his sweet disposition, his kind words, his charitable deeds, his good citizenship and his participation in community affairs. But, if he has never obeyed the gospel of Christ he is in a lost condition. When a person as previously described passes from this life, his peers are apt to say, "Well, he was not a member of any church but he certainly was a good man, worthy of salvation."

The basic difference between a moralist who is not a Christian and a Christian is morally clean is found in their relationship with God. The moralist exclaims that he deserves to be saved upon his own meritorious goodness. This attitude was found in the Pharisees "who trusted in themselves that they were righteous, and despised others"; and, is found in the words of a self righteous individual as recorded in Luke 18:9 – 12), "The Pharisee stood and prayed thus with himself, 'God, I thank You that I am not like other men-extortioners, unjust, adulterers, or even as this tax collector. 'I fast twice a week; I give tithes of all that I possess." The Christian admits his inability to save himself and submits to the will of God. He cries out, "God, be thou merciful to me a sinner" (Luke 18:13). If one moralist can be saved without the blood of Christ, then it must be concluded that all moralists can be saved. If this be true, Christ died in vain. There was no need for his crucifixion on Calvary.

Surely, if any moralist could have been saved without the vicarious death of Christ, the man Cornelius would have been. It is rather doubtful that any living person would have been more moral in character than Cornelius. He was a centurion in the Roman army. This meant that he was a Gentile. He was a devout man and one that feared God. He was a benevolent individual and was habitual in his prayers to God. He is referred to as a righteous man and one who enjoyed an excellent reputation, even among the Jews (Acts 10:1, 2, 22). In spite of such high standards, Cornelius was instructed by an angel of the Lord to "Send men to Joppa, and call for Simon whose surname is Peter, 'who will tell you words by which you and all your household will be saved' (Acts 11:13, 14). This morally upright person needed to hear the gospel of Christ in order that he might be saved. It is no different today. God is no respecter of person. He saves all men alike and in like manner – through the blood of Jesus Christ (Acts 10:34; Ephesians 1:7). God requires faith, repentance, and baptism on the part of the alien sinner in order to receive remission of sins (Hebrews 11:6; Acts 17:30; Acts 2:38). If we are saved, it is not by our own goodness but by God's grace (Ephesians 2:5, 8).

"THERE WILL BE NO INVITATION SONGS ON THE DAY OF JUDGEMENT"

The title of this article is a quotation taken from brother Wayne Jackson's 'A New Testament Commentary' and his remarks on Luke 12:35-48 regarding the watchful and foolish servants (I do recommend this one volume commentary by our beloved brother). Now this statement of truth I have known but just had never thought of it in this manner. The emphasis is on the necessity of being prepared when our Lord returns to claim His own and to judge each individual as taught in Matthew 25:31-46; 2 Corinthians 5:10 and Romans 2:6. Procrastination is a work of the devil. We have all heard the saying, "the road to hell is paved with good intentions." We are taught in Proverbs 27:1: "Do not boast about tomorrow, For you do not know what a day may bring forth." The people that the inspired writer James spoke about in chapter 4:13-17 had made 'big plans' about their future business but they had left God out of their proposed endeavors; so they were informed as follows: "Whereas you do not know what will happen tomorrow. For what is your life? It is even a vapor that appears for a little time and then vanishes away. Instead you ought to say, "If the Lord wills, we shall live and do this or that." In the immediate context you have this statement: "Therefore, to him who knows to do good and does not do it, to them it is sin." Since we do not have the promise of tomorrow we should always include in our thoughts and plans, "If the Lord wills" we shall "do this or that."

The Heavenly Father desires "all men to be saved and to come to the knowledge of the truth" (I Timothy 2:4). "The Lord is not slack concerning His promise, as some count slackness, but is longsuffering toward us, not willing that any should perish but that all should come to repentance" (2 Peter 3:9). God gave His Son to die for the sins of the world (John 3:16); and the good news about His death, burial and resurrection "is the power of God to salvation for everyone who believes, for the Jew first and also for the Greek" (Romans 1:16). Faith in Jesus as being the divine Son of God comes through the "word of God" (Romans 10:17; John 20:30, 31). This living active faith motives one to repent of sins and be immersed into Jesus Christ for the remission of sins (Acts 2:36-38).

There is danger in delay. A person should obey the commands of the gospel when they are first learned. The exhortation in Hebrews 4:7 can be applied here: "Today, if you will hear His voice, Do not harden you hearts." Over the years we have had a practice of singing a song of encouragement in our worship assemblies to give opportunity for people to make known their desire, that is, to complete their obedience based on their confession of faith in Jesus Christ as being the Son of God. One song that used to be sung during the evening assemblies as well as during gospel meetings was "O Why Not Tonight" No doubt scores of sinners have responded during the singing of that grand old hymn. The lyrics really stress the need to give one's life to Jesus while there is time. Remember, there will be no invitation songs sung on the judgment day!

O WHY NOT TONIGHT?

O do not let the word depart, And close thine eye against the light;
Poor sinner, harden not thy heart, Be saved, O tonight.

Tomorrow's sun may never rise To bless thy long deluded sight,
This is the time, O then be wise, Be saved o tonight.

Our God in pity lingers still, And wilt thou thus His love requite?
Renounce at once thy stubborn will: Be saved O tonight.

Our blessed Lord refuses none Who would to Him their souls unite;
Believe, obey the work is done; Be saved O tonight.

Chorus
O why not tonight? O why not tonight?
Wilt thou be saved? Then why not tonight?

— Elizabeth H. Reed, Faith Publishing House,
Evening Light Songs, 1949, edited 1987.

THE GIVING OF THANKS

Our blessed Lord taught, "Ask, and it will be given to you; seek, and you will find; knock, and it will be opened to you. "For everyone who asks receives, and he who seeks finds, and to him who knocks it will be opened" (Matthew 7:7, 8). The apostle wrote in Philippians 4:6, "Be anxious for nothing, but in everything by prayer and supplication, with thanksgiving, let your request be made to God..." As children of God we have the words of Jesus and the Holy Spirit (through Paul) informing us that we have the wonderful privilege of asking, making supplications and requests and our God will hear us. The fact is we probably ask more in our prayers than we do in the giving of thanks for His infinite grace through which He bestows an abundance of blessings upon us. For example, brethren often fail to give thanks for the food that is about to be eaten. A brother is usually requested to "ask the blessing" or to "bless the food".

And so many times the brother will ask the lord to "bless this food to the nourishment of our bodies and our bodies in your service" and there is nothing wrong in that request. But what we often fail to do is to express our gratitude for the food that we have received as a blessing from God. It is on this point that I would like to emphasize so that we all might be mindful of our need to give thanks, not only for our food but for all the blessings of life that God has given us. The writer James states that "Every good gift and every perfect gift is from above, and comes down from the Father of lights, with whom there is no variation or shadow of turning" (James 1:17).

Concerning the giving of thanks specifically for our food, consider the example of Jesus Christ. In the feeding of the four thousand men plus women and children Matthew wrote, "And He took the seven loaves and the fish and gave thanks, broke them and gave them to His disciples; and the disciples gave to the multitude" (Matthew 15:36). On another occasion when He fed the five thousand, John wrote, "And Jesus took the loaves, and when He had given thanks He distributed them to the disciples, and the disciples to those sitting down; and likewise of the fish, as much as they wanted" (John 6:11, 23). Then there is the example of the apostle Paul giving thanks before he ate food that had been given as a blessing from God. He was on his way to Rome as a prisoner and the boat in which he was traveling was in serious trouble and was about to sink. The people on board had not eaten in fourteen days and Paul encouraged them to take nourishment. In Acts 27:35 we read, "And when he had said these things, he took bread and gave thanks to God in the presence of them all; and when he had broken it he began to eat." In matters of judgment Paul wrote the following in Romans 14:6, "...He who eats, eats to the Lord, for he gives God thanks; and he who does not eat, to the Lord he does not eat, and gives God thanks." The apostle later wrote in I Timothy 4:4, 5, "For every creature of God is good, and nothing is to be refused if it is received with thanksgiving; for it is sanctified by the word of God and prayer." In our prayer before our meals let it be one of thanksgiving for the food that we are about to receive along with other expressions of praise and requests.

THE WAY THAT IS SAFE
AND CANNOT BE WRONG

Several years ago we lived in Savannah, Georgia. It was a new experience for us to watch those huge ships entering the mouth of the Savannah River and traveling several miles inland to the state docks. It didn't seem possible that the massive ships could achieve such a feat. However we learned that a channel had been dredged in the middle of the river for a safe passage for the ships. And as long as the captains of the ships steered their vessels in the channel there was safety. It was not necessary to know where all the hidden dangers were beneath the surface of the water; but it was essential to possess knowledge of the safe way to travel. This principle is very applicable in the study of the New Testament of Jesus Christ.

Jesus taught men to enter the "narrow gate" and walk in the "difficult" way (Matthew 7:13, 14). "There is a way that seems right to a man, But its end is the way of death" declared the wise man in Proverbs 14:12. We should therefore seek out the way that is infallibly safe and cannot be wrong in religious matters. We suggest the following aspects of this way that is revealed in the Word of God.

1. It cannot be wrong to accept the Holy Scriptures as being the inspired Word of God (II Timothy 3:16, 17; II Peter 1:3, 21).

2. It cannot be wrong to believe in God and in His Son Jesus Christ (Hebrews 11:6; John 8:24; Matthew 16:16).

3. It cannot be wrong for sinners to repent of their sins (Acts 17:30, 31; II Peter 3:9).

4. It cannot be wrong to be baptized for the remission of sins, having confessed one's faith in Jesus Christ (Romans 10:10; Acts 2:38; Acts 8:35-39).

5. It cannot be wrong to be immersed in water instead of being sprinkled (John 3:23; Romans 6:3, 4; Colossians 2:12).

6. It cannot be wrong to have an obedient faith instead of a faith only religion (Matthew 7:21; Hebrews 5:8, 9; James 2:14 – 26).

7. It cannot be wrong to wear the name of Christ (Christian) rather than names that honor men and/or movements (Acts 11:26; 26:28; I Peter 4:16; Romans 16:16).

8. It cannot be wrong to sing praises to God in worship without the addition of instruments of music (Ephesians 5:19; Colossians 3:16; Hebrews 2:12; 13:15).

9. It cannot be wrong to partake of the Lord's Supper upon the first day of every week (I Corinthians 11:23- 30; 16:1, 2; Acts 20::7).

10. It cannot be wrong to be faithful in attendance to the periods of worship (Acts 2:42; Hebrews 10:24, 25; James 4:17).

11. 11. It cannot be wrong to be pure in heart and live a faithful Christian life (Matthew 5:8; Hebrews 12:14; Revelation 2:10).

We need to possess the wisdom of following the safe way wherein is assurance and security. Why take a risk when the safe way can be learned and followed by all who choose to do so. Jesus said, "I am the way, the truth, and the life. No one comes to the Father except through me" (John 14:6). The infallible Word of God provides us the infallibly safe way through Jesus Christ that cannot be wrong and when He returns, we shall be judged by it (John 12:48).

"THIS WORLD HAS MANY CHOICES; ETERNITY HAS ONLY TWO"

The title of this article is found in the words of a religious song that I have heard over the radio several times. It is a moving song. One that really makes you think. God made man in His image and one likeness is that man has the ability to make choices in life. Adam and Eve made the wrong one and introduced sin to the human family (Genesis 2 & 3; Romans 5:12). The Israelites were required to choose to serve or Baal or God (I Kings 18:20, 21). Jesus invites mankind to come to him and He will give rest to all who decide to do so (Matthew 11:28 - 30). Our Lord also presents to us two gates to enter and two ways to travel in this life (Matthew 7:13, 14). The decision an individual makes will determine the direction he will travel in this life and eventually where he will be in eternity. In this life we all make decisions small and great from day to day. Some of our decisions will bring joy to our heart while others cause sadness and unpleasant consequences. The young couple that commits fornication often affects adversely the conscience of one and perhaps both parties. And sometimes a child is the result of such an immoral deed and shame is felt among members of both families. Pity the person who becomes addicted to some form of drugs and destroys both body and mind. In a moment of anger a life is taken and the guilty party has to endure the consequence by spending his life in prison or death. On the other hand a young person gives his life to God and commits his life to serving His Lord and Master. Life is enjoyed and the morning of each day is received as being beautiful and appreciated. Love is found in the heart of Christian young lady and marriage follows after a courtship with someone she will spend a lifetime with as they rear their children in the way of the Lord. In spite of the hardships and challenges in life they encounter, happiness is found in living for Jesus Christ and serving others. A young man decides that his true desire in life is to live in a foreign country and preach the gospel of Christ, and to train people to become productive citizens. As long as a person has the mental ability and breath resides in his body, decisions can be made. But the time will come when the capability to decide will cease.

Eventually the spirit of man will take flight and the body dies (James 2:26). The spirit returns to God and the body goes back to dust from whence it came (Ecclesiastes 12:7). The power to choose where we will be in eternity is past. We will have no power to have control over matters. In life there is the ability to do things our way and to make decisions but not so in eternity. That has already been determined by the choice one made while living. In Matthew 25:31-46 Jesus makes it very clear that now He is the only one who has the power to decide where one will be in eternity. To those who gave their lives to Jesus and served Him faithfully in life they will hear this sweet invitation, "Come, you blessed of My Father, inherit the kingdom prepared for you from the foundation of the world" (V. 34). But to the majority who decided not to believe in and serve the Lord Jesus Christ, these terrible words will be heard, "Depart me, you cursed, into the everlasting fire prepared for the devil and his angels" (V.41).

My dear friend if you will confess Jesus Christ is the Son of the Living God, He will confess you one day before His Father and the angels in heaven (Matthew 10:32, 33). And as a penitent believer, you should be immersed into Jesus Christ for the remission of your sins (Acts 2:36-38). It is my prayer that you will decide to confess Him now because if you do not, there is coming a day in which all mankind will confess Him but then it will be too late (Philippians 2: 9- 11). When Jesus comes again and sits on the throne of His glory, judgment will have begun. Then it will the sheep or the goats, right or left, saved or lost, heaven or hell. Please make the choice to live for Jesus in this life if you have not already done so in order that you may live with Him in eternity. This is my earnest plea and prayer for you.

WHAT HAPPENED TO
THE BRAZEN SERPENT?

The children of Israel became very discouraged and impatient as they traveled from Mount Hor by the way of the Red Sea to compass the land of Edom. They began to speak against God and His servant Moses. Complaints could be heard as to why God had brought them out in the wilderness to perish. Because of this display of a lack of faith, fiery serpents were sent among the people and many of them died that day. The children of Israel cried to Moses to ask God for mercy and deliverance. God instructed Moses to make a fiery serpent and put in on a standard. Those individuals bitten by the serpents could look upon the brazen serpent that Moses had built and be spared from certain death (Numbers 21:4-9).

This act of God's grace and salvation from death was a type of that greater deliverance from eternal ruin and destruction. Jesus said, "And as Moses lifted up the serpent in the wilderness, even so must the Son of Man be lifted up, that whoever believes in Him should not perish but have eternal life" (John 3:14,15). The brazen serpent certainly became something sacred to all those Israelites who were spared from death.

But what happened to the brazen serpent erected by Moses? Some seven hundred years later we find that Hezekiah began to reign as a king in Judah. In his desire to walk in the likeness of David, he made every effort to please God. "He removed the high places, and brake the pillars, and cut down the Asherah: and he brake in pieces the brazen serpent that Moses had made; for unto those days the children of Israel did burn incense to it; and he called it Nehushtan" (2 Kings 18:4). That which had been sacred had become an object of superstitious homage. There is nothing definite as to the length of time involved in such idolatrous worship but it must have been for many years. And there is do doubt that this was the same brazen serpent and not an imitation because the Bible reads, "...and he brake in pieces the brazen serpent that Moses had made." Man is prone to worship the creature rather than the Creator (Romans 1:25). It may be the golden calf that Aaron made or the golden calves that Jeroboam set up at Dan and Bethel (Numbers 32; I Kings 12:28,29). Even that which was ordained of God can become a snare and a temptation to the people. This was true in the case of the brazen serpent.

Have you wondered why we do not have the ancient relics (the Ark of the Covenant, etc.) in our possession? Did you ever desire to see a true likeness of Jesus Christ? People are still searching for Noah's ark. How about the cross on which Jesus was crucified? And then there is the robe of Christ. Men want something tangible to touch and see. So, there appears from time to time something like the 'Shroud of Turin' in order for people's faith to be strengthened. But, we do not need to have that which is material in order to have faith and assurance. Christianity is based on faith. Paul wrote in 2 Corinthians 5:7, "For we walk by faith, not by sight." Jesus said, "Thomas, because you have seen Me, you have believed. Blessed are those who have not seen and yet have believed." Faith in God and the Lord Jesus Christ is essential for salvation (Hebrews 11:6; John 8:24). There were witnesses to the life and works of Jesus and by the guidance of the Holy Spirit they wrote down all that is necessary to produce faith in our hearts (John 20:30,31). It is through the Word of God that saving faith is found and secured (Romans 10:17).

It would appear that in the divine providence of God those items previously mentioned, along with others have not been preserved for us to have and see today. God knows that man's basic nature never changes. There would be the likelihood for mankind to do exactly what Israel did regarding the brazen serpent and that is of worshiping the inanimate object instead of the Lord God.

WHEN CAN A PERSON BE BAPTIZED?

In this question we are not presently concerning ourselves with the 'when' as in learning the steps of obedience to the commands given by the Lord when one has heard the gospel of Christ and desires to give oneself to Jesus. Certainly we would all agree that a person who becomes a believer in Christ and is penitent of sins should be baptized without further delay. This is brought out by the fact that we have no promise of another opportunity. The ancient writer declared by inspiration, "Do not boast about tomorrow, For you do not know what a day may bring forth" (Proverbs 27:1). We have always encouraged a person to obey the gospel when it is first learned. There is always the danger of the devil hindering one's obedience by delaying a decision.

Our main thrust in this article is to observe that the Bible nowhere asserts that there is a specific day of the week when one is to be baptized. It is surprising to learn that some feel the only time (and day) when a person can be scripturally immersed is during a period of worship on the first day of the week. It may be that we have not made it as clear as we should in regards to the 'when' a person can be baptized. The only time some members witness a baptism is during worship on Sunday. Young people may therefore conclude that this is the only scriptural time for one to be immersed.

In the book of Acts we have several examples of people obeying the commandments of the gospel of Christ. The people on the day of Pentecost were baptized on the first day of the week; however, since there were about 3,000 people being immersed, we can conclude that it took several hours to accomplish this feat (Acts 2:36-41). It is not revealed on what day the people of Samaria were baptized (Acts 8:12, 13). We certainly could state that the Ethiopian nobleman was not baptized during a worship assembly since he was riding in his chariot when he learned of Jesus through the preaching of Philip (Acts 8:26-39). Lydia and her household were baptized on a Sabbath day which would be the seventh day (Saturday) of the week (Acts 16:13-15). It was sometime after midnight that the Philippian jailer and his household were baptized. Luke said that it was "the same hour of the night" (Acts 16:25, 30-34).

If all the baptisms recorded in the book of Acts occurred on the first day of the week during worship, we could conclude that this would give credence to the understanding that all baptisms should be performed on that particular day of the week. But such is not the case as found in these examples. Therefore we can immerse believers anytime of the day on any day of the week. The emphasis is not on the 'when' with reference to the time of the day, rather it is the 'when' people learn the truth.

We have baptized scores of individuals during the week days, following a home Bible study late in the evening or during the night. It is usually the case that deep emotions are evident when people have made the decision to give their lives to Christ. There is normally a very close relationship between the teacher and student that contributes to the joy of such an experience.

In conclusion, we urge all to be baptized upon learning of Christ. Any gospel preacher would be happy to assist you regardless of the time of any day during the week. The most important thing is to do it now while the mercy of God lingers.

WHEN WAS SAUL SAVED?

Luke, the inspired historian, records the conversion of Saul in Acts chapter nine. In chapters 22 and 26, Paul reviews his conversion while making a defense of his character and work. When someone is asked when Saul was saved, they usually respond, "When he saw the Lord on the road to Damascus." A famous country singer released a song during his life entitled, "I Saw the Light". No doubt, many have claimed to have 'seen the light' while asserting that they were saved at that moment in time. But, was Saul really saved when he saw a light on the road to Damascus? You are urged to read again these three chapters in the book of Acts to learn the truth of the matter. Please study carefully the following observations:

1. If Saul was saved on the road to Damascus, he did not know it because he asked, "Lord, what do You want me to do?" (Acts 9:6) There is no denial that Saul, at this time, became a believer in Jesus Christ. But, was he saved? If so, what was the significance of the question, "Lord, what do You want me to do?"

2. If Saul was saved when he saw the Lord on the Damascus road, the Lord himself did not know it because he told Saul to "Arise and go into the city, and you will be told what you must do." Certainly, this would have been the opportune time for the Lord to have informed Saul of his salvation if he had been saved at this point in the process of his conversion.

3. Further, if Saul was saved while on the road to Damascus, the disciple Ananias, whom the Lord had sent to Saul, did not know for he said to Saul, "And now why are you waiting? Arise and be baptized, and wash away your sins, calling on the name of the Lord" (Acts 22:16). Saul had believed in Christ. He had been a penitent person as indicated by his actions, "And he was three days without sight, and neither ate nor drank" (Acts 9:9). In verse eleven of the same chapter we read that during this period of time Saul was constant in prayer. Yet, when Ananais came to Saul, he was still unsaved. We know this because Ananias instructed Saul to "Arise and be baptized, and wash away your sins..." (Acts 22:16). How could sins be washed away if there were no sins? It would have been completely unnecessary to tell a person to obey a command in order to have his sins forgiven if in fact his sins had already been forgiven.

4. Finally, Paul did not understand his sins had been remitted on the road to Damascus because he obeyed the requirements given by the Lord through Ananias. How do we know this to be true? Later, when Paul wrote to the brethren in Rome he said, "Or do you not know that as many of us (plural pronoun, including Paul) as were baptized into Christ Jesus were baptized into His death? Therefore we (plural pronoun) were buried with Him through baptism into death, that just as Christ was raised from the dead by the glory of the Father, even so we (plural pronoun) also should walk in newness of life" (Romans 6:3,4). When was Saul baptized "into Christ Jesus"? It was when he was instructed by Ananias to do so. It was then that his sins were washed away by the blood of Jesus Christ, the Lamb of God (John 1:29; Revelation 1:5).

It is very interesting to note that neither faith nor repentance were mentioned in this example of a person's conversion to the Lord but both prerequisites were necessarily implied; yet, the very command that was given by Ananias, that is water baptism, remains controversial in the religious world today. Also, there were other reasons why the Lord appeared to Saul as he traveled to Damascus. Namely, that the Lord was going to send him to preach the gospel to the Gentiles and that Saul was going to suffer for the name of the Lord. It is important to understand that in order to be qualified as an apostle, Saul had to have seen the Lord following His resurrection (Please read Acts 9:15, 16; 26:16- 18).

WHO ARE MY BROTHERS AND SISTERS IN JESUS CHRIST?

The young men were roommates at a small Christian college during the 1950s. It was a time of unrest in the churches of Christ because of the differences in the understanding what the Bible taught regarding cooperation among congregations and the care of orphans. There were debates over the issues and articles written in the major publications in the brotherhood regarding these subjects. Eventually brethren parted ways and a division came into being, affecting the relationship among even the best of friends and family members. The roommates went their separate ways over these doctrinal differences. Years later they were talking over the telephone and one of the former roommates invited his friend to come by and see him sometimes where he taught at one of our Christian colleges. The other former roommate declined and that is when the first gentleman said to his friend "We can meet somewhere else than on the college campus for we are still brethren." His ultra conservative friend replied, "I don't know about that."

When I was born into the Elliott family I had two brothers and a sister awaiting my arrival. I would have another brother who was born a couple of years later. I did not choose my siblings. I didn't even choose my parents. In contrast, when I was born of water and the Spirit (John 3:3, 5) I became a brother to all of God's family who had responded to the grace of our Heavenly Father by being immersed as a penitent believer in the name of Jesus Christ for the remission of their sins (Acts 2:36-38). It was the Lord who saved us by His blood (Revelation 1:5; Ephesians 1:7) and added us to His spiritual body (Acts 2:47). While we have a part in choosing God to be our Father we do not have anything to do with choosing our brothers and sisters in Christ. It is often the case that some brethren are living immorally; some may have quit attending the assemblies while others have joined sectarian bodies and some of my brethren have chosen not to associate with me because of doctrinal differences, nevertheless, they are still my brothers and sisters.

When the prodigal son in Luke 15 went to that far country of dissipation and sin, he remained his father's son and a brother to his father's oldest son. It is wonderful to know that he repented and returned to his forgiving and merciful father. It is hard to imagine the sin of a member of the Corinthian congregation who was having a sexual relationship with his father wife. The brethren were instructed by Paul to discipline him for such sinful actions and not to have any fellowship with him. But Paul still referred to this man as a "brother" (1 Corinthians 5:1, 5, 7, 11). The apostle Paul later wrote that the brethren were to forgive and comfort this brother and that implied he had repented of his sins. Paul further instructed the brethren "to reaffirm your love to him" (2 Corinthians 2: 5-8). In 2 Thessalonians 3:6-15, Paul informed the brethren to withdraw fellowship from certain ones who would not work and who would "not obey our word in this epistle and do not keep company with him, that he may be ashamed. Yet do not count him as an enemy, but admonish him as a brother" (Emphasis, mine, RE).

It is of great importance that we observe closely the teaching of Paul as found in Galatians 3:26, 27: "For you are all sons of God through faith in Christ Jesus. For as many of you as were baptized into Christ have put on Christ." It is through the system of faith revealed in the Holy Scriptures and by an obedient faith in the Son of God that a penitent person becomes a child of God by being baptized into Christ where there is salvation (2 Timothy 2:10). It was our Lord Jesus Christ who declared: "He who believes and is baptized will be saved..." (Mark 16:16). The Holy Spirit clearly revealed through the preaching of the apostle Peter that baptism for the penitent believer was "for the remission of sins" (Acts 2:38). The emphasis is placed on the one being immersed and not on the one doing the immersing of the believer. And the place where the immersion takes place is matter of indifference whether it is in a baptistery, a pond or a river. When I preached for a congregation in Savannah, Georgia back in the late 1950s, I met a preacher from a conservative Christian Church located in a nearby city. He desired to make a change and become identified with the churches of Christ. He gave me a tract that he had written on the subject of "The Plan of Salvation" which I read. I could have removed his name from the tract and placed my name there because every point that he made on this subject was supported by the Word of God. Years later while preaching in a small town in southeast Alabama I became acquainted with a preacher who had left an independent Methodist church and was worshiping with the body of Christ. He informed me that he had always taught that baptism was essential for salvation and he immersed people for that reason.

Over the years we have learned of various religious groups in different countries that immerse believers for the remission of sins. Granted that the majority of denominations do not believe that baptism has anything to do with being saved from sins; however, we must realize that there are exceptions to that general rule. And we understand that many who are immersed in the name of Jesus Christ for the remission of their sins may also have become members of religious organizations that are not mentioned in the New Testament. But the fact is, since they obeyed the same commands as a believer in Christ as is common among us, we must conclude that they became children of God and thus our brothers and sisters. Brethren in error, yes, but they are our brothers and sisters in Christ. What they need to do is to leave any and all religious institutions that are not mentioned in the Holy Scriptures and become identified with other baptized believers and worship and serve God in the one body which is the church of our Lord Jesus Christ (Colossians 1:18; Ephesians 1:22, 23).

I have often said that I may not know all my brothers and sisters in Christ but I do know, according to the teaching of my Lord and His apostles, who my brethren are. More than that, I cannot say. Jesus Christ is the judge and He will deal with all God's children as to our faithfulness or unfaithfulness as pertaining to His Word and the manner of life that we have lived (John 12:48; Matthew 25:31-46).

WHO SHOULD NOT BE BAPTIZED?

This not the usual question one asks relative to such an important matter. Often the question is raised, "Who should be baptized?" However we can, by dealing with the question, "Who Should Not Be Baptized?" give answer as to who should be baptized.

First of all, infants should not be baptized. Children, while being born in a world of sin and being subject to sin are not born sinners. There is a difference. Sin is not something one inherits but rather it is something one does, "Whoever commits sin also commits lawlessness, and sin is lawlessness" (I John 3:4). While a child inherits the consequence of Adam's sin, he is not born totally depraved as per the teaching of John Calvin. The prophet Ezekiel explained it this way: "The soul who sins shall die. The son shall not bear the guilt of the father...'" (Ezekiel 18:20).

Second, young children who are not mature enough mentally to grasp the teaching relative to Jesus, his coming, his purpose for dying, his sonship and an awareness of right and wrong in their lives should not be baptized. The age of 'accountability' varies with individual children. There must be the acceptance of God's grace in this matter. God does not impute sin to those children who are in the years of innocence. This is the time for parents to teach and train their sons and daughters in the way of the Lord (Proverbs 22:6; Ephesians 6:4; II Timothy 3:14, 15).

Third, the individual who does not believe in Christ should not be baptized. It would be foolish to immerse an unbeliever. Jesus taught that for an alien sinner to be saved he must "believe and be baptized" (KJV, Mark 16:16). The person who does not believe is judged already (John 3:18). We can see why Paul did not instruct the Philippian jailor to be baptized when he asked, "Sirs, what must I do to be saved?" It was needful that the jailor first learn of Jesus through the word (Acts 16:30-32). Faith in Christ was produced in his heart by the preaching of the inspired word of God (Romans 10:17; Acts 16:34).

Fourth, the person who is impenitent should not be baptized. One could be immersed a thousand times but if there is not true repentance in his heart, such would not avail him anything. There has to be a radical change in the desire and will of the heart before one can be saved (Acts 17:30, 2 Peter 3:9). Man may not know absolutely the intent of another's heart but God does. Peter commanded the people on Pentecost to "Repent, and let every one of you be baptized in the name of Jesus Christ for the remission of sins..." (Acts 2:38). True repentance will lead to a reformed manner of life (Matthew 3:8).

Fifth, no one should be baptized who refuses to confess the name of Jesus. This confession is the outgrowth of one's faith. What one believes in his heart he confesses with his mouth (Romans 10:9, 10). No wonder the nobleman from Ethiopia exclaimed, "I believe that Jesus Christ is the Son of God" (Acts 8:37). There have been cases wherein people knew of the divinity of Jesus but refused to confess it (John 12:42, 43). Such people are not suitable candidates for scriptural baptism. Even Jesus will deny such moral cowards before His Father in heaven (Matthew 10:33).

Well, you may ask, 'Who should be baptized?' Those individuals who are mature enough to understand the facts and commands of the gospel, who are believers in the sonship of Christ, who are willing to repent of their sins and who will confess their faith in Jesus Christ. These are the fit subjects for scriptural baptism. "And now why are you waiting? Arise and be baptized, and wash away your sins, calling on the name of the Lord" (Acts 22:16).

Section 3

LESSONS FROM NATURE

A TRAGEDY, INDEED

The beautiful and scenic valley was filled with people from various areas of the country. The grandeur and splendor of the mountains was over-whelming. The river that rushed hurriedly by was clear and cool. A relaxed atmosphere prevailed. A person could forget the cares of life in such a lovely place. Then, the tragedy began to unfold.

The unusually heavy rains fell in torrents. The streams began to empty into the river that was already swollen with too much water. The indication was evident that severe flooding was to occur. Local officials frantically warned the inhabitants of this beautiful valley of the impending danger. They were met with mixed reactions. Many of the people moved quickly to higher elevation. However, one official stated that some persons would not move because hey already had the steaks on the grill. Others inquired as to how high the water might get. This official mentioned that he and his men did not have the time to argue with the people about the matter but had to move quickly to other parties to give them warning of the dangers. The rest of this story reveals that after some ten inches of rain, the results were simply terrifying. The rushing mighty waters crushed everything in its path. The greatest loss was the unfortunate deaths of so many people, including those who had been sufficiently warned but decided not to heed that message of an imminent danger approaching them.

My friends, the Bible is filled with warnings from the Garden of Eden right on down through the book of Revelation. If there is one message that is loud and clear to the human family it is to repent or perish. Ask those people who lived in the days of righteous Noah. Inquire of the Israelites who fell in the wilderness. "Prepare to meet your God, O Israel!" was the warning given to the people by the prophet Amos (Amos 4:12). God was going to punish them for their disobedience and warning them to turn from their evil ways and come back to Him. John the Baptist preached the message of repentance (Matthew 3:1, 2). Paul and other early preachers of the gospel informed the lost of Jesus Christ "and the judgment to come" (Acts 24:25). The majority of the seven churches of Asia were warned to repent of their sins (Revelation, chapters 2 & 3). The believers on the day of Pentecost were taught to repent and be baptized for the remission of sins (Acts 2:36-38). Repentance is required of all men (Acts 17:30). The erring Christian is taught to repent and confess his sins (Acts 8:22; I John 1:6-10).

Today, warnings are constantly and faithfully sounded by the children of God that Christ is coming again to save eternally His church; and, to render "vengeance on those who do not know God and on those who do not obey the gospel of our Lord Jesus Christ" (II Thessalonians 1:8). As to the when Jesus is coming again we are not sure but of the fact that he is coming again, we know (Matthew 24:36; John 14:1-3). There is a limit to this warning. Force cannot be used. Man is a being of choice. The decision is left up to the sinner. When the warning has been given and the ones warned reject the message of doom, their blood will be upon their own hands (Ezekiel 33:7-9).

The tragedy of lost souls in eternity will be of greater consequence than any natural disaster known to mankind.

"Careless soul, why will you linger,
Wand'ring from the fold of God?
Hear you not the invitation?
O Prepare to meet thou God."

— *J. H. Stanley*

CHANGE COMES FROM WITHIN

There is an oak tree in the downtown section of the city where I live that is one of the most beautiful trees I have ever seen, especially in the autumn of the year. For years, I have observed this stately tree as its leaves have turned from dark green to a maroon color. One day, my wife and I were driving by the tree and she commented that the leaves had not begun to change. I replied, "Oh, yes they have. They are turning from the inside first" (that is the peculiarity of this particular tree). Then, she could see the color of the leaves, beginning next to the trunk of the tree. When the process of change was completed, this oak tree became one of the most beautiful trees you could see in autumn.

The transformation of a person from a vile sinner to a pure saint of the Lord occurs in a similar fashion. Faith in the Lord Jesus Christ and repentance from sin changes the heart of a person (Acts 15:9). Paul informs us that the brethren in Rome had "obeyed from the heart that form of doctrine", "thus having been set free from sin", they became "slaves of righteousness" (Romans 6:1-4; 17, 18). Underneath the outward appearance of a Christian, there is a change occurring. Sanctification begins in the heart, the inner man. As a person thinks, so he becomes (Proverbs 23:7). Our daily Christian living and our worship to God begin in our hearts. Without love, nothing else matters. The first and greatest command is to love God with all of our being (Matthew 22:37, 38).

When Jesus said, "I desire mercy and not sacrifice" (Matthew 9:13), He was not implying that sacrifices were unnecessary. He was expressing the great truth that the attitude of the heart was much more important. Remember the words of Samuel that he stated to King Saul, "Behold, to obey is better than sacrifice, and to heed than the fat of rams" (I Samuel 15:22, 23). He was not relegating animal sacrifices as being unimportant; rather, he was emphasizing that the spiritual condition of the heart was of greater importance. The letter of the law minus love is of no value. Love without manifesting itself in obedience to the will of the Lord is unacceptable (John 14:15).

Jesus taught, "Blessed are the pure in heart, For they shall see God" (Matthew 5:8). The inspired writer of Hebrews exhorted, "Pursue peace with all people, and holiness, without which no one will see the Lord" (12:14). Holiness of life is predicated on a pure heart. Our actions are determined by what we are in our hearts. We cannot think one way and live an entirely different life. It is truly a short distance between the heart of a person and one's life. If the source is pure, the product will be holy. No wonder the wise man said, "Keep your heart with all diligence, for out of it springs the issues of life" (Proverbs 4:23). Therefore, it is most important that we fill our hearts with that which will govern our very lives. Paul instructs us in this matter as found in Philippians 4:8, "Finally, brethren, whatever things are true, whatever things are noble, whatever things are pure, whatever things are of good report, if there is any virtue and if there is anything praiseworthy – meditate on these things." Sometimes, the observation is made regarding a Christian in this manner, "She is such a beautiful person." And, it is not because of the outward appearance but it is that there has been a change made, one that began from the inside and permeated the very life of that individual. The transformation takes time but when it is completed, God will have produced a beautiful life that is conformed to the image of His Son (Romans 8:29).

CLOUDS

For several weeks we have experienced a real 'monsoon' season in the southeast section of our country. But I don't remember enjoying looking at the clouds in their various sizes and shapes since my childhood. Even the sunsets have been enhanced as the sun rays are seen beaming around a magnificent cloud. Some of the cumulous clouds reach perhaps 20 to 30 thousand feet in height. The beautiful blue sky at times has been filled with soft pillows of clouds. Other clouds that hang low and are darker in color have for their background the larger whiter clouds. Some clouds hide the sun and make for cooler weather while working in the yard or in the field. Then there are storm clouds that bring lightning and loud bursts of thunder and heavy rains and sometimes hail. On some days the entire sky is overcast with clouds that can make a person feel depressed. But, all in all, clouds are beautiful and they make believers appreciate God's creation. The Psalmist declared, "The heavens declare the glory of God; And the firmament shows His handiwork" (Psalms 19:1). You need to stop for awhile from your busy schedule and look upwards to the beautiful scenes not made with man's hands.

It is amazing how often we read about clouds in the Bible in connection with important persons and events. Here is a list of just a few times clouds are mentioned in both the Old and New Testament.

1. God set a rainbow in the clouds (Genesis 9:13).

2. A pillar of cloud guided the Israelites during the day on their exodus from Egypt (Exodus 13:21).

3. The glory of God often appeared in a cloud (Exodus 16:10; 19:9; Numbers 11:25).

4. A cloud covered Mount Sinai when God called for Moses, Aaron, Nadab, Abihu and seventy of Israel to come up and meet with Him there (Exodus 24:15-18).

5. A cloud filled the Holy Place and the house of the Lord when the glory (Divine Presence) of God appeared (I Kings 8:10-13). This is called the Shekhinah.

6. "A day of clouds" is mentioned when God speaks of punishment on Egypt, Ethiopia and other enemies of Israel (Ezekiel 30:1-4).

7. Job describes how rain is formed from the drawing up of the water "Which the clouds drop down and pours abundantly on man" (Job 36:27, 28).

8. Daniel wrote of the time when "One like the Son of Man, Coming with the clouds of heaven! He came to the Ancient of Days, And they brought Him near before Him" (Daniel 7:13, 14).

9. "A bright cloud overshadowed them" on the Mount of Transfiguration when God said, "This is my beloved Son, in whom I am well pleased. Hear Him!" (Matthew 17:5).

10. At the Lord's judgment upon the city of Jerusalem the "Son of Man" is depicted as "coming on the clouds of heaven with power and great glory" (Matthew 24:30).

11. Luke wrote about the ascension of Jesus in Acts 1:9, "Now when He had spoken these things, while they watched, He was taken up, and a cloud received Him out of their sight."

12. The apostle wrote that the Israelites "all were baptized into Moses in the cloud and in the sea" (I Corinthians 10:1, 2).

13. Paul, in giving encouragement to the Thessalonians regarding their loved ones who died in Christ, wrote of the second coming of the Lord in this manner, "Then we who are alive and remain shall be caught up together with them in the clouds to meet the Lord in the air. And thus we shall always be with the Lord" (I Thessalonians 4:13-18).

14. Both Peter and Jude wrote harshly concerning false teachers who would lead Christians astray as being like "clouds carried by tempest" and "clouds without water, carried about by the winds" (II Peter 2:17; Jude 12).

15. The apostle John wrote that the Lord Jesus Christ was "coming with clouds" (Revelation 1:7).

16. John also "saw still another mighty angel coming down from heaven, clothed with a cloud" (Revelation 10:1).

17. In the highly figurative book of Revelation John wrote, "Then I looked, and behold, a white cloud, and on the cloud sat One like the Son of Man, having on His head a golden crown, and in His

hand a sharp sickle." This was regarding the reaping of the earth's harvest, a matter of punishment (Revelation 14:14-16).

Sanford F. Bennett in 1867 wrote the beautiful lyrics of the song "Sweet By and By" and the first stanza tells us that "There's a land that is fairer than day, And by faith we can see it afar; For the Father waits over the way, To prepare us a dwelling place there." In the book of Revelation we read that "The city had no need of the sun or of the moon to shine in it, for the glory of God illuminated it. The Lamb is its light" (21:23). Also "There shall be no night there: They need no lamp nor light of the sun, for the Lord God gives them light. And they shall reign forever and ever" (22:5). It is necessarily implied that no clouds, especially storm clouds, will be there as the beautiful hymn "O They Tell Me of a Home" teaches:

"O they tell me of a home far beyond the skies,
O they tell me of a home far away;
O they tell me of a home where no storm clouds rise,
O they tell me of an unclouded day.

O they tell me of a home where my friends have gone,
O they tell me of that land far away
Where the tree of life in eternal bloom
Sheds it fragrance thro the unclouded day.

O they tell me of the King in His beauty there,
And they tell me that mine eyes shall behold,
Where he sit on the throne that is whiter than snow,
In the city that is made of gold.

O they tell me that He smiles on His children there,
And His smile drives their sorrows away;
And they tell me that no tears ever come again,
In that lovely land of unclouded day.

O the land of cloudless day,
O the land of an unclouded sky;
O they tell me of a home, where no storm clouds rise,
O they tell me of an unclouded day."

— *Josiah K. Alwood, Copyright, 1993, Howard Publishing Co.*

EARTHQUAKES

The devastating earthquakes that occur in various countries from time to time and destroy cities and kill thousands of people makes us realize more and more the uncertainty of life. The magnitude of destruction wrought by such force is overwhelming. There is a Scripture I want to mention presently that deals with a particular earthquake.

In the sixteenth chapter of the book of Acts, the account is given of the conversion of a Philippian jailor and his household. The jailor, a gentile, was a non-believer in the deity of Jesus Christ. The day that Paul and Silas were beaten and cast into prison was perhaps an ordinary one for the jailor. While the day may have started out like any other day for this particular person, it certainly did not end in a common fashion. Something transpired that transformed the life of this Roman citizen and the lives of his loved ones. Something drastically happened. An earthquake occurred in this man's life. It was a literal tremor, a movement of the earth that the shook the foundation of the building that housed those people in the prison. The jailor was awakened by this event and was about to take his own life because he thought his prisoners had escaped. Paul prevented this tragedy by shouting, "Do yourself no harm; for we are all here!" It was at this time that the jailor sprang forth and asked the most important question:" Sirs, what must I do to be saved?"

After hearing and believing the gospel, this man and his family were baptized into Jesus Christ for the remission of their sins (Acts 16:30-34; Mark 16:15, 16). The jailor began the day unsaved but concluded it by being redeemed by the blood of the Lamb. Something wonderful came out of what seemed to be a truly horrible experience in his life.

Into every life, sometime, somewhere, somehow, 'earthquakes' occur. Not necessarily literal, physical movements of the earth, but events that can help to change our lives, if we accept them in a positive manner. These 'earthquakes' come in various forms. There was the death of a teenage son that caused his parents to turn to Jesus. A man was operated on and it was discovered that he had cancer. He repented of sins and came back to the Lord. Three months later he died. The person who lost all his material wealth realized for the first time that he had been trusting in the wrong values in life. He sought then the true riches in Christ.

Tragedies and trials can become blessings in disguise if we permit God to work in our lives (Romans 8:28). David stated "Before I was afflicted I went astray; But now I observe thy word." He even declared, "It is good for me that I have been afflicted; that I may learn Your statues" (Psalms 119:67, 71).

The gospel of Christ is God's power to save (Romans 1:16). But, 'earthquakes' that come into our lives can and often do motivate people to realize their plight in life without God. It is then that we should seek the salvation that is the Savior.

FARMERS, FAITH, AND THE FATHER

Virginia and I had watched the growing of winter wheat beginning in late summer of 2010 until the spring of 2011. You see, when we are approaching our home we leave the city limits and pass through a portion of a farm that is located on both sides of County Road 12 or Powell Road. We then turn south for a short distance and once again we are in the city limits of Prattville, Alabama where we make our home. Presently we are observing how fast the soybeans and the purple hull peas are growing so rapidly since we have finally received some wonderful and much needed rain. Though I have never farmed on such a level, I have had gardens in most places where we have lived. In fact, in one town I had 30 long rows of various vegetables. One morning I pulled 300 ears of sweet corn for Virginia to prepare and freeze for later consumption by our family of six. But I do enjoy watching the crops grow to maturity so the farmers can harvest them.

Farmers, bless their hearts, have to be people of great faith. Faith that in the future when the seeds are planted the sun will warm the earth and that the rains will fall to aid the seed to germinate and then to water the plants in order for them to grow until the harvest time. Patience in the ploughman is predicated upon faith, faith that the God of the universe will supply the needed environment for there to be a harvest. The biblical writer James wrote in James 5:7, "Therefore be patient, brethren unto the coming of the Lord. See how the farmer waits for the precious fruit of the earth, waiting patiently for it until it receives the early and latter rain." Farming is certainly a calculated risk because if there is not enough moisture for the plant to grow, or, if there is too much water there will a disaster and not a harvest.

The writer James also declared in chapter 1 and verse 17 of his epistle, "Every good gift and every perfect gift is from above, and comes down from the Father of lights, with whom there is no variation or shadow of turning." There are two points to consider from this passage. The first is that God the Father is the source of all of life's blessings. We will agree that the needed ingredients for the harvest of the various crops are the warmth from the sun

118

and the rain that falls upon the earth. Second, when God says something you can 'bank' on it. The Lord Jesus made this declaration as found in Matthew 5:45, "(F)or He makes His sun rise on the evil and on the good, and sends rain on the just and on the unjust." Thus all men are recipients of the physical blessings from the Heavenly Father, the Creator of the universe. Following the universal flood God made a promise when He said, "While the earth remains, Seedtime and harvest, Cold and heat, Winter and summer, And day and night Shall not cease" (Genesis 8:22). There are times when we have cold days in the summer and hot days in the winter but the fact is that as long as the earth exists there will be the different seasons of the year for the planting and the harvest of the various crops by the farmers.

While driving by the acres of winter wheat one day we saw a man combining the wheat and I told my wife that I needed to take pictures of that beautiful scene. When we arrived home I got my camera and back to the field I went. I parked my truck and started to walk near the combine to take a picture of it and when I did the operator stopped and motioned for me to come near and so I did. Then he pushed the door opened and asked me to join him. I was really surprised at his offer but I hurried to the machine and climbed up in the cab with the gentleman. This was my first ever ride in such a giant of farm machinery. After we introduced ourselves I began to take pictures.

I could not help but think of this poem as we harvested the beautiful wheat:

> "Back of the loaf is the snowy flour,
> Back of the flour, the mill;
> Back of the mill are the wheat and shower
> And the sun and the Father's will."
>
> — *Maltbie D. Babcock (1858-1901)*

That is the very reason why we all should express our gratitude to God before we eat our food like the apostle Paul did as recorded in Acts 27:35, "And when he had said these things, he took bread and gave thanks to God in the presence of them all; and when he had broken it he began to eat." He recognized that it was God who had blessed them with the food that they were about to eat.

How truly blessed we are in this land wherein we live. God has been good to us as a nation of people and we should never forget His grace in providing our freedom and the physical and material blessings we enjoy.

It was in the year of 1893 when Katherine Lee Bates, age 33, an English professor at Wellesley College made a train trip to Colorado Springs, Colorado to teach summer classes when she was inspired to write the following poem because of the beautiful scenery she saw while traveling. I just believe that she was greatly motivated to write certain lines in her poem when she saw the magnificent fields of wheat in the state of Kansas. Here is the first stanza of that poem:

AMERICA THE BEAUTIFUL

"O beautiful for spacious skies,
For amber waves of grain,
For purple mountain majesties
Above the fruited plain!
America! America!
God shed His grace on thee,
And crown thy good with brotherhood
From sea to shining sea!"

— *Katie Lee Bates, 1893, Wikipedia Free Encyclopedia*

GLOBAL WARMING

The debate continues. Extremes are evident. Politics divide. The panic button is being pushed. Who shall we believe? Is there not a middle ground somewhere? Books have been written on the pollution of our planet and our atmosphere. A movie has been made to warn people of the impending danger of such pollutions. A former vice-president of our nation has been awarded the Nobel Prize for his efforts to warn us of global warning if we continue to destroy the purity of the very air that we breathe. Yet, there are reputable scientists and meteorologists who strongly disagree with several of his arguments and conclusions. They explain that we are in a cycle of weather changes that has been going on for centuries. And here I sit as a novice and endeavoring to understand matters that are often too great for my finite mind.

I live in the area of our nation where the drought is the most severe. Our water supply is diminishing rapidly. I have witnessed the failure of so many of the crops planted by our farmers. The cattlemen are having great difficulty in finding food for their stock because the pastures have burned up due to the lack of moisture. I watched on the television the powerful fires that scorched the land and burned the houses in Colorado. The tragedies caused by natural occurrences and man-made, could we not understand that such might be possible as we consider the reasons for changes in our weather? I know that as humans we do pollute our environment. We all have witnessed this fact. It is good that we are becoming more aware of this problem.

While not trying to diminish the need to clean up our polluted land, water and air, I want to mention another 'global warming' that the world in general has no interest in whatsoever. We go about our everyday activities without considering the fact that there is coming a time when this life will come to end. We buy and sell and get gain without fully realizing that life is like a vapor that last only for a short time (See James 4:13-17). Many are the persons, who like the scoffers mentioned by Peter, reason that since there was a yesterday there will also be a tomorrow and things will continue as they have since the beginning of time. But read very carefully the words of the apostle

Peter in 2 Peter 3:5- 7:"For this they willfully forget: that by the word of God the heavens were of old, and the earth standing out of water and in the water, by which the world that then existed perished, being flooded with water. But the heavens and the earth which are now preserved for fire until the day of judgment and perdition of ungodly men. And then Peter continues, "But the day of the Lord will come as a thief in the night, in which the heavens will pass away with a great noise, and the elements will melt with fervent heat; both the earth and the works that are in it will be burned up. Therefore, since all these things will be dissolved, what manner of persons ought you to be in holy conduct and godliness, looking for and hasting the coming of the day of God, because of which the heavens will be dissolved, being on fire, and the elements will melt with fervent heat?" (Vs 10-12).

Sin is the pollution of the soul. And unless a person has this stain removed from his soul by the cleansing blood of the Lamb and our Savior Jesus Christ (Revelation 1:5), he will suffer the inevitable consequence of such terrible fate. Now this is the 'global warming' that we should be prepared for by "denying ungodliness and worldly lusts" and living "soberly, righteously, and godly in the present age, looking for the blessed hope and glorious appearing of our great God and Savior Jesus Christ" (Titus 2:12, 13).

HE SHALL BE LIKE A TREE PLANTED BY THE RIVERS OF WATER

There were times while taking my morning walks on Saint Simons Island, Georgia that the sun rays could not reach me because of the beautiful oak trees with their overhanging limbs covering the street below. Trees are one of God's most beautiful creations and especially these particular trees laden down with Spanish moss. The trees on the island are so respected that the streets are built around them. I have often thought of this poem we had to memorize in school many years ago.

Trees

"I think that I shall never see
A poem lovely as a tree.
A tree whose hungry mouth is prest
Against the earth's sweet flowing breast;
A tree that looks at God all day,
And lifts her leafy arms to pray;
A tree that may in Summer wear
A nest of robins in her hair;
Upon whose bosom snow has lain;
Who intimately lives with rain.
Poems are made by fools like me,
But only God can make a tree."

— Alfred Joyce Kilmer (1886-1918)
(Wikipedia Free Encyclopedia)

Psalm one is a favorite of scores of saints. Therein is a contrast between a godly and an ungodly person. It is of the believer in God that demands our attention in this article. Undoubtedly David is the writer and he informs us that this man is blessed; that is to say he is happy and fortunate. This is one of several 'beatitudes' mentioned in this book. Please observe that the negative is first mentioned as pertaining to this man's character. He "walks not in the counsel of the ungodly, Nor stands in the path of sinners, Nor sits in the seat of the scornful." This means that he does not habitually seek the advice/counsel of those individuals who would influence him to do evil. He does not associate with sinners in such a manner that others would consider him one of the 'in groups'. And certainly he would never join the ungodly scoffers of all that is good and sit with them in their devilish fellowship and participate in their evil doings.

This blessed man is one whose "delight is in the law of the Lord, And in His law he meditates day and night." "Law" would not only be the Ten Commandments but would include the first five books of the Old Testament and the words of the prophets who spoke by the guidance of the Holy Spirit as mentioned in 2 Peter 1:20, 21: "(K)nowing this first, that no prophecy of scripture is of any private interpretation, for prophecy never came by the will of man, but holy men of God spoke as they were moved by the Holy Spirit." This man of God takes great pleasure and satisfaction in having access to the Word of God to read and to meditate on its message for his spiritual growth and well being. The writer in Psalms 119:47, 48 & 97 expresses the same in this manner: "And I will delight myself in Your commandments, Which I love. My hands also I will lift up to Your commandments, Which I love, And I will meditate on Your statutes." "Oh, how I love Your law! It is my meditation all the day." Such an attitude should permeate the very life of a disciple of Jesus Christ (John 8:31, 32; 2 Timothy 2:15).

The Psalmist compares this blessed child of God to one of His creations: "He shall be like a tree planted by the rivers of water, That brings forth its fruit in its season, Whose leaf also shall not wither; And what he does shall prosper."

Notice that the tree was planted by someone. It did not accidentally grow in that location. The seed (Word of God) that is planted in the good ground (heart) "is able to save your souls" (Luke 8:11; James 1:21). The moisture from the rivers (channels) provides the nourishment to keep the tree healthy and strong and enables it to bear fruit to be enjoyed by all. Even in times of drought the leaves stay green because water is nearby. The Lord God blessed Israel in various ways when the people served him faithfully. The land produced bountiful crops; the herds multiplied; wives gave birth to children and there was food to eat. The Holy Scriptures contain manifold promises to the children of God who trusts in Him. Jesus taught this as recorded in Matthew 6:33: "But seek first the kingdom of God and His righteousness, and all these things shall be added to you." I Corinthians 3:21: "Therefore let no one boast in men. For all things are yours." 2 Corinthians 9:6: "But this I say: He who sows sparingly will also reap sparingly, and he who sows bountifully will also reap bountifully." The righteous man will "bear much fruit" as he is led by the Spirit (John 15:8; Galatians 5:22, 23).

Because Christ dwells in the heart of the righteous man by faith, he will be "rooted and grounded in love" (Ephesians 3:17). This 'tap root' of faith in Jesus Christ and in the knowledge of His Word, will prevent him from being "tossed to and fro and carried about with every wind of doctrine" (Ephesians 4:11-16). He will "be steadfast, immovable, always abounding in the work of the Lord" (1 Corinthians 15:58). This is one version of an old folk song that should express the conviction of every Christian.

"Jesus is my Savior, I shall not be moved;
In His love and favor, I shall not be moved,
Just like a tree that's planted by the waters, Lord, I shall not be moved.
In my Christ abiding, I shall not be moved;
In His love I'm hiding, I shall not be moved,
Just like a tree that's planted by the waters, Lord, I shall not be moved.
If I trust Him ever, I shall not be moved;
He will fail me never, I shall not be moved,
Just like a tree that's planted by the waters, Lord, I shall not be moved."
On His word I'm feeding, I shall not be moved;
He's the One that's leading, I shall not be moved,
Just like a tree that's planted by the waters, Lord, I shall not be moved.
Chorus
I shall not be, I shall not be moved;
I shall not be, I shall not be moved;
Just like a tree that's planted by the waters, Lord, I shall not be moved.

THE HONEYBEE AND THE BUZZARD

Surely we all have some knowledge regarding this insect and this fowl. Both have been placed here on this earth for different purposes as designed by the Creator, God Almighty. While their functions are vital, they are radical in contrast. The buzzard is rather despised by the human family. We esteem this bird as being unsightly in appearance and undesirable because of its work, the devouring of dead carcasses. Yet, in the balance of nature, this scavenger has a rightful place in our environment. The honeybee, on the other hand, is well thought of and respected. While we dislike the sting of such a small insect, we do appreciate the delicious honey that it makes for us. The bee can be seen visiting the beautiful flowers and various blooms in the vegetative kingdom. No wonder the honey that this bee makes is so sweet.

Strangely enough, the buzzard and the honeybee remind us of the various attitudes and dispositions found in different people. First of all, some folk enjoy dwelling on the ungodly, the gossip, the hearsay, the ugly, the bad, the filthy, the hurtful, and the immoral. They seem to get their kicks over telling or hearing a good piece of juicy slander. And, the worse it stinks, the better they like it. This old world is filled with individuals who love filthiness. The Bible refers to people who "speak foolishness" and whose "heart will work iniquity" (Isaiah 32:6). Paul writes of the unrighteous in this manner, "Their throat is an open tomb;; With their tongues they have practiced deceit; the poison of asps is under their lips: whose mouth is full of cursing and bitterness" (Romans 3:13, 14). Their ultimate end is eternal perdition, for Jesus said in Matthew 12:36, 37, "But I say to you that every idle word men shall speak, they will give account of it in the day of judgment. For by your words you will be justified, and by your words you will be condemned."

We are grateful however that there are many Christians who love the good and the beautiful things of life. They think upon that which is pure, honest, just, true, lovely, and of good report (Philippians 4:8). They feed upon the word of God that is "Sweeter also than honey and the honeycomb" (Psalms 19:10). They know that "Pleasant words are like honeycomb, Sweetness to the soul, and health to the bones" (Proverbs 16:24). They "love life" and endeavor to "see good days"; therefore, they "refrain his tongue from evil" (I Peter 3:10).

The question therefore is, "To be or not to be". That is, are you soaring over dead carcasses and seeking the corrupt; or, are you feasting upon the beautiful and the good? Let us all 'be' (live) like the honeybee and not the buzzard!

THE CHANGING OF THE SEASONS: GOD'S FAITHFULNESS

Several years ago Virginia and I were in the extreme northeastern section of the state of Georgia working with a congregation that met in the small community of Tiger near the city of Clayton. It was in the autumn of the year and the color of the foliage was radiant in their assorted colors. While driving along the highway we noticed a large pumpkin patch so we stopped and found one pumpkin that someone had painted a face on it. Autumn is perhaps my favorite season of the year. While spring is alive with beautiful flowers and the budding of the leaves on various trees, autumn produces more color than one might imagine. Yet, I enjoy all the seasons of the year because each one presents evidence that there is a Supreme Architect with infinite wisdom and almighty power who had the power to create and set in motion this amazing universe in which we live.

It was following the universal deluge and after Noah and his family left the ark that this great man of faith offered burnt offerings that were acceptable unto God that our Creator made this promise (Genesis 8:20:22):

> *"While the earth remains,*
> *Seedtime and harvest,*
> *Cold and heat,*
> *Winter and summer,*
> *And day and night*
> *Shall not cease."*

So as long as the earth remains we have this precious promise from God that there will be the changing of the seasons of the year. You can depend on God faithfulness because it is impossible for Him to lie (Titus 1:2; Hebrews 6:18). The Psalmist declared in Psalm 19:1-4:

> *"The heavens declare the glory of God;*
> *And the firmament shows His handiwork.*

Day unto day utters speech,
And night unto night reveals knowledge.
There is no speech nor language
Where their voice is not heard.
Their line has gone out through all the earth,
And their words to the end of the world."

As believers in God we worship and praise Him and not the beauties He has created for us to enjoy each season of the year.

"TO THE OCEANS, WHITE WITH FOAM"

During our family gatherings on Saint Simons Island, Georgia, it has been my habit to arise early in the mornings and walk on the beach down to the pier and the village where I would buy a cup of coffee, eat breakfast and read the daily newspaper. Being from the hill country of northwest Georgia I am still fascinated by the appearance of the Atlantic Ocean. When the tide comes in the waves would hit the rocks and splash over them. The white caps were beautiful. Often I would express my deepest gratitude to God for His marvelous creation. Both the heavens and the earth with its seas declare the glory of God (Psalms 19). The book of nature indeed proves that there is a Supreme Architect who designed this universe (Romans 1:20). Though not a world traveler I have seen some of the beauties of our country with its mountains in the southeast and in the western part of our nation, the Gulf of Mexico and the Atlantic Ocean. With all the faults that exist in our United States of America I do believe as a citizen that we live in the greatest nation on earth.

The pilgrims and early settlers sought freedom to worship God in this new land while settlers in the South American countries sought gold. Our governmental leaders possessed a faith in the Creator of the universe. There is no doubt but that the Lord God has richly blessed this land and its people. The wise man declared that "Righteousness exalts a nation, But sin is a reproach to any people" (Proverbs 14:34). While sin and disbelief have always been in existence, our modern day society has strayed greatly from a faith in God and from His moral standard for human conduct. Atheism is growing daily; sexual perversion is common place; dishonesty and corruption are widely accepted and exist among many of our political and civic leaders; the killing of unborn children is considered acceptable since it is legal; adultery is prevalent among marriage partners and fornication among teens and adults abounds nationwide. Man has become a law unto himself (Judges 21:25). The Word of God is no longer reverend even among some religious groups.

The blood of thousands of our men and women who have fought for our country and our freedom flows like a mighty river; yet, we are using this freedom to destroy the moral fiber of our people. It has become a license to do as we please without considering what God would have us to be as a nation of people. Eventually we will reap as we have been sowing (Galatians 6:7, 8). It is most important that we give heed to the following warnings: "The wicked shall be turned into hell, And all the nations that forget God" and "Now consider this, you who forget God, Lest I tear you in pieces" (Psalm 9:17; 50:22).

The story is told about a student who wanted to fool his professor in some way. He held a bird in his hand and asked the professor, "What do I have in my hand?" The professor replied, "It is a bird." The student asked, "What color is it?" "It is a red bird" answered the professor. Then the student asked, "Is it dead or alive?" The wise old professor said, "The power of life or death is in your hand?" The power to revive faith in God and His standard of morals and ethics is in our hands. May the lyrics of the beautiful song 'God Bless America' written by Irving Berlin ever be our desire, hope and prayer.

God Bless America

While the storm clouds gather far across the sea,
Let us swear allegiance to a land that's free,
Let us all be grateful for a land so fair,
As we raise our voices in a solemn prayer.
"God Bless America, Land that I love.
Stand beside her, and guide her
Thru the night with a light from above.
From the mountains, to the prairies,
To the oceans, white with foam,
God bless America, My home sweet home.

— *Irvin Berlin, 1918, Wikipedia Encyclopedia*

THE VINE AND THE BRANCHES

"I am the vine, you are the branches" (John 15:5). There are various speculations expressed relative to the setting of this well known parable spoken by the Lord. Some have suggested that Jesus saw a vine growing on the side of a wall. Others think it may have been the vineyards nearby, while others mention that Jesus had just instituted the supper that contained fruit of the vine. Nevertheless, he uses something very common to bring forth some vital lessons to His disciples. The Bible is replete with natures' symbolisms and made applicable in spiritual matters. Jesus has been referred to as being a rock, a stone and presently in our study as being the vine. Basically speaking, this parable of the vine and the branches in John 15 deals with the various relationships of Jesus with others.

First of all, we observe Christ's relationship with His Father. The Lord said: "I am the true vine, and My Father is the vinedresser" (John 15:1). This would indicate that God is the proprietor as well as being the vinedresser. It is God who is spoken of as being the one who does the pruning and the purging of the branches. The prominent and prevalent attitude of Jesus toward His Father is always a submissive one (John 6:38). Jesus is the "true vine". Israel of old had been "a noble vine" of God in ages past which was only a figure of the true vine, Jesus Christ (Jeremiah 2:21; Hebrews 9:24).

Second, there is Christ's relationship toward man. "I am the vine, you are the branches" (John 15:5). Jesus is the vine and the individual disciples are the branches; not nations, institutions or denominations. Jesus said, "If anyone does not abide in Me, he is cast out as a branch, and is withered" (John 15:6). Herein we learn of the vital connection between Christ and His disciples. Jesus is spoken of as being the head of the body (Ephesians 5:23). The branches must have the vine in order to live; however, the vine can exist without the branches.

"For without Me you can do nothing" (John 15:5). "In Christ" speaks of human redemption. The cleansing agent is the word of the Lord. "You are already clean because of the word which I have spoken to you" (John 15:3;

Ephesians 5:26: James 1:18). The apostle Paul taught that we are "baptized into Christ Jesus" (Romans 6:3; Galatians 3:26, 27). "In Christ" means that the Christian is in God because Christ is in God and God is in Christ (John 14:20). The branch abiding in the vine is conditional as we learn in this parable. The symbolism must not be pressed beyond its intended meaning. The clear teaching in the scriptures is that man has the ability to make choices.

Third, the parable suggests the relationship of Christ toward good works. Good, productive branches are pruned in order to bear more fruit (John 15:2). Meritorious works of mortal man are meaningless. The works ordained of God are essential and are the outgrowth of an obedient faith (Ephesians 2:10; James 2:14-26). The outward evidence of a Christian's union with Christ is seen by the fruit one bears. The inward bond of union which is the cause of fruitfulness is love (John 15:10). The Christian's life is to glorify God (John 15:8; Matthew 5:16). Specifically, we can bring glory to God by leading others to Christ and by living in such a manner as to manifest the fruit of the Spirit (John 15:8; Matthew 28:19; Galatians 5:22, 23).

Fourth, there is Christ's relationship or lack of relationship with severed branches. Unproductive branches are taken away (John 15:2, 6). This is positive proof that a child of God can so sin as to be eternally lost. The precept of this doctrine is herein presented as well as an example of the same in the person of Judas Iscariot (John 13:2). If the continuing in Christ is conditional and present, so is the purging and casting off of the branches. The final punishment of the unproductive branches shall occur when "The Son of man will send out His angels, and they will gather out of His kingdom all things that offend, and those who practice lawlessness, and will cast them into the furnace of fire. There will be weeping and gnashing of teeth" (Matthew 13:41, 42).

It was in the spring time when sap flows freely that I cut off some branches from a grape vine. Later I observed the life giving fluid actually flowing from the vine to the ground. There was a certain sadness that filled my heart as I contemplated this parable of our Lord. How tragic it is for Christians to sever their ties with the Lord through unfaithfulness. We can only live as long as we sustain the right relationship with Jesus Christ our Savior.

WAS IT A SIGN FROM HEAVEN?

It was about seven o'clock one morning recently when I looked out the glass door toward the backyard and the utility house and I saw something that I had never seen before since moving into this house in the year of 2004. Shinning brightly on the side of the utility house was a circle with a bright cross in the middle of it. I couldn't believe what I was seeing so I walked hurriedly to my office and got my camera and took some pictures of that scene. I wanted my wife to see what I had seen so she would not think that I was having a hallucination. I thought to myself, people around the world are always 'seeing' the face of Jesus in the clouds and even sometimes in pancakes. Of course certain religionists are always seeing the likeness of Mary, the mother of Jesus, in various places and on different substances. So why could I not be the fortunate one this time to have a 'sign from heaven' and in this case, a cross. Now I know the cross I saw was not the traditional one on which the Lord was crucified but nevertheless, it was a cross. You can envision that if you turn this cross just a bit, it would be the kind that we believe Jesus was placed on and crucified. The cross that I saw is called Crux Decussata. "Crux Decussata comes from decus, Latin for 'distinction', 'honour', 'glory' and 'grace'." I must point out that the side of the utility house that had the circle and cross on it was facing west and I was looking east toward the rising of the sun. But was it a sign from heaven?

Man's nature never changes. We have a strong desire to see in order to believe. When Jesus Christ walked upon this earth, he taught people about the coming of the kingdom of God and performing miracles; there were certain unbelievers who requested that Jesus perform a 'sign' for them, seemingly just to satisfy their curiosity. In fact some of His hearers (the Pharisees) had accused Him of performing miracles by the power of Beelzebub and not by the power of the Holy Spirit (Matthew 12:24-32). They also said to Jesus, "Teacher, we want to see a sign from You" (Matthew 12:38). The writer Mark record states it in this manner: "Then the Pharisees came out and began to dispute with Him, seeking from Him a sign from heaven, testing Him"

(8:11). So you can plainly understand that their request was not made in sincerity and from honest hearts. The reply from the Lord came swiftly: "But He answered and said to them, "An evil and adulterous generation seeks after a sign, and no sign will be given to it except the sign of the prophet Jonah" (Matthew 12:39, 40). Jesus spoke in reference to His resurrection from the dead. If the people of His day would not believe in Him because of His miracles and teaching, there remained no further evidence to be given. Jesus knew that even if a dead person returned to the world of the living, such would not necessarily cause faith to be found in the hard hearts of some people. While Jesus lived under the Old Covenant, the Jewish populace was to adhere to the writings of "Moses and the prophets" (Luke 16:27-31).

The apostle John summed up the basic reason (though Jesus often responded because of compassion) for the signs/miracles performed while he was alive. "And truly Jesus did many other signs in the presence of His disciples, which are not written in this book; but these are written that you may believe that Jesus is the Christ, the Son of God, and that believing you may have life in His name" (John 20:30, 31). After the resurrection of our Lord, He sent His apostles on a world wide mission to preach the good news of His death for the sins of the world and His resurrection (Matthew 28:19, 20; Mark 16:15, 16). "And they went out and preached everywhere, the Lord working with them and confirming the word through the accompanying signs. Amen" (Mark 16:20). The Hebrew writer had reference to the teaching of the Lord and the apostles and the reason for the miraculous signs in their work: "How shall we escape if we neglect so great a salvation, which at the first began to be spoken by the Lord, and was confirmed to us by those who heard Him, God also bearing witness both with signs and wonders, with various miracles, and gifts of the Holy Spirit, according to His own will" (Hebrews 2:3, 4)? The word "confirm" means "to establish the truth, accuracy, validity, or genuineness of; corroborate; verify." So the deity of Jesus was established by His signs and wonders; and, the word that the Holy Spirit gave to the apostles was confirmed by miracles. Therefore, there is no longer a necessity for 'signs from heaven' or from any other source. Today we do not need any likeness of Jesus, a shroud, pieces of His cross or perhaps His robe. When Thomas saw Jesus following His resurrection, Jesus said to him, "Thomas, because you have seen Me, you have believed. Blessed are those who have not seen and yet have believed" (John 20:29). The faith we have comes from the word of God and not from any 'signs from heaven' (Romans 10:17). The apostle Paul declared in 2 Corinthians 5:7, "For we walk by faith, not by sight." The Christian's faith rests upon objective truth found in the inspired word of God, and not by subjective feelings that might arise from seeing 'signs from heaven'.

Oh, my 'sign from heaven' occurred when the rays of the morning sun shined on a window on my house and was reflected then to the utility house. The reason that this had never occurred before was because there had been a Bradford pear tree shielding the sun rays from doing such but my neighbor had the tree removed several months ago. It is amazing how the reflection of the sun rays on the window pane and frame caused the circle and a cross to appear on my utility house. Maybe the major reason was to say to me that X marks the spot where I need to do some painting just below the window on the utility house.

WHEN IT RAINS, IT POURS

Well, many folk have prayed for rain because of the drought condition in the southeastern section of our country and the good Lord sent it. The problem was that some areas were flooded. I am reminded of the story of some brethren in west Texas who became greatly concerned about the extreme drought conditions in their part of the world. They decided to obtain the services of a preacher to come and pray for rain. Finally they found a city preacher to come out and pray for rain. He came and prayed fervently for the Lord to send rain upon the arid land. After a couple of days had passed the rain began to fall. In fact it rained until all the land was flooded and the situation became very serious. The brethren became very concerned again because all their properties were inundated with water. They came together to discuss what they should do. One brother was heard to have said, "That is what we get by having a preacher to pray for rain who knew nothing about agriculture."

You know life is much like that. There are times of peace, joy, happiness and good health. These are mountain top experiences. But in a moment of time things can radically change. The prophet Elijah was successful on Mount Carmel but in a short time he was to be found in a deep valley of discouragement and he desired to die (1 Kings 18; 19:4). This mighty man of God was human after all and not unlike ourselves (James 5:17). The good times do not test our strength and faith. It is when the tragedies of life occur. It is when death invades our home. It is when a loved one is diagnosed with a terminal disease. It is when the ill winds of discouragement and despair howl strongly across the depths of our inner being. It is when you pray for a friend or a loved one to get well and doesn't and he dies. It is when you lose your job and you have to look elsewhere for employment. And there are dozens of other reasons why your heart becomes burdened down with anxiety and sadness.

Please excuse the personal experiences but I must mention some of them. My lovely bride has and is presently experiencing some health problems; there was the sudden death of a dear friend that has overwhelmed me; a telephone call this morning informed me that a brother-in-law was critically injured yesterday in an automobile accident. Life is not a bed of roses. Sometimes the valleys in life are deep and long. But it is not a time to give up. Blaming God and leaving the Lord would not be answer. Gold refined by fire rids the dross and makes it purer (I Peter 1:7). I think of this passage in Proverbs 24:10, "If you faint in the day of adversity, Your strength is small" in connection to that which I am now discussing. There was a time when many of the disciples of the Lord left Him and He asked His own apostles, "Do you also want to go away?" It was then that Simon Peter answered, "Lord, to whom shall we go? You have the words of eternal life. "Also we have come to believe and know You are the Christ, the Son of the living God" (John 6:66-69). It is in the valleys of life that I need Him. He has never forsaken me and why should I forsake him. He is my Rock and my salvation. He is my Hightower; my shelter in the time of the storms. He gives me comfort in the night. His strength is greatly manifested in weakness. I often requested of Him to bestow His grace upon me so that I might see the sun beyond the overcast and the silver lining behind every cloud. And His grace is sufficient for me. A moving verse is found in James 4:6 which is a simple but a very profound statement, "But He gives more grace." Listen to this precious promise of our Heavenly Father, "Call upon Me in the day of trouble; I will deliver you, and you shall glorify me" (Psalm 50:15). The following hymn explains best what I am trying to say:

HE GIVETH MORE GRACE

He giveth more grace as our burdens grow greater,
He sendeth more strength as our labors increase;
To added afflictions He addeth His mercy,
To multiplied trials He multiplies peace.
When we have exhausted our store of endurance,
When our strength has failed ere the day is half done,
When we reach the end of our hoarded resources
Our father's full giving is only begun.
Fear not that thy need shall exceed His provision,
Our God ever yearns His resources to share;
Lean hard on the arm everlasting, availing,
The Father both thee and thy load will upbear.
His love has no limits, His grace has no measure,
His power no boundary known unto men;
For out of His infinite riches in Jesus
He giveth, and giveth, and giveth again.

— Annie J. Flint (1866-1932)
THE TRIUMPHANT STORY of ANNIE JOHNSON FLINT By Rowland V. Bingham

Section 4

MARRIAGE AND THE FAMILY

A FATHER'S FAILURE

"O my son Absalom—my son, my son Absalom—if only I had died in your place! O Absalom my son, my son!" (2 Samuel 18:33) Here is an exceedingly bitter cry. It is one of the saddest passages in the entire Bible. One would think that such was the cry of a mother who had lost the dearest thing on earth to her, a child. But no, it is the bitter cry of a man weeping for his son who had been killed. Absalom, the son of David had been slain while leading his forces against his father, the King of Israel. David had instructed Joab and his men to deal gently with his son (2 Samuel 18:5). But they slew the young man anyway (2 Samuel 18:14, 15). In the rearing of his son Absalom David was indeed a failure.

But wherein had David failed? We must be fair and note that in other ventures in life, David was not a failure. In fact in many things he was very successful. We observe that David rose rapidly in rank. We saw him first as a shepherd boy. He possessed a brilliant mind and fortitude. As a courageous lad he went out to meet and defeat the great giant Goliath in battle. David was a many sided man. He was not only a shepherd but a poet, a singer and later to become the King of Israel. A man like this will usually do good in any situation. While as king much wealth was accumulated in the treasury. The enemies had been defeated. The time was called the 'Golden Age of Israel.' David provided the proper foundation upon which his son Solomon eventually erected the temple. But in what did this successful man fail?

He failed as a father. David paid a great price for his success. When David looked over his life he saw it too. It cost him many hours of sorrow. Our text in 2 Samuel 18:31-33 reveals only one time of his weeping. His son was killed while rebelling against him. Many fathers are like David today. They too will pay the price. Some men are successful at building fortunes but completely unsuccessful at building men.

One might ask: why did David take this failure so hard? Because of his tender love for his son he had lost. Fathers are not supposed to do much weeping it is often thought by misinformed individuals. We should understand

141

however that often fathers are just as devoted to their children as mothers. David also takes his failure hard because his loss was without remedy. We may blunder in some things and correct them next time but there is no next time in the rearing of children. David could have said, "I would make Absalom a different boy if I could only have my time over with him." No wonder he cried. David took failure hard because he knew he lost his son hopelessly. Absalom was gone for good. He could not be brought back again. Death always produces this feeling when we lose loved ones. David lost his son needlessly. If he had been the right kind of a father, perhaps he could have saved his son. Many a father carries this accusation in his bosom.

The story is told about a father who took his little child into the field one afternoon and it being a hot day he laid down in the shade of a beautiful tree. The little child ran about gathering wild flowers and little bits of grass and coming to his father and would cry, "Look how pretty!" At last the father fell asleep and while he was sleeping the child wandered away. When the father awoke his first thought was, "Where is my child?" He looked around but he could not see him. He shouted at the top of his voice but all he heard was an echo. Running to a little hill he looked around and shouted again. There was no response. Then going to a steep cliff at some distance he looked down and there, far below on the rocks and briars he saw the mangled form of his precious child. He rushed to the spot and took up the lifeless corpse and hugged it to his bosom and accused himself of being the murderer of his child. While he was sleeping and neglecting for a just a short time his child had wandered over the precipice.

Such depicts so many fathers and mothers today. While their children are wandering closer and closer to the edge of the cliff and to certain destruction, parents are asleep regarding the moral and spiritual welfare of their offsprings. Often parents contribute to the downfall of their children because of their own way of life. Some fathers drink, gamble and are unfaithful to their marriage vows; and then they wonder what went wrong in the rearing of their children. King David was crushed beneath the burden of thought that he had lost his son Absalom for all eternity. It should be noted that providing the daily necessities for one's family is not enough. More important is the rearing of children in the nurture and admonition of the Lord (Ephesians 6:4). Money may provide for the body but not for the soul. Money may buy groceries but not character.

Another question to ponder is why was David a failure as a father? When John was born, the question was raised, "What kind of child will this be?"

(Luke 1:66) It is required of parents to train children in the way of the Lord (Proverbs 22:6). David undoubtedly shifted his responsibilities to someone else. He had many obligations, cares, troubles and political problems but he should not have neglected his son. Perhaps Absalom never thought about going to David with his broken toy and he never thought about going to him with his broken heart. David gave him everything but himself. Many fathers are like that today. David in his sins concerning Bathsheba could have influenced his son, adversely so. David repented and returned from the far country of sin but Absalom never came back from that land of sorrow.

Fathers, you should consider your responsibilities toward your children before it is eternally too late. Lead your loved ones in the way of the Savior Jesus Christ. Make every effort to save your family from sin and an everlasting separation from the God of heaven. You cannot afford to lose your sons and daughters.

ARE ALL THE CHILDREN IN?

When our children reached the age of sixteen and began to date, my wife and I began to stay awake later at night. It was a new experience for us to see a son drive out of the driveway with a relatively new car and wonder if either the son or the car would make it back in one piece; or, to see our young daughter being ushered by a young man to an awaiting vehicle in the driveway. We, of course, made a number of mistakes in dealing with our children as they matured through their teenage years; however, here are some suggestions that will be beneficial both to parents and to teenagers.

1. Teach your children the high moral standard of purity revealed in the Holy Scriptures. This information will arm them against such sins as fornication and drunkenness.

2. Keep the door of communication open between you and your children. Parents must conduct themselves in such a manner as to motivate trust in the hearts of young people toward parents. The attitudes of self-righteousness, perfection and distrust will never get the door of communication opened in the first place.

3. Do not condemn the whole child because of one mistake. What if the Lord acted like many parents in this matter? We would all stand condemned.

4. Know the young person your son/daughter is dating. You know that evil companionships corrupt good morals.

5. Know where your young people are going on a date. This is the parent's right. In case of an accident, you would be able to locate them easier.

6. Know when they will return. It may be old-fashioned, but I believe young people need rules and regulations in this area of their lives. Surely both parties involved can agree upon a suitable time. It is a policy in our home that if a child is to be out later than expected a telephone call is to be forthcoming.

7. Parents should trust their children unless and until they are proven unworthy of trust. Honesty and fairness in dealing with each other contribute greatly to complete trust.

8. Pray for the physical and spiritual welfare of your children. Some parents manifest little, if any, concern about their children's dating habits and associates. The providential care of the Heavenly Father is with His children as they live for Him.

9. Parents must recognize the importance of setting the proper example before their children. Young people quickly detect our saying one thing and doing another. If you tell your children not to drink alcoholic beverages, you had better set the proper example for them to emulate.

10. Parents need to tell their teenagers that they love them. We all perhaps have the seen the sign that asks, "Have you hugged your child today?" There is no substitute for parental love. If we truly love our children, we will not permit them to have their way all the time.

11. Be willing to admit your mistakes. We encourage our children to confess their wrongs, but parents are very slow to do the same when in the wrong. It isn't easy to say anytime, "I'm sorry, I have made a mistake," especially with reference to our children. But if we will, our children will respect us for doing so. Many parents project an attitude that they have never made a mistake and expect perfection from their children.

12. There are two qualities needed among parents in the rearing of their children—especially teenagers. They are patience and understanding. Some parents are woefully lacking in both of these characteristics. We cannot expect our children to mature in a short time. During the years when a son/daughter is struggling to become an adult, scores of mistakes will be made. They will face problems peculiar to this age. That is when parents must learn to be patient and understanding.

13. Remember that the material things of life are the least important. We make a mistake by showering our children with everything they want. Love, happiness, emotional stability and a sense of security cannot be bought with a car, beautiful clothes and plenty of money.

14. All your efforts to rear your children in the way of the Lord will bring happiness in later years. It is then that you can truly say, "It has been worth it." If you plant a peach orchard, it takes years before you can enjoy the fruits of your labor.

Did you know that one of the sweetest sounds in the world was the opening and closing of the kitchen door? Often at night, while waiting for the children, my wife and I would be happy to hear them come in one at a time, opening and closing the kitchen door. Often my wife would ask, "Are all the children in?" And I would say, "Yes, all the children are in."

By the grace of God, as we reach our heavenly home, and as the ceaseless ages roll by, it will be wonderful to be able to answer her question, "Are all the children in?" With an answer, "Yes, they are all in." Let us make every effort to live right in obedience to God and carry our children with us to that place prepared for the redeemed.

ARE YOU MARRIED?

My wife and I were eating lunch recently at a local restaurant. The server was a petite pretty young lady, exceptionally nice, and attended to our every need. I said to Virginia that I hoped she was as good and pleasant in every way as she was in her demeanor toward us. As we were finishing our lunch and she approached our table, I noticed some kind of ring on her left hand so I asked, "Are you married?" There was a slight pause before she answered and then she replied, "No, I suppose you could say I am engaged. My boy friend and I have been living together for five years and we have one child." While I was disappointed, I was not surprised. I offered to marry them for just a free lunch but she refused my offer.

The complete disregard toward the teaching of the Word of God concerning marriage is not a gray matter. It is either black or white. Living together without the marriage vows is a violation of God's law; or, it really doesn't matter at all because there are no rules governing such cohabitation of unmarried couples. Sad to say, married couples are now in the minority in this country. People who are living in what the Bible calls fornication should straighten out their own lives before condemning couples of the same sex who are marrying one another; now having said that, it is to be understood in no uncertain terms that practicing homosexuality is not a gray matter. Either it is condemned in the Holy Scriptures or it is allowed. That is to say, it is either a black or white issue. There is no neutral position.

And when it comes to politics and the leaders in our national government, it is not a black or white issue where race or ethnicity is concerned. The reason being, I heard a white leader say that he saw nothing wrong with men marrying men and women marrying women. Soon after that I heard another national leader who was black say that he condoned 'gay marriages'. The real issue therefore is whether or not the Word of God commends or condemns such life styles and then it becomes a black or white issue morally speaking and not a gray one. Bible believers understand God's design for marriage, that is, one man for one woman.

You perhaps have noticed that I have not given all the biblical passages that speak out against homosexuality. That can be done in another article. It is rather useless to quote and/or read scriptures to someone who does not respect the inspired Word of God. The unbelieving world cares very little, if any, for the teachings of the Bible. How would you react to someone quoting verses to you from the Quran (Koran)? The belief of an individual determines his manner of life. Carnality produces a perverted way of living in the individuals who choose not to believe in God, His Son and in His Holy Word.

How sad it is that people who know what the scriptures teach on the sanctity of marriage but choose instead to live in all manner of sexual immorality. The same principle applies today in this important matter regarding the individuals who do not "receive the love of the truth, that they might be saved." A great man of God wrote: "And for this reason God will send them strong delusion, that they should believe the lie, that they all may be condemned who did not believe the truth but had pleasure in unrighteousness" (From the ancient writings of Paul as found in the book of 2 Thessalonians 2:10, 11). "Righteousness exalts a nation, But sin is a reproach to any people" (Proverbs 14:34).

CELEBRATING OUR 55TH WEDDING ANNIVERSARY
(August 19, 2005)

My, it was a hot summer evening (without AC) on Friday, August 19, 1955 in the church building in Wildwood, Florida when Virginia and I made our vows to "love and cherish one another" and to live together "until death us do part" 'They say' that a group of singers sang some beautiful songs but I don't think I heard them. I barely remember brother Orvel Boyd saying something about marriage and asking us to repeat the vows that he read. But he must have really 'tied the knot' because by God's grace and Providence we are still living together as husband and wife. And that says a great deal for Virginia. Bless her heart. We were both twenty years old and we had completed our sophomore year at Alabama Christian College and now I was marrying her without any financial security. I was as poor 'as Job's turkey' (and I understand that is really poor). I even had to borrow a car from a friend to make the trip to Wildwood because the old 1948 Plymouth was not mechanically able to make such a long trip from Montgomery. It had to be love for such a lovely lady like Virginia to marry a poor boy like me because it could not have been for money since I had very little and without a promise of additional funds. But the Lord God has blessed us and provided for us over the past fifty-five years. He has given us three sons and a daughter, along with nine grandchildren. And we are still working regularly with a congregation of Jesus Christ. Perhaps our example will be a source of encouragement to young couples and the unmarried men and women who plan to marry and that is, you can have a successful marriage in this modern age when marital infidelity and divorce are rampant by being guided by the true manual for marriage and that is God's Word.

The 1947 trailer was only 28 feet long and 8 feet wide. You talk about close communion! It was so small that I had to go outside to change my mind. One night it was raining and the roof was leaking right over my bed and a rain drop hit me on my knee. I started to write a song with the title: "Rain Drops

Falling on My Bed" but I never did. I probably would have made plenty of money if I had written it that night. The 'front door' could not be locked which concerned my new bride. The water to the kitchen came through a water hose from the adjacent house and we had to use the bathroom in the Home EC building which was next to our 'new home' on the campus of Alabama Christian College in Montgomery, Alabama. But God has been good to us and He has blessed us abundantly. We are now rich materially and spiritually. We praise Him and thank Him every day!!

CULTIVATING MARITAL LOVE

A few years ago I visited a very fine Christian couple who lived in a community several miles from my home. After a cordial welcome and a conversation on a variety of subjects, the husband informed me of the problems existing in their son's marriage. As I listened, it was easy to detect the deep sadness that filled the hearts of these parents. This brother mentioned that he had been concerned for some time since he thought that his son and daughter- in-law had not been trying to improve their relationship. He said, "Love that is not cultivated will soon die." I could not forget that statement that was filled with many pertinent points regarding the necessity of permitting love to mature.

In oriental countries a custom has been in times past for the parents to select their children's future mates. It seems that the couple enters marriage with a nominal amount of affection but with the passing of the years that love is cultivated and matures. Whereas so many of our young folk in our society get married in the heat of passion and their love subsides in a few years. The present divorce rate is proof that there is a wholesale failure in our marriages in this country. There is real need to cultivate marital love.

Webster's New Word Dictionary defines the word *cultivate* as follows:

1. *to prepare and use soil, land, etc for growing crops; till*
2. *to break up the surface soil around (plants) in order to destroy weeds, prevent crusting, and preserve moisture...*
3. *to improve or develop (plants) by various horticultural techniques*
4. *to improve by care, training; or study; refine (to cultivate one's mind)*
5. *to seek to develop familiarity with; give one's attention to; pursue.*

Especially in this analogy, attention should be given to definition number two, that is, "to break up the surface soil around (plants) in order to destroy weeds, prevent crusting and preserve moisture."

Certainly in marriage there is the constant need to eliminate the negatives that would destroy the proper relationship between the husband and the wife.

151

Every effort must be made to keep the marriage from "crusting". Love will become hard if not cultivated. Also care must be given in preserving and maturing marital love. This requires the obtaining of wisdom; knowledge and training to develop (cultivate) this love. A very wise man wrote: "The plainest man that can convince a woman that he is really in love with her has done more to make her in love with him than the handsomest man, if he can produce no such conviction. For the love of a woman is a shoot, not a seed. And flourishes most vigorously only when grafted on that love which is rooted in the breast of another" (Charles Caleb Colton, 1780-1832, GIGA Quotes). I want to mention some suggestions that will enable marital love to be cultivated and to mature with the passing of the years.

First of all, husbands and wives should learn early in their marriage relationship to give themselves totally to each other. Love is something that must be given away in order to receive it. This is true in every aspect of marriage including the sexual relationship (See I Corinthians 7:1-6). Marriage is not a fifty-fifty relationship but it is the giving of oneself one hundred percent to making the marriage successful, happy and enjoyable.

Second, there is the need to be unselfish in marriage. Paul wrote that loves "does not seek its own" (I Corinthians 13:5). It would be wonderful if each partner sought the other's good and welfare at all times. But if one is not careful self will be the focal point in every deed. And this is when trouble arises. Selfishness suppresses service for others. It is probable that most marital problems can be traced to this root sin of self-centeredness.

Third, love should be expressed both by words and actions. While it is good for the husband to bring an occasionally gift home for his wife, however, there is no substitute for those beautiful words, "I love you." Often the husband is reluctant to verbalize his feelings for his wife. True love can also be best understood by its characteristics. Henry Drummond mentioned several of them in his book, "The Greatest Thing In the World." They are: "Patience, kindness, generosity, humility, courtesy, unselfishness, good temper, guilelessness, and sincerity". Of course the apostle Paul wrote of such characteristics of love nearly two thousand years ago as is found in I Corinthians 13:4-8).

Fourth, one needs to learn not to hold grudges. There is real trouble brewing when a tea kettle cannot release the steam that has been created by the heat of a fire. A husband or a wife who harbors resentment will eventually explode emotionally. The advice of the apostle Paul is worthy of heeding in the marriage relationship: "Be angry, and do not sin: do not let the sun go down on your wrath" (Ephesians 4:26). Sure there will be disagreements in marriage but how beautiful it is when there is forgiveness and reconciliation. When one has been wrong there is the need to say, "I am sorry". And the response should be, "I forgive you."

Fifth, before problems have become so great and seemingly insurmountable, help should be sought from a trusted friend. This assistance may be found in the person of an elder, a preacher or a Christian friend. There may be the need of seeking the help of someone who is trained professionally in marriage counseling. The institution of marriage is so precious in the sight of God that every effort should be made to save this relationship.

In closing, the point should be emphasized that when two people truly love the Lord, their love for one another will become stronger. The reason being, when the husband and wife draw nearer to God, they are drawn nearer to one another. This is a fact that cannot be denied. The result is inevitable.

I assisted in the funeral service on one occasion of a man who, had he lived one more week, he and his wife would have celebrated their sixty-sixth wedding anniversary. How wonderful that two people could learn to live together for such a long time. They had truly cultivated their love over the years to the degree that only death could separate them. That was exactly what God had planned in His design for marriage (See Matthew 19:4-6; I Corinthians 7:39). My wife and I have been married for fifty-eight years. I can truly say with all sincerity that I love her more now than I did when we were joined together in a simple but beautiful wedding ceremony on a very warm August night in 1955. Our love for one another has brought us closer together as we have faced many difficulties and disappointments as well as the good times along life's way. There are scores of couples who will testify to the fact that marriage can be successful.

And they should be examples worthy of emulation by the young couples who have just begun their journey in life together as husband and wife.

THE DEATH OF A CHILD

First of all there was the news of the deaths of eight students in Enterprise, Alabama when a tornado destroyed their high school building. Then there was the bus accident in Atlanta, Georgia that took the lives of four college students as well as the bus drivers. Later it was learned that the fifth student died due to the injuries suffered in the terrible accident. One of the greatest fears that parents have is the possibility that a child might be killed in some accident or that some disease might take the life of a beloved son or daughter. I remember well when the telephone rang late one night and a close Christian friend informed me that his fifteen year old daughter had been killed in an automobile wreck. It was not an easy task to face the parents who were dear friends of mine and members of the local church where I was serving as a preacher. I went with the father so he could identify his precious child. It was a heart rendering experience. It was thirty four years ago that I had to go alone to identify my baby brother, age 35, who had been killed by a car so I would be able to tell my mother that it was indeed her precious son. My mother had already lost her oldest son in World War II at the tender age of 19. Most parents would be willing to precede their children in death. It seems so unnatural that the younger generation should die before the older one.

One of the students killed by the tornado was a member of the church of Christ and active in the youth group in the local congregation. She was only sixteen years old. Her picture in the newspaper showed her to be a very attractive young lady and her smile depicted her as being one with an outstanding personality. Her friends in school had many nice things to say about her. A gospel preacher and Chaplin for the Enterprise Police Department identified her when she was pulled from the rubbish of the building. He and the youth minister had many good things to say about her at the funeral service. I know personally that speaking at the funeral service of a young person is very difficult because of the emotions involved, not only as a friend and preacher but as a parent. It is easy to "weep with those who weep" (Romans 12:15) because you know that but by the grace of God that could be you looking at the lifeless body of your child in the casket. Young people do not fully comprehend the concern that parents have with their safety and welfare and cannot until they themselves become parents. A friend of the teenager who was killed spoke highly of her and the one thing that stood out in my mind was this: "She had a smile that could brighten anyone's day", and, "How she loved God and how she wanted everyone to know him, too." Now that last statement means all the world to Christian parents. How wonderful that in her youth this teenager had remembered her Creator (Ecclesiastes 12:1, 2). In their great loss her parents know that they cannot recall their daughter back from the grave but they have the blessed assurance that they can go where she now resides and that is with the Lord (2 Samuel 12:23). I do not know how Christian parents deal with the loss of a child, regardless of his/her age, who dies unprepared to meet the Lord in eternity. I remember hearing of a well known gospel preacher in my home state of Georgia whose son was burned to death in a hotel fire in the city of Atlanta.

His son was not a Christian. It was said that the father's hair turned grey in a short period of time. And there was the story of faithful gospel preacher in another state whose unbelieving son was killed while engaged in an unlawful activity. It was reported that the preacher said mournfully and in deep sorrow that "while I was busy conducting Bible studies in various homes I neglected my own son." Please forgive the personal experiences but when my three siblings died, the main concern I had was whether or not they were children of God. I visited my last brother one week before he suffered a hard death. I knew, because of the circumstances, this would most likely be the last time I would see him in this life. As I embraced him and as we both wept, I said to him that I could accept his death but only if he was right with the Lord. I spoke at the funeral of my brother and I was able to do so because he had fallen asleep in Jesus.

I would encourage all parents to give their lives to Jesus and serve Him faithfully and bring your children up "in the training and admonition of the Lord" (Ephesians 6:4). Children should come to realize that Christian parents never grow too old but they continue to pray for their physical and spiritual welfare. The old familiar song, "Will the Circle Be Unbroken" has a real meaning to it when family members enter eternity. All Christian parents desire to go heaven and take their children with them. It is by experience and factual knowledge that we understand that life is so fragile and death is a certainty (Hebrews 9:27). The grim reaper is no respecter of person or age. There is no assurance of tomorrow (Proverbs 27:1). It is only in the Son of God that we have eternal life (I John 5:11, 12). Jesus Christ died on Calvary that we could "have redemption through His blood, the forgiveness of sins, according to the riches of His grace" (Ephesians 1:7). He gave His life for us and the least we can do is to give our lives to Him.

ELI, A GOOD MAN BUT A BAD FATHER

One unique aspect of the Bible is that the inspired writers pointed out the weak characteristics as well as the strong in various individuals. It is revealed that Peter, a pillar of the early church, denied the Lord (Matthew 27:69-75). David, a man after God's own heart, committed adultery and had a man killed (2 Samuel 11:1-5, 14-21). Even the great man of faith, Abraham, spoke a falsehood regarding his wife Sarah (Genesis 12:13). Thus it is not strange that the Holy Scriptures reveal to us the faults of Eli, a high priest of God, as well as his good points. Let us now consider the positive side and strengths of this great man.

First of all, Eli was a descendant of Aaron through Ithamar, the youngest of his sons (compare Leviticus 10:1, 2, 12 with I Kings 2:27; 2 Samuel 8:17 and I Chronicles 24:3). He was the first of the line of Ithamar who held the office of high priest. Besides being a high priest he was also a judge. In this capacity he judged Israel for forty years (I Samuel 4:18). He took a genuine interest in the training of the young boy Samuel. It was Eli who told Hannah that her petition for a male child had been granted by the Lord God (I Samuel 1:17). His submissive attitude toward the judgment of God against him must also be noted. When informed by Samuel he simply stated, "It is the Lord. Let Him do what seems good to Him" (I Samuel 3:18). In so many ways Eli was a very good man; however, there was an area in which he as a failure and that was as a father.

The sons of Eli, Hophni and Phinehas brought shame and ruin to their father and sin to a degenerate priesthood. They knew not the Lord (I Samuel 2:12). Legally they had the right to take a portion of meat from the people but they went beyond this and even extracted meat which was to be offered as a sacrifice to God (See Leviticus 7:31-35; 8:31; II Chronicles 35:13). Their legal due as priests was the right shoulder and the wave breast, consecrated to God by the burning of fat upon the altar (Leviticus 3:5; 7:31, 34). Such action by these sons of Eli distressed the people. Their sin was flagrant and vile, calculated to awaken the intense disgust and abhorrence of every pure and reverent mind.

They were the basest of sinners in that they, as priests, committed adultery with the women who served in the house of God (I Samuel 2:22). In their sinful ways, they encouraged others to do the same (I Samuel 2:24).

Eli was a failure as a father. The primary responsibility of rearing children in the way of the Lord is in the home. Actually, Paul places the duty on the shoulders of the father who is the head of the home (Ephesians 6:4). A great fault today is that many fathers do not fulfill this obligation. Children often associate with evil companions who influence them in a worldly and sinful manner (I Corinthians 15:33). Eli's sons were not strong enough to counteract the evil tendencies of the age and their father erred in not taking precautions adequate to the occasion. Many children of good men sometimes become godless because of the absorption of parents in public affairs and business. Children learn more of Christianity from what they observe of their parents probably more than any other source. On the other hand there is no greater encouragement for a child to despise Christianity than a discovery of insincerity and hypocrisy in the lives of their parents.

An outstanding weakness of Eli was that while knowing the sins of his sons he did not restrain them (I Samuel 3:13). A man may possess many amiable qualities and be on the whole a good man and yet be mocked by some defect which mars his character, prevents his usefulness, and makes him the unintentional cause of much mischief. Eli's reproof was not administered in proper time. Early childhood is the time to teach and to train. A little plant may be easily rooted up but when it has grown into a tree it can only be removed by extraordinary efforts. Eli was weak, gentle and easy-going. He should have disciplined his sons before it became impossible to do so. It was said of Adonijah, the son of Haggith, that "his father had not rebuked him at any time by saying, "Why have you done so" (I Kings 1:6)? It would seem that the reproof Eli gave his sons was not given with sufficient earnestness. After learning of their terrible sins, he said to them, "Why do you do such things? For I hear of your evil dealings from all the people. "No, my sons! For it is not a good report that I hear. You make the Lord's people transgress" (I Samuel 2:23, 24). His reproof was not pointed enough and specific. It was too general and in indefinite terms, just those things he had heard that his sons had done. There seemed to be no real sufficient determination to correct the evil ways of Hophni and Phinehas. Someone has said, "Indulgence never produces gratitude or love in the heart of a child."

Another observation of the reproof given by Eli was that it was not followed by adequate chastisement. It was specifically stated that his sons "did not heed the voice of their father..." (I Samuel 2:25). The Law of Moses in the case of disobedient children was very severe (Deuteronomy 21:18-21). Eli seemingly made no effort to prevent the continuance of their evil ways. Eli as a father, high priest, and judge was guilty of disobedience (I Samuel 3:13). Hophni and Phinehas were hardened in heart and rebellious in spirit. Solomon wrote that "Harsh discipline is for him who forsakes the way, And he who hates correction will die" (Proverbs 15:10).

The ultimate end for Eli and his sons is recorded in I Samuel 4:10-18. Hophni and Phinehas were killed in battle. Eli being an old man fell and broke his neck and died when he heard about their deaths. Also the ark of God was taken by the Philistines. There was shame, degradation and ruin for all. Eventually the priesthood was taken away from the house of Eli (I Samuel 2:27- 31; I Kings 2:27).

Parents can save themselves from many heartaches and sorrows in later life by following God's instruction to bring up their children in the way of the Lord. May God abundantly and richly bless all those parents who are endeavoring to this very thing in this crooked and perverse generation.

FLAUNTING FORNICATION

No, it wasn't a young husband who had just learned that his wife had given birth to their first child and he was so excited that he proudly exclaimed to all in the waiting room that he was the father of a baby boy. No, that was not the case at all; rather, it was a young man who stood in front of TV cameras, raising his right arm and with glee in his eyes announced to the whole world that he was the father of child born to a former Playboy Bunny. His supporters shouted with approval. You see there had been a question as to who the father was of this baby which had been born out of wedlock. The mother had died suddenly and she had not revealed which man had fathered the child. It may have been the case that she really did not know herself who the father was.

A famous movie actor divorced his wife and began to co-habit with another movie star. There was a mix feeling about these two well known actors. What about the hurt that his ex-wife was experiencing over their marriage breakup but soon the ugliness was forgotten and now the unmarried couple is interviewed on national television and is praised for their involvement in the making of another movie. Forget about the fact that they are unmarried and are living in violation of the marriage laws given by the Creator of mankind.

Then there is the case of a rich heiress who videoed herself and her partner committing fornication. I am reminded of the example of the Israelite who was very brazen in bringing his Midianite woman before Moses and the congregation of the children of Israel and taking her into a tent and committed fornication with her. It was then that Phinehas the son of Eleazer, the son of Aaron took a javelin and thrust both of them through with it. Because of his action the plague which God had sent among the people was stopped; however, twenty-four thousand Israelites died due to their committing harlotry with the women of Moab (Numbers 25:1-9). Webster's New World Dictionary defines 'flaunt' as meaning, "1. to make a gaudy, ostentatious, conspicuous, impudent, or defiant display. 2. to flutter or wave freely. To show proudly, defiantly or impudently (to flaunt one's guilt..." Such acts as displayed by the rich heiress and the Israelite showed contempt for God's laws regarding the need to avoid the sin of fornication.

Recently in a major city in a western state the local school system invited a psychologist to speak to students in the twelve to fourteen age groups about sexual mores. He encouraged the boys and girls to engage in sex in their young age. This educated person explained more in detail as to what he meant when he encouraged these youth to be active in sexual exploitation when he said that it could be between male and female or of the same sex. It really didn't matter to him as long as they enjoyed themselves. In other words there should be no restrictions regarding with whom and how it was to be done. Now wasn't that nice of the school to require these young students to hear such advice from a person of education and influence. "The Greek word for 'fornication' (porneia) could include any sexual sin committed after the betrothal contract. ...In Biblical usage, 'fornication' can mean any sexual congress outside monogamous marriage. It thus includes not only premarital sex, but also adultery, homosexual acts, incest, remarriage after un-Biblical divorce, and sexual acts with animals, all of which are explicitly forbidden in the law as given through Moses (Leviticus 20:10-21). Christ expanded the prohibition against adultery to include even sexual lusting (Matthew 5:28)." (Dr. Henry M. Morris, "Fornication," in ChristianAnswers.net at: http://www.christiananswers.net/). How sad that some educators in our public school system would actually encourage our children to violate the Word of God regarding sexual impurities.

We have been informed that married people are in the minority. Couples who live together without conforming to the marriage laws are more numerous than the couples who are legally married. Unmarried couples living together have increased ten times over the past few years than in previous ones.

We live in a world where darkness reigns. In this so called 'Christian Nation' sin abounds profusely. Where there is no law to be obeyed regarding morality each person can do as he/she pleases. Virginity went out of style many years ago. Our youth are being taught by precepts and examples that sex is acceptable outside of the marriage relationship.

Our modern day society is much like the pagans in the Roman Empire when the apostle Paul wrote the book of Romans. He described in chapter 1, verse 29, the immorality of the people, "Being filled with all unrighteousness, sexual immorality,, wickedness, covetousness, maliciousness; full of envy, murder, strife, deceit, evil-mindedness; they are; whisperers..." Even among members of the church in Corinth there was a brother who was guilty of fornication in that he was living with his father's wife (his step-mother, no doubt) (I Corinthians 5:1).

The believer in Christ is taught that the body is sacred and should be used only in a pure manner in serving the Lord. Paul writes in I Corinthians 6:13, 18, "Meats for the belly, and the belly for meats: but God shall destroy both it and them. Now the body is not for fornication, but for the Lord; and the Lord for the body." "Flee fornication. Every sin that a man doeth is without the body; but he that committeth fornication sinneth against his own body" (KJV). Fornication is described as a work of the flesh and they that practice such sin shall not "inherit the kingdom of God" (Galatians 5:19, 20). We are taught to "Mortify therefore your members which are upon the earth, Fornication, uncleanness..." (KJV, Colossians 3:5). Paul instructs the Christian to "abstain from fornication" (KJV, I Thessalonians 4:3). In Jude 1:7 we have this warning, "Even as Sodom and Gomorrha, and the cities about them in like manner, giving themselves over to fornication, and going after strange flesh, are set forth for an example, suffering the vengeance of eternal fire" (KJV).

The apostle Paul exhorted Timothy to "Flee also youthful lusts; but pursue righteousness, faith, love, peace with those who call on the Lord out of a pure heart" (2 Timothy 2:22). This is the opposite of the culture in which we find ourselves as Christians. The believer in Jesus will make every effort to keep oneself pure in heart and body. We cannot expect citizens of the kingdom of darkness to comply with the teachings of the Word of God regarding the purity of life. In Hebrews 12:14 we read, "Pursue peace with all people, and holiness, without which no one will see the Lord." In the Sermon on the Mount, Jesus spoke regarding purity when he said, "Blessed are the pure in heart, For they shall see God" (Matthew 5:8). A pure heart makes for a holy way of life. As one thinks in his heart he becomes (Proverbs 23:7). It is therefore most important that parents teach their children regarding sexual sins and the need to keep oneself pure. Elders must make sure that biblical lessons are taught by preachers and teachers regarding these important matters so that our young people will be properly informed of God's desire for them to be pure both in heart and body.

GODLY FATHERS

One of life's greatest blessings and challenges for a man is fatherhood. This relationship involves the greatest joys and demands the best one has to give and often will include many sorrows. A godly father loves his wife and is loyal to his marital vows (Ephesians 5:25). He desires the best for his children. A father is industrious. He labors to provide for his family and the needs of others who lack the material things of life (I Timothy 5:8; Ephesians 4:28).

The greatest contribution a father can make to his family is leadership in spiritual matters. In every age, the head of the family has been required of God to provide the proper direction regarding religious training. Modern fathers are most likely to leave this responsibility to the wife and mother. However, Paul exhorted: "And you fathers, provoke not your children to wrath: but nurture them in the chastening and admonition of the Lord' (Ephesians 6:4). It is a tremendous requirement to make sure one's children are taught of God but the rewards are everlasting. A Christian father may not be able to give very much materially to his children but the legacy of having a father who loved his family and the Lord, surpasses everything else. The greatest inheritance a Christian father can leave is one that is rich in faith in God and the Lord Jesus Christ.

We should never underestimate the love that a father possesses in his heart for his children. His emotions may not be as noticeable as the mother; yet, the feelings are just as deep. Most fathers would give their lives on behalf of their families. Their hearts are filled with deep gratitude when they witness their children succeeding in life. The Christian father rejoices greatly when his children obey the gospel of Jesus Christ. My father will be remembered for being a fine Christian gentleman. Also, the legacy of having a good name has meant more to me than all the riches of this world. It was the wise man of old who wrote: "A good name is to be chosen rather than great riches, Loving favor rather than silver and gold" (Proverbs 22:1); and, "A good name is better than precious ointment..." (Ecclesiastes 7:1).

Godly fathers are rare in this modern society. But, we should always be thankful for the ones who are. Truly, you are blessed indeed if you have/had a Christian father who placed Christ first in his life. His influence in your life and even in the lives of his grandchildren will be felt for many years to come. Say, have you hugged your father recently?

DEAR OLD DAD

"So often we praise our mothers here and merit all their ways.
We so ignore the fact that Dad he, too, deserves some praise.
Who strives to earn the daily bread? To keep all healthy—glad?
Isn't he that gets so little praise and that is dear old Dad.
To praise our mothers, that is good (this they may deserve)
Yet why so slack in praising Dad and keep in reserve?
Let's measure their equalities—give merits, praise, when due.
Start pinning laurels on your Dad, He's done a lot for you.

— *Eva Gilbert Shaver, The Speaker's Treasury of 400 Poems, Croft M. Pentz*

"IS THE YOUNG MAN SAFE?"

Absalom, son of David, king of Israel, had become an insurrectionist and was actually fighting against the armies of his father. David had commanded Joab, Abishai and Ittai, leaders of his forces to "deal gently for my sake with the young man, even with Absalom." Later, the story reveals that a messenger comes to King David from the battlefield. He is asked by a concerned father, "Is the young man Absalom safe?" Eventually, David learns of the death of his son and cries aloud, "O my son Absalom—my son, my son Absalom—if only I had died in your place! O Absalom my son, my son (II Samuel 18:29, 33). Today, we might ask the question, as did David, 'Is the young man safe?'

Youth must, first of all, answer that question. Man is a being of choice. Many of our youth are in trouble simply because they decided to be. Absalom was basically a selfish person. He felt that the world owned him something and he was out to collect. Such an attitude causes unhappiness. Jesus taught that true happiness comes from serving others. He declared, "Just as the Son of Man did not come to be served, but to serve, and to give His life a ransom for many." (Matthew 20:28). Paul exclaimed that he was a "debtor" to all men because he possessed the knowledge of the gospel of Christ (Romans 1:14). In matters of morality, the final decision has to be made by the individual. A person's decisions determine the direction in life one will travel and eventually his/her eternal destiny. One should seek strength and guidance from God in deciding what is right and wrong (II Timothy 3:16, 17; Philippians 4:13).

Second, one's associates contribute to the answer of the question, 'Is the young man safe?" In II Samuel 15:1-6, it is stated that Absalom stole the hearts (affections) of his fellowmen by offering them something that he could not give them. Friends exert a tremendous amount of influence upon a young person.

"Evil companionship corrupts good habits" is just as true today as when Paul wrote the statement in I Corinthians 15:33. Social pressure by one's peers often encourages wrongdoing. Youth must be especially careful in choosing bosom buddies. Even older people should make every effort to set the proper example before our youth. Often, by ungodly living, adults encourage adolescents to go astray.

Third, parents are more directly responsible than others for the spiritual safety of their sons and daughters. David made a journey to the far country of sin in the case of Uriah the Hittite and his wife, Bathsheba (II Samuel 11-12:15). David was truly penitent of his sins as is clearly taught in Psalms 51. However, there is no absolute way to measure the negative influence such sins had in the lives of his children, especially Absalom. Parents need to realize that their children look to them for guidance and example in matters pertaining to godly living. And yet, there are parents who sin in every conceivable manner and then wonder later in life how they went wrong in rearing their children. Many parents fail in providing spiritual training for their offsprings in spite of the Lord's instructions to "bring them up in the nurture and admonition of the Lord" (KJV, Ephesians 6:4). Delinquent parents contribute greatly to the downfall of youth and probably more so than any other source of influence in our society. 'Is the young man safe?' Consider seriously the question, 'Am I encouraging our young men and women to live right'?

LESSONS FOR PARENTS IN ECCLESIASTES 12:1

"Remember now your Creator in the days of your youth, Before the difficult days come, And the years draw near when you say, "I have no pleasure in time.""

This passage of scripture is ordinarily used in encouraging young people to remember God and to give their lives to the Lord; however, I believe there are several lessons contained in this text that would be applicable for parents.

First of all, parents should remember that children are not ours to rear as we choose to do so. The Psalmist declared," Behold children are a heritage from the Lord…" (Psalm 127:3). We should have the same attitude of Hannah when she made this vow to God, "O Lord of hosts, if You will indeed look on the affliction of Your maidservant and remember me, and not forget Your maidservant, but will give Your maidservant a male child, then I will give him to the Lord all the days of his life, and no razor shall come upon his head" (I Samuel 1:11). Our attitude should be same, that is, when God gives us children, we should give them back to Him by rearing them in the "training and admonition of the Lord" (Ephesians 6:4).

Second, youth is the time to teach our children of God and Jesus Christ. Their hearts are receptive and not filled with prejudice. Children trust their parents and they can be impressed with the teaching they receive from the Word of God. Jochebed, the mother of Moses, must have greatly influenced him while he was in her care. It was in his adulthood that this man of God made an important decision as is recorded in Hebrews 11:24-25, "By faith Moses, when he became of age, refused to be called the son of Pharaoh's daughter, choosing rather to suffer affliction with the people of God than to enjoy the passing pleasures of sin." Then there is the case of Timothy who was greatly influenced in his youth to give his life to Christ. The apostle wrote concerning who taught Timothy the Word of God as found in the book of 2 Timothy: "When I call to remembrance the genuine faith that is in you, which dwelt first in your grandmother Lois and your mother Eunice, and I am persuaded in you also' (2 Timothy 1:5). "And that from childhood you have known the Holy Scriptures, which are able to make you wise for salvation through faith which is in Christ Jesus" (2 Timothy 3:15).

Third, parents should realize that soon the difficult (evil) days will come. Parents will not always be around to help their children in making the decision as to what is right or wrong. It is when the child is at home that parents must prepare them to be able to face the "difficult days" when they are away from home. There is the example of a young soldier in the Far East when the time came for him and his buddies to have a period of 'rest and relaxation'. The decision was made by the majority of the soldiers to go to a town and commit sins of immorality and drunkenness. The young Christian soldier refused to follow the crowd because he remembered that his parents were praying for him and his safety. He also remembered the lessons from the Word of God relative to keeping his body pure (I Timothy 4:12).

Fourth, parents know their children are growing older and will soon leave home in a matter of a few years. It is during the age of innocence that children should be influenced to give their lives to the Lord. Youth is not the only time to "remember God" but it is the best time. The case is, the older a child becomes, the more difficult it is to make the decision to obey the gospel. The reason being, Satan can harden the heart through the deceitfulness of sin (Hebrews 3:12, 13).

In conclusion, the inspired writer states in this text that there is a point of no return. There are many influences such as higher education that can destroy the young person's belief in God as being the Creator of the universe and can cause one to become an agnostic or even an atheist. The practice of sin can hardened the heart of an individual that he will have no desire to repent and return to God. Because of the influence of evil companions, a son or a daughter can be led astray (I Corinthians 15:33). Many a young adult no longer has any pleasure in the former years when he was at home and associating with friends who were Christians and all were attending the various assemblies of the church. It is sad to say that not all stories about 'prodigal' children end well as did the one in Luke chapter fifteen.

A PIECE OF CLAY

I took a piece of plastic clay
And idly fashioned it one day,
And as my fingers pressed it still,
It moved and yielded at my will.
I came again when days were past;
The bit of clay was hard at last,
The form I gave it still it bore,
But I could change that form no more.
I took a piece of living clay,
And gently formed it day by day,
And molded with my power and art
A young child's soft and yielding heart.
I came again when days were gone;
It was a man I looked upon;
That early impress still he wore,
And I could change it never more.

— *Author Unknown*

MOTHERHOOD

It is always good to remember a godly mother. Jesus while on the cross of shame and suffering thought of His mother and instructed John to care for her after His death (John 19:26, 27). One of the sweetest words in any language is 'Mother'. A dictionary is not necessary to possess an understanding of such a meaningful term. Not all mothers are wives but they should be and not all wives are mothers but God permitting they can be. One of the primary purposes of marriage is the propagating of the human race (Genesis 1:27). The role of motherhood should never be taken lightly nor should the status of being a mother be made light of in this modern age. There is no greater relation for a woman to sustain in this life than being a Christian mother.

Perhaps the crowning act of creation by the Lord God was the forming of woman from the side of man. God saw that it was not good for man to be alone thus He gave to him a help suitable for him. Adam later named this woman "Eve" because she was the "mother of all living" (Genesis 2:18-25; 3:20). The wise man taught that "He who finds a wife finds a good thing"" and that "a prudent wife is from the Lord" (Proverbs 18:22; 19:14). In the bringing forth of a child the husband and wife truly become one flesh. There is the binding together of the two. Motherhood is the highest honor given to woman. No matter what else she may do in life it should be secondary to her being the kind of mother that God desires.

A mother is greatly responsible for the spiritual training of her children (Proverbs 22:6). Her influence is great for good or bad. Abraham Lincoln said of his mother, "All that I am, or hope to be, I owe to my angel mother". An old Spanish proverb states that "An ounce of mother is worth a pound of clergy."

Most of us have heard the old saying that "The hand that rocks the cradle rules the world". No doubt Queen Jezebel exerted a tremendous amount of evil influence on her husband Ahab and their wicked son Ahaziah (I Kings 16:30; 22:52, 53). Several years ago "Ma Barker" trained her sons to rob, steal and to kill. It was said that the infamous Nero had a murderess for a mother.

However, the Bible is replete with examples of godly mothers who influenced their loved ones to live for the Lord. Jochebed, the mother of Moses, guided that young heart in the right way because when he became an adult, he "refused to be called the son of Pharaoh's daughter; choosing rather to suffer affliction with the people of God than to enjoy the passing pleasure of sin." (Numbers 26:59; Hebrews 11:24, 25). No doubt students of the Bible know of the beautiful story of Hannah and how she received a son from the Lord. This wonderful woman had promised that she would give the child to the Lord as long as he lived (V.28). Hannah named her son Samuel. This young boy, at a tender age, was carried to the house of God to be taught and trained by Eli the high priest of God (I Samuel 1). Samuel became one of the truly outstanding leaders in Israel, serving God and his people as prophet, priest and judge. If there were more Hannahs in the homes there would be more preachers in the pulpits.

Jedidah was the wife of the wicked king Amon but she was also the mother of the young and good Josiah (2 Kings 22:1)). In contrast to the wickedness of his father it is said of Josiah that "he did that which was right in the sight of the Lord,, and walked in all the ways of his father David; he did not turn aside to the right hand or to the left" (2 Kings 22:2). We must conclude that his good mother and perhaps Jeremiah the prophet exerted a godly influence upon Josiah. Then consider the mother John the Baptist, Elizabeth, who walked righteous before God, "walking in all the commandments and ordinances of the Lord blameless" (Luke 1:6). We also learn that she was determined to name her son John (Luke1:13, 60) Mary, the mother of Jesus, was blessed greatly by having been chosen of God to give birth to the Son of God (Luke 1:42). Mary was a typical mother in many ways. For instance she treasured in her heart the things said about the baby Jesus and later the things which he said (Luke 2:19, 51). Finally we mention the grandmother and mother of Timothy. These two godly women, Lois and Eunice, had taught Timothy from his earliest childhood "the Holy Scriptures, which are able to make you wise for salvation through faith which is in Christ Jesus" (2 Timothy 1:5; 3:14, 15). These are some of the godly mothers mentioned in the Bible who are worthy of imitation by Christian mothers today.

A virtuous mother is industrious as is brought out by the passage of scripture in Proverbs 31:10-31. Certainly the daily chores of a mother are demanding. She is also considerate of the needs of others in her community. Dorcas was one who was "full of good works and charitable deeds" (Acts 9:36, 39). The widow who was to be enrolled by the church must have been "well reported for good work...if she has relieved the afflicted, if she has diligently followed every good work" (I Timothy 5:10). Also the Christian mother and wife will be hospitable. Again from I Timothy 5:10, "if she has lodged strangers, if she has washed the saints' feet" From Hebrews 13:2, "Do not forget to entertain strangers, for by so doing some have unwittingly entertained angels." The Shunammite woman manifested a wonderful attitude of such hospitality in regards to the prophet Elisha as recorded in 2 Kings 4:8-37. This quality of hospitality makes the home pleasant where people love to visit.

We need always to show our respect and honor to our mother whether they are living or have died (Ephesians 6:1, 2). We can do this by living for the Lord and being the proper influence for good among our peers.

DEDICATED TO MOTHERS IN THE HOMES

So long as there are homes to which
Men turn—at close of day,
So long as there are homes where
Children are, and women stay,
If faith and love and loyalty are found
Across those sills,
A stricken nation can recover
From grievous ills.
So long as there are homes where
Fires burn, and there is bread,
So long as there are homes where
Lamps are lit—and prayers are said,
Though a people falter in darkness,
And nations grope,
With God himself back of these little homes,
We still have hope

— *Grace Noll Crowell*
"There Are Homes"
from Light of the Years,
Copyright, 1936

ONE OF THE GREATEST FEARS OF PARENTS: THE DEATH OF A CHILD

I write as a father. It was on Friday night, October 2, 1987, that I received a call from a dear Christian friend of mine informing me that his teenage daughter had been killed in a car wreck. He asked me if I would go with him to Montgomery so he could identify the body of his precious child. My wife and I hurried over to his house to try to comfort him, his wife and family in their deep despair and grief in the loss of their child that had been so full of life only a few hours earlier. It was about 2:00 a.m. by the time we reach the place where his daughter was being held since she died in the car wreck. Because I knew the teenager and loved her dearly, it was hard enough for me emotionally and I just couldn't imagine how difficult it was for this grieving father to do what he had to do. But in 1973 when my younger brother, age 35, was killed in another state while walking across a four lane highway, I had to go to the local funeral home in my hometown to identify him and I knew how difficult that was for me. But, the thought of having a child to get killed and to leave this world and into eternity, surely would be one of the greatest crosses to bear in this life.

In recent days we have learned of several young people being killed in automobile accidents. One was a precious and sweet Christian teenage girl who lived in Decatur, Alabama. I read an email of sympathy and in it the individual asked "Why, God, why?" And it is not necessarily wrong to ask "Why." We are but as little children who might ask their parents the same when they did not understand the reason the hurt they were feeling in their hearts when something bad had happened to them. I could say to you that when God created the universe He set in order certain laws like gravity. When an evil person or an innocent child falls from a 10 story building, the results will be the same. And, when two vehicles traveling at certain speeds collide, serious injuries or deaths may occur. As being able to answer all the "whys", I cannot. It becomes most difficult to deal with when bad things happen to good people, especially fine Christian young people.

David, in the depths of despair, asked, "Why do You stand afar off, O Lord? Why do you hide in times of trouble" (Psalm 10:1)? Again he asked, "How long, O Lord? Will You forget me forever? How long will You hide Your face from me? How long shall I take counsel in my soul, Having sorrow in my heart daily? How long will my enemy be exalted over me? In his humanity, he asked these questions but he knew in his heart that the God of the universe cared for him and was with him. So he expressed his inner feelings in this manner, "But I have trusted in Your mercy; My heart shall rejoice in Your salvation. I will sing to the Lord, Because He has dealt bountifully with me" (Psalm 13:5, 6).

Then consider Job who "was blameless and upright and one who feared God and shunned evil"; and, "was the greatest of all the people of the East." God asked Satan, "Have you considered My servant Job, that there is none like him on the earth, a blameless and upright man, one who fears God and shuns evil?" (Job 1:1, 3, 8). Yet he lost so much of his earthly possessions, had sores all over his body; but, to me, the greatest loss of all were the deaths of his children (Job 1:18, 19). How does a parent deal with such an overwhelming catastrophe? I am amazed that Job could have continued to live but he did. When you read the entire book you will find that Job did have questions that he presented to God but his example of endurance has given encouragement throughout the centuries to believers when tragedies strike their families and loved ones. Consider these responses of Job to his great grief: "Then Job arose, tore his robe, and shaved his head; and he fell to the ground and worshiped. And he said: "Naked I came from my mother's womb, And naked shall I return there. The Lord gave, and the Lord has taken away; Blessed be the name of the Lord." "But he said to her, "You speak as one of the foolish women speaks. Shall we indeed accept good from God, and shall we not accept adversity?" In all this Job did not sin with his lips." "But He knows the way that I take; When He has tested me, I shall come forth as gold." (Job 1:20, 21; 2:10; 23:10). To me, the outstanding statement that Job made in dealing with his lack of understanding of the "whys" relating to his losses is found in chapter 13 and in verse 15: "Though He slay me, yet will I trust Him" (KJV). In this life we may never know all the answers to the "whys" as to the trials, tribulations, disappointments, difficulties and deaths that occur in our lives but we can trust in Him who knows all things and can work out everything to our eternal welfare (Romans 8:28).

"SET YOUR HOUSE IN ORDER"

It was during the fourteenth year of Hezekiah's reign in Judah that the king became "sick and near death." Isaiah, the prophet of God, instructed him to "set your house in order, for you shall die and not live'" (2 Kings 20:1) King Hezekiah prayed to God to permit him to live. By the grace of God, he was granted an additional fifteen years to his life. The king was approximately forty years of age at the time of his illness and the pronouncement of his impending death. This must have been a tremendous shock to him. Death is common among infants and aged men expect to die; but, a man in his prime and vigor of life is reluctant to face the reality of dying.

There is a great truth and fact held in common by all men and that is, death is inevitable. The Preacher wrote in Ecclesiastes 9:5, "For the living know that they shall die." The inspired writer declared in Hebrews 9:27, "And as it is appointed for men to die once, but after this the judgment." In view of this fact, man should set his house in order, that is, to prepare for the final stroke that shall remove him from among the living. But, what is it to set one's house in order?

It is stated that after his counsel had been rejected, Ahithophel went to his house to "put his household in order, and hanged himself and died; and he was buried in his father's tomb" (II Samuel 17:23). It is not exactly clear as to the understanding of the phrase that he "put his household in order"; however, it may be that his financial and worldly affairs were included in his actions. Normally, this is the accepted view as experience has taught us. When there is an extended illness, men hasten to prepare a will and arrange for their family in matters of monetary interest. There are times when death comes so swiftly that there is no time for such transactions. Procrastination has caused many heartaches and family feuds when the grim reaper gives no forewarning.

There is another view of setting one's house in order that is of greater importance than the worldly affairs and that is the moral and spiritual aspects of a man's life We can set our house in order by having a right relationship with God. As we often say, 'this is the bottom line'. The wise man said it in this fashion, "Let us hear the conclusion of the whole matter: Fear God and keep His commandments, For this is man's all. For God will bring every work into judgment, Including every secret thing, Whether good or evil" (Ecclesiastes 12:13, 14). As a penitent believer one should be baptized into Christ for the remission of sins (Acts 2:36-38; Galatians 3:26, 27). In living a faithful Christian life one can rest assured that his house is in order regardless of how and when death overtakes him (Revelation 2:10; 14:13. So we should not neglect those people who are touched by our life. We need to express our love to our mate and to our children. We should influence our family in the way of the Lord; treat our neighbors fairly and honestly; teach the lost of Jesus and care for the widows, orphans and the indigent people. Now is the time for us to set our house in order.

HOW TO LIVE

How to live
And not how to die
Is the great theme
Of the Book of books.
However, if we,
Trust the God of Peace,
Follow the Prince of Peace
Obey the gospel of peace,
And, if possible, live in peace
With man,
We are assured of a peaceful departure,
And a safe landing on the golden shore.
It is when we learn how to LIVE
That we learn HOW TO DIE.

— *Frank L. Cox, Minister's Monthly*

SOME SINS OF SONS AND DAUGHTERS

In the book of Ecclesiastes 11:9-11 the preacher wrote an exhortation that is much needed today for our young people: "Rejoice, O young man, in your youth, And let your heart cheer you in the days of your youth, Walk in the ways of your heart, And in the sight of your eyes; But know that for all these God will bring you into judgment. Therefore remove sorrow from your heart, And put away evil from your flesh, For childhood and youth are vanity". There are some prevalent and prominent sins to be found among some young men and women that need to be exposed and examined. Following are a few of such shortcomings.

Generally speaking there is a lack of reverence and respect for parents. Piety (respect) should be learned and practiced first in the home (I Timothy 5:4).

The apostle Paul taught that children should "Honor your father and mother" (Ephesians 6:1-3). The lack of respect for parents will bring on another transgression, that is, a failure to obey parental authority. Before there can be obedience there has to be the recognition of the father as being the rightful head of the home. If this relationship is not properly understood children will not obey their parents. Of course, there would be exceptions where the father is dead, absent from the home or should a father absolutely refuse to discipline the children. In every age God has placed the husband (father) as being the rightful head and leader of the family unit. This is, no doubt, the reason why Paul specified the father in Ephesians 6:4 when he wrote: "And you fathers, do not provoke your children to wrath, but bring them up in the training and admonition of the Lord." The Bible teaches that children are to obey their parents: "Children, obey your parents in the Lord, for this is right" (Ephesians 6:1). Even Jesus was in subjection to His earthly parents (Luke 2:51). The sin of being "disobedient to parents" is listed among such sins as "fornication, wickedness, covetousness, maliciousness, full of envy, murder" (Romans 1:28-32, ASV).

There is a great need today for proper discipline in the home. Certainly there is the positive aspect of discipline which involves teaching and training; however, there is the corrective side which should be administered when disobedience occurs among sons and daughters. This disciplinary action may come in various forms. But it must be done in order to establish and maintain respect for parental authority in the home. The wise man wrote in Proverbs 13:24: "He who spares his rod hates his son; but he who loves him disciplines him promptly (early)." There is still a need for some 'hickory tea' to be applied to the lower part of a child's anatomy even in our modern age. The Lord God chastises His children out of love and earthly fathers should do the same in order to manifest their love for their children (Hebrews 12:5-9). Pity the poor children who never receive any correction from their parents. These same young people may grow up with emotional problems because of the lack of discipline in the home. Children should realize that discipline is proof of their parents' love and concern for them. The basic reason for the lack of respect for authority in our schools and elsewhere can be traced directly to the break-down of the proper training in the home. If a child does not learn respect and obedience in the home it is unlikely that it will be learned anywhere.

In this age of plenty and prosperity, there seems to be a lack of gratitude for parents and the material blessings. One of the prevalent sins of the Gentiles as mentioned in Romans 1:21 was "although they knew God, they did not glorify Him as God, nor were thankful..." Parents have unknowingly contributed to this sin of ingratitude. Many fathers and mothers were reared when times were hard.

The attitude that "I want my child to have all the things that I didn't have" can actually be detrimental in the rearing of children. Too many physical and material blessings bestowed upon children can produce a lack of gratitude among the young people. Certainly, sons and daughters should express both my actions and words their thankfulness to parents who have provided for them the daily necessities and even the luxuries of life.

Some young people are not always honest with their parents. For example a son may tell his parents that he is going to one place some evening while planning to go elsewhere. A young lady may inform her parents that she and her date were at a place of entertainment when actually they were in a different location. Young people need to deal honestly with their fathers and mothers. The Bible teaches that God hates "a lying tongue" (Proverbs 6:17). Paul instructed Christians in this manner: "Do not lie one to one another" (Colossians 3:9). The final abiding place for all liars is "in the lake which burns with fire and brimstone" (Revelation 21:8). If young folk demand truth and honesty from adults they must understand that the same is required and expected of them.

Finally, young people need to understand that the decision to do right or wrong is eventually theirs to make. Sure, parents are to teach and train children in the way of the Lord (Proverbs 22:6); but, in the final analysis, the young man and woman must be responsible for the decision either to stand for the right or submit to sin. Simply possessing the proper knowledge of what is right and what is wrong is not conviction. It is when one is really put to the test and is able to resist evil and to do right that one's true convictions are seen. This is an individual matter. When one has been properly taught and still commits wrong, one should not then blame someone else for the deed done. Young people should count the cost and be willing to live with the decision made, whether it is be right or wrong. A lack of maturity will cause one to habitually blame parents for mistakes made when the decision is left up to the son or daughter.

Of course, the Lord wants sons and daughters to "Remember now your Creator in the days of your youth..." (Ecclesiastes 12:2). It is wonderful to know of young people who obey their Savior and dedicate their lives to God who loved them enough to give His only begotten Son to die on Calvary for the sins of the world (John 3:16).

SOME SYMPTOMS OF A SECULAR SOCIETY

First of all, it is best that we define three of the words in the heading of this article. The word 'symptoms' as used in the medical field can be described as indicators of an underlying health problem. For example, if someone is experiencing chronic fatigue, this may indicate a serious heart problem. In spiritual matters, a member of the church who is habitually absent from the worship assemblies may indicate that there is a lack of love for the Lord which is a real 'heart problem'. The word 'society' is defined as: "A society, or a human society, is a group of people involved with each other through persistent relations, or a large social grouping sharing the same geographical or social territory, subject to the same political authority and dominant cultural expectations. Human societies are characterized by patterns of relationships (social relations) between individuals who share a distinctive culture and institutions; a given society may be described as the sum total of such relationships among its constituent members. In the social sciences, a larger society often evinces stratification and/or dominance patterns in subgroups" (Wikipedia Free Encyclopedia). The following definition is one of the best that I could find regarding the word 'secular' (adjective) but in this case I will use the word 'secularization' (noun) to aid in our understanding of the word 'secular':

> "Secularization refers to the historical process in which religion loses social and cultural significance. As a result of secularization the role of religion in modern societies becomes restricted. In secularized societies faith lacks cultural authority, religious organizations have little social power, and public life proceeds without reference to the supernatural. Secularization captures a long-term societal change, but it has consequences for religion itself. In Western countries, where it has been most pronounced, it has made the connection to their Christian heritage more tenuous. Yet secularization is important beyond the formerly Christian West, given that many of the forces that first sustained it there affect other societies as well."

> — *Frank J. Lechner*

It is generally understood that a structure is no stronger than its foundation. This is true of civil governments and nations. When the foundation has been weakened, society is most likely to crumple, decay and implode. In Psalm 11:3 we read, "If the foundations are destroyed, What can the righteous do?" The foundation of any civilization is the family unit. Someone has rightly said, "As the home goes, so goes the nation." In our country, the traditional understanding of marriage and the home is under attack by Satan and our secular society. Biblically speaking, marriage is the joining together of a man and a woman as husband and wife (See Genesis 2:20-25; Matthew 19:4-6 & Ephesians 5:22-33). This is God's design for marriage and the home and believers in His Holy Word are bound by the will of the Heavenly Father in this important matter.

But decisions are being made by governmental officials and judges as well as citizens in various states in our nation to the contrary of what we refer to as a 'traditional marriage'. Note the following: "On Tuesday, November 6, 2012, voters in Maine, Maryland and Washington approved the legalization of same-sex marriage in their states. In addition, voters in Minnesota rejected a state constitutional amendment to define marriage as an opposite-sex union. Same-sex marriage is already legal in Massachusetts (2004), Connecticut (2008), Iowa (2009), Vermont (2009), New Hampshire (2010) and Washington, D.C. (2010). In addition, California continues to recognize same-sex marriages that were performed between June 16 and November 4, 2008, the period in which same-sex marriage was legal in California." The 'Gay Movement' is becoming more and more influential in our society. Even some mainline denominations are ordaining 'gays' to be bishops and preachers. Some 'Pastors' are performing marriages of same-sex couples. The movies and television programs are presenting same-sex marriage as an alternate and acceptable lifestyle. Not a few school systems are using text books to influence our children that 'two fathers' or 'two mothers' are normal and that parents should not object to such teaching in the classrooms. Biblical passages found in Romans 1:18-32; 1 Corinthians 6:9- 11; Jude 7 clearly condemn such life styles.

We also have learned that married couples are now in the minority. There are more young adults 'living together' rather than choosing to go through a marriage ceremony. Again, the movies and television programs are projecting this arrangement as being acceptable in our modern society. The Holy Spirit had the apostle Paul to write in Galatians 5:19-21 that "fornication" (illicit sexual intercourse) is one sin mentioned among others as being classified as "works of the flesh" and "that those who practice such things will not inherit the kingdom of God." "Other signs of cultural decay are accepted with little notice. According to data from the Centers for Disease Control and Prevention, 40 percent of babies born in America are born to unmarried women."

In this 'secular society', "there have been 53 million abortions performed in the United States since Roe v. Wade was decided back in 1973. While the number of abortions is down, on the average, there have been approximately 1.21 million abortions in America each year." One may call that which is growing in a pregnant woman's womb a fetus or whatever; but, the fact is, it is a living being, an unborn child. God's attitude concerning abortion is found in Proverbs 6:16, 17: "These are six things the Lord hates, Yes, seven are an abomination to Him: A proud look, A lying tongue, Hands that shed innocent blood..."

Our teens are being taught in many of our schools (even in lower grades) on how to have 'safe sex' while the objections of parents are being rejected. Some liberal-minded professionals, including educators and doctors, believe that teenage girls should have the right to purchase "emergency contraceptive pills, generally sold in the U.S. as Plan B-Step or Next Choice." "These pills contain a synthetic hormone similar to birth control pills, prevent ovulation – and, therefore pregnancy – about 85 percent of the time when taken within 72 hours of unprotected sex." John, the apostle of love, was instructed by the Lord to write these word, "But the cowardly, unbelieving, abominable, murderers, sexually immoral, sorcerers, idolaters, and all liars shall have their part in the lake which burns with fire and brimstone, which is the second death" (Revelation 21:8).

Cal Thomas, a well known columnist writes, "There is no longer any cultural corrective because we have abandoned the concept of objective truth. Nothing is right or wrong, because that suggests a standard by which right and wrong might be defined. Personal choice is the new 'standard,' which is no standard at all. One might as well develop individual weights and measures. This is the age of pluralism, inclusivism and tolerance wherein individuals have the right to believe whatever they choose, morally, doctrinally, etc." But this is not anything new. In Judges 21:25, we read, "In those days there was no king in Israel; everyone did what was right in his own eyes."

A growing number of people, especially young people, no longer believe in God or religion. "An October poll from the Pew Forum on Religion and Public Life drew attention to the rise of the religiously unaffiliated—now 1 out of 5 adults and 1 out of 3 adults under 30." Atheists, the ACLU and other liberal groups are continuing to make impact on our nation's scene with their objections to anything pertaining to 'Christianity'. My friend, America is not a 'Christian nation'. Believers in God, Jesus Christ and the Bible are in for a real battle against the forces of evil that are prevalent in our nation.

There are other 'symptoms' we could discuss that are indicators of the deplorable condition in our country but we shall mention only these presently. In closing, please read carefully the following from the Word of God: "Righteousness exalts a nation, but sin is a reproach to any people" (Proverbs 14:34). "The wicked shall be turned into hell, And all the nations that forget God" (Psalm 9:17). The passage in 2 Chronicles 7:14 had reference to God's chosen people at that time which was the nation of Israel; however, the directives, principles and promises can be applied to the present condition in our country today. "If My people who are called by My name will humble themselves, and pray and seek My face, and turn from their wicked ways, then I will hear from heaven, and will forgive their sin and heal their land."

WORKS CITED

Wikipedia, the free encyclopedia

Thomas, Cal, Newspaper Article, Gay Marriages, etc

The National Law Review, Employment and HR: United States: Results of State Voter Referendums On Same-Sex Marriage: Implications for Employee Benefit Plans, McDermott Will & Emery

Christianity Today, December, 2012

Article by Joseph S. Adams, Jacob Mattinson, Todd A. Solomon and Brian J. Tiemann

Merica, Dan, CNN

Yudell, Michael, Article, Tuesday, November 27, 2012

Bible, New King James Version

THIS GLOBE IS NOT SO GOLDEN

The world in itself and of itself is not getting any better. The truth of the matter is mankind, without God, is becoming worse. God's wonderful creation, the human race, had lost its golden glow with the introduction of sin into the world. With the passing of time, it repented God that he had made man in His image because of the terrible blight of sin that had tarnished the golden innocence of His creation (Genesis, chapters 6 and 7). Think about it, only eight souls were saved from the vast multitude of people who lived on this globe when God deluged the earth with water. There was a new beginning but it was not long before the sins of those who lived in Sodom and Gomorrah and were guilty of sexual perversions caused God to destroy those cities with fire and brimstone (Genesis 19). Societies over the centuries that have forgotten God have suffered the inevitable consequences. The Psalmist wrote, "The wicked shall be turned to hell, and all the nations that forget God" (Psalm 9:17).

The populace of our great nation has not learned the lesson that we eventually reap as we have sown in moral issues (Galatians 6:6, 7). The devil has an agenda and it is slowly but surely being carried out by influential individuals and organizations. In fact the television and movie industries are doing what they can to influence the citizens of our country to accept the lifestyle of the homosexual, bi-sexual and transsexual. I might also mention that many major newspapers are doing what they can to assist in propagating this same agenda. The Montgomery Advertiser, in the January 17, 2006 edition, had for its leading stories on page 1 and the first page of section D, the awards given at the Golden Globes on Monday night, January 16, 2006. The movie, 'Brokeback Mountain' won four awards including best picture and best director. This movie is about the romance of two cowboys. Having two rugged cowboys portrayed as homosexuals was not by mere chance but by design. Someone has said that Marlboro used a rugged cowboy to encourage people to smoke because it was a 'manly' thing to do. That person later died with cancer. How many 'manly' homosexuals have died with aids? But

'Brokeback Mountain' was not the only movie dealing with sexual perversion that received awards during the Golden Globes ceremony. Read carefully the following:

> "It was a triumphant night for films dealing with homosexuality and transsexuality. Along with victories for "Brokeback Mountain," acting honors went to Felicity Huffman in a gender- bending role as a man preparing for sex-change surgery in "Transamerica" and Philip Seymour Hoffman as gay author Truman Capote in "Capote."
>
> — Montgomery Advertiser, page 1 D, January 17, 2006

Felicity Huffman made it clear in her acceptance speech that we all should accept the lifestyles of those persons portrayed by the actors in the various films when she said: "I know as actors our job is usually to shed our skins, but I think as people our job is to become who we really are and so I would like to salute the men and women who brave ostracism, alienation and a life lived on the margins to become who they really are", (Montgomery Advertiser, page 1 D, January 17, 2006). She received a thunderous applause at the conclusion of her remarks. The actors of the TV series Will and Grace were recognized during the Golden Globes ceremony.

Each person had something to say about being in the series. One of the actors said that the television industry needed "more gays." He had portrayed a 'gay' in the series. He also received a thunderous applause for his remarks. The president of the gay-rights group Human Rights Campaign commented on the six awards given to movies with gay or transsexual central characters: "It was a historic night." "I think it says a lot about where we're going as a country" (Montgomery Advertiser, page 1 D, January 18, 2006).

Now, that last statement concerns me greatly. It may be later than we think. A generation ago the subject of homosexuality was spoken of in whispers by most Bible believers. We could not perceive of the publicity that would be given to such a movement among our citizenry. But that is the manner in which changes are made, gradually but aggressive. Now we are confronted with a moral issue that can and most likely will become one of the major thrust of a persecution against believers in Christ. To people who do not respect God's Word, passages of scriptures that condemn such sexual perversion will have little or no effect upon their beliefs and actions (Romans 1:26, 27; I Corinthians 6:9- 11; Jude 7). The kingdom of darkness is governed by a different law and ruler. As the saying goes, I am not a prophet or a son of a prophet but I do believe that believers in Christ will be the blunt of a direct onslaught by Satan and his forces concerning this matter. In fact the time may come that the very words that I am writing will be the evidence presented to a court of law that I am filled with prejudice, hatred and have violated the civil rights of others and I will be found guilty of violating a law of the land in so doing. Preachers will be a definite target of this attack because of what they teach and preach from the pulpit regarding the sin of sexual perversion. It not only may happen but it has happened in other countries like Canada, the Netherlands and other countries in Europe.

We should all pray daily that righteousness might prevail in our nation. The wise man wrote centuries ago that "Righteousness exalts a nation, but sin is a reproach to any people" (Proverbs 14:34). Let us join forces with others in an effort to change the direction that our country is headed in moral issues. Let us place our trust in the Heavenly Father who still rules in the affairs of men and rely upon His strength and grace to sustain us in the time of need (Daniel 4:17). We are not better than our brothers in sisters in Christ who suffered tremendously for their faith in Christ (Revelation 2:10). And remember these words of the apostle Paul who endured so much for the cause of Christ, "Finally, my brethren, be strong in the Lord and in the power of His might. Put on the whole armor of God, that you may be able to stand against the wiles of the devil. For we do not wrestle against flesh and blood, but against principalities, against powers, against the rulers of the darkness of this age, against spiritual host of wickedness in the heavenly places. Therefore take up the whole armor of God, that you may be able to withstand in the evil day, and having done all, to stand" (Ephesians 6:10 – 13).

TWO WRONGS HAVE THE RIGHT

But, the two wrongs do not make one right. The reason being, the wrongs are not right, singularly or collectively. Now permit me to explain what I mean by all this jargon.

On Sunday, October 17, 2004, the Montgomery Advertiser carried an article pertaining to a protest led by an extremist group from the state of Kansas that occurred in Montgomery, Alabama on Saturday, October 16, 2004. The group was comprised of some of the members of the Westboro Baptist Church in Topeka, Kansas. Their basic message in sermon and in songs was that God hates the homosexuals. They also "Thank God for Ivan", believing that it was punishment sent from God for the immorality that exists in our country. Also that "God hates America." A daughter of the preacher of this church explained that the signs and slogans are "about the United States' enabling of the homosexual lifestyle." Some of the songs and comments expressed the belief of this group that "the Sept. 11, 2001, terrorist attacks were God's wrath on homosexuals." The beliefs of this radical group are not representative of the religious community in our nation. In fact, such extremism is injurious to an understanding of the nature of God and an acceptance of the Bible as being divinely inspired of God. Such ignorance and misguided zeal give fuel to the secular society to ridicule believers in Jesus Christ as being the only savior of mankind and God the Father being the Creator of heaven and earth. But, these zealots have the right in this country to express their religious beliefs and teachings. For this we are indeed thankful.

The truth of the matter is, God loves the homosexual but He hates the sin. In the great Roman treatise concerning the infinite grace of God, it is easy to understand how much God detest the sin of homosexuality. In chapter 1: 18 - 32, we learn that the "wrath of God is revealed from heaven against all ungodliness and unrighteousness of men, who suppress the truth in unrighteousness, because what may be known of God is manifest in them, for God has shown it to them." The heathen populace did not "glorify God" and became steeped in idolatry. Because of their willfulness in rejecting God, He "gave them up to uncleanness, in the lusts of their hearts, to dishonor their bodies among themselves." "God gave them up to vile passions. For even their women exchanged the natural use of what is against nature. Likewise also the men, leaving the natural use to the woman, burned in their lust for one another, men with men committing what is shameful, and receiving in themselves the penalty of their error which was due. And even as they did not like to retain God in their knowledge, God gave them over to a debased mind, to do those things which are not fitting; being filled with all unrighteousness, sexual immorality..." One can plainly understand from a casual reading of this passage that God condemns the sins of sexual perversion, including homosexuality.

However, the Holy Spirit guided the apostle Paul to write in the same book of Romans, chapter 5, verses 6 – 10, "For when we were still without strength, in due time Christ died for the ungodly. For scarcely for a righteous man will one die; yet perhaps for a good man someone would even dare to die. But God demonstrates His own love toward us, in that while we were still sinners, Christ died for us. Much more then, having now been justified by His blood, we shall be saved from wrath through Him. For if when we were enemies we were reconciled to God through the death of His Son, much more, having been reconciled, we shall be saved by His life." The "ungodly" in verse 6, the "sinners" in verse 8 and the "enemies" mentioned in verse 10 would involve all of mankind, including the homosexuals. "God so loved the world that He gave His only begotten Son, that whoever believes in Him should not perish but have everlasting life" (John 3:16). It was by the grace of God that Jesus died "for everyone" (Hebrews 2:9). No greater truth can be found in the Holy Scriptures than this, that God loved/loves the human family, including those who were/are guilty of sexual sins.

On the other hand, the second group present on the occasion previously mentioned, was comprised of those who believe that the homosexual way of life is right and should be accepted by society even to the point of making it legal for persons of the same sex to be married. Under the picture of two women hugging one another on page 4c of the Montgomery Advertiser, it reads that one woman "embraces her wife". Yes, you read that correctly, a woman who "embraces her wife" (emphasis mine, RE).

There are many passages in the Bible, including Romans 1:18-34; I Corinthians 6:19–20, that prove beyond a shadow of doubt the homoerotic lifestyle is sinful in the mind of God. Also, when the design of marriage and the relationship of man and woman are considered in view of the infinite wisdom of God, one has to conclude that same sex marriages and the homoerotic lifestyle are expressly forbidden in the Holy Scriptures. In Genesis 1:26 – 28, we read the following, "Then God said, "Let us make man in Our image, according to Our likeness..." "So God created man in His own image, in the image of God He created him; male and female He created them. Then God blessed them, and God said to them, "Be fruitful and multiply: fill the earth and subdue it..." One can plainly see that God made man (generic term) male and female. God did not make one entity with dual personalities but two entities, male and female. It is also understood that the male and female should have children in order to "fill the earth". Two people of the same sex cannot accomplish what God intended for the male and female (in marriage) to do. In chapter two of the book of Genesis we find more details concerning the making of man and woman by Almighty God.

Notice in verses 20 – 25, "So Adam gave names to all cattle, to the birds of the air, and to every beast of the field. But for Adam there was not found a helper comparable to him. And the Lord God caused a deep sleep to fall on Adam, and he slept; and He took one of his ribs, and closed up the flesh in its place Then the rib which the Lord God had taken from man He made into a woman, and He brought her to the man. And Adam said: "This is now bone of my bones and flesh of my flesh; She shall be call woman, because she was taken out of man." "Therefore a man shall leave his father and mother and be joined to his wife, and they shall become one flesh. And they were both naked, the man and his wife, and were not ashamed." After God made man, there was not to be found among the animal kingdom a help-meet (companion) suitable for Adam. God caused the man to fall into a sleep and God took a part of man and made the woman. For all time to come, the truth was stated that the man should leave his parents and cleave to his wife. It is easy to understand that the institution of marriage by God consisted of a man marrying a woman. That is God's design for mankind. Any arrangement contrary to this is a perversion of God's plan originating from His infinite wisdom and love.

The eternal Word (God, the Son) was involved in the making of the man and woman in the Garden of Eden. John declared this so in John 1:3, "All things were made through Him, and without Him nothing was made that was made." The apostle Paul expressed it in this manner, "He is the image of the invisible God, the firstborn over all creation. For by Him all things were created that are in heaven and that are on earth, visible and invisible, whether thrones or dominions or principalities or powers. All things were created through Him and for Him" (Colossians 1:16, 17). Jesus gave credence to the story of creation and in particular to the making of man and woman as recorded in Matthew 19:4 – 6, "And He answered and said to them, "Have you not read that He who made them at the beginning 'made them male and female,' "and said 'For this reason a man shall leave his father and mother and be joined to his wife, and the two shall become one flesh'? "So then, they are no longer two but one flesh. Therefore what God has joined together, let not man separate."

It is clear that God (including God the Son) made male and female and that the man (male) should be joined to his wife (female) thus becoming one flesh. And since God joins them (male and female) in marriage, man has no right to separate the two of them. It takes professional (?) help for a person to misunderstand God's design in marriage, that is, one man for one woman. Individuals who believe in God and have respect for His Word have no alternative but to accept God's design and plan for marriage that involves a man and a woman. We must also conclude that Jesus did have much to say about homosexuality when it is understood that man and woman were made by Him in the very beginning and that they were the only suitable candidates for the marriage relationship.

Yes, the two groups that confronted one another during the protest on October 16, 2004 had the right to express themselves; but, the truth of the matter is that neither group was right because each stood in violation of what the Holy Scriptures teach regarding God's love for all of mankind and His design for the male and female in the holy estate of matrimony.

WEDDINGS AND MARRIAGE

The month of June is normally a time for weddings. You can see pictures in the local newspapers of a number of couples who have 'tied the knot' and they look so happy and blissful. Young love is simply a beautiful thing. It makes the world go around. It makes 'old timers' reflect over the intervening years when they went through the same experience. Isn't life wonderful?

In the midst of so much 'gloom and doom' it is good for us all to pause and consider some lighter moments regarding matrimony and the time honored event that we call a wedding. In my years of preaching I have performed several weddings for young couples. There have been some unusual happenings that occurred before, during and after the actual ceremony. I must begin with my own personal experience. I went all the way to Wildwood, Florida, to meet who I hoped would be my future in-laws. Now brother Sam Slaughter was an impressive looking gentleman from the old school. He had worked for the Seaboard Airline Railroad for many years when I first met him. He also had cattle on his farm that was located between Wildwood and Oxford, just off of U. S. Highway 301. I finally got up enough courage to ask him if I could marry his daughter. Well, would you like to know what he asked me in return? Out of the blue he asked, "Can you hitch up a team of mules?" My integrity was immediately tested. I had to reply in the negative. Brother Sam later said to brother Orvel Boyd in my presence, "Here this young man wants to marry my daughter and he can't even hitch up a team of mules." Now I have never understood the connection between hitching a team of mules and marrying the love of my life. I really think he wanted to know if I knew how to provide for his middle daughter. I did go ahead and marry his daughter and to this day I still don't know how to hitch up a team of mules.

I have been requested to perform wedding ceremonies for many couples but never in this fashion. I was visiting in the hospital in the city where I was preaching when a lady who was employed by the hospital approached me in the hall. Now this lady was a member of a congregation in a different city and she knew me and I had seen her on occasions during gospel meetings, etc. She walked up to me and the first words she spoke to me were, "Will you marry me?" Now I had never been asked exactly that way before, not even when I was single. I knew what she meant but having a sense of humor I had some difficulty in answering her in a collective manner but I did and I said I would.

The ceremony that I have used over the years has been a traditional one. I remember on one occasion the young lady said to me during the rehearsal that she did not want the part of the vows used that had her to repeat "to obey" her prospective husband. I didn't use it and I don't think she did. Someone didn't obey someone because the marriage failed after a few years.

In one wedding the father of the bride was unable, because of sickness, to give his lovely daughter in marriage so her brother was chosen to do the honor. During the rehearsal I instructed him how to bring his sister down to front of the auditorium and where they should stand in front of me. I then instructed him to reply to my question 'Who giveth this woman to be married to this man?' in this manner, 'Her father and her mother.' He smiled and took this responsibility rather lightly and I reminded him that things would be quite different during the actual ceremony so we went over this part again. It was a beautiful wedding with the men in their tuxedos and the ladies in their lovely dresses. When the time for the bride to enter, her brother escorted down to where they stood in front of the wedding party. I had some choice words about marriage and the sanctity of the home and when I had finished; I looked the bride's brother in the eyes and asked in a very solemn manner, 'Who giveth this woman to be married to this man?' In all seriousness and without any hesitation he replied "Mama and Daddy" and with that he turned and sat down. Well, the groom and the bride were grinning from ear to ear and the entire wedding party was about to laugh out loud and there I stood trying my best to carrying on with the ceremony. The gentleman had no inclinations to be so formal when referring to his parents as 'Her father and her mother.' But I have learned whether while preaching, conducting a wedding or whatever, you have to learn to 'roll with the punches' and carrying on the best you can, and of course, with a sense of humor.

But on the serious side of matters I want to mention that in preaching for two different congregations recently I had three ladies to walk up to me and mention that I had married them. Two were from the same congregation. The first lady said, 'You married me thirty-nine years ago and we are still together and I love you for it." The second one informed me that I had performed her wedding ceremony thirty years ago. A younger sister in Christ and her husband reminded me that I performed their wedding twenty-five years ago.

The lady introduced me to a son, a handsome young man, age twenty two. I could mention several couples that I performed their wedding ceremony many years ago and who remain married to this day. Most of my friends who attended the same Christian college that I did and who married are still living together with their mates. They are proud grandparents and in some cases even great- grandparents. My wife and I, the Lord willing, will celebrate our fifty third wedding anniversary this year (August 19, 2008). I pray that my generation will not be the last to believe that this sacred and beautiful relationship is for life. I trust there are scores of young Christian men and women who will hold marriage in high esteem as God has intended. Our Lord Jesus Christ in answering a question said, "Have you not read that He who made them at the beginning 'made them male and female,' "and said, 'For this reason a man shall leave his father and mother and be joined to his wife, and the two shall become one flesh'?" "So then they are no longer two but one flesh, Therefore what God has joined together, let not man separate" (Matthew 19:4-6).

To Be One With Each Other

What greater thing is there for two human souls than to feel that they are joined together to strengthen each other in all labour, to minister to each other in all sorrow, to share with each other in all gladness, to be one with each other in the silent unspoken memories?

— George Eliot [Mary Anne Evans] (1819 – 1880)
http://www.classicallovepoems.com
Wikipedia, the free encyclopedia

"WHAT DO YOU MEAN BY THIS SERVICE?"

"And it shall be, when your children say to you, 'What do you mean by this service'" (Exodus 12:26)? Because of the hardness of the heart of Pharaoh the children of Israel were still held captive in the land of Egypt. Now the Lord God was to bring yet one more plague upon the Egyptians and that was the death of the firstborn of both man and beast. Moses and Israel were instructed as to the details of their duties in this, the beginning of a great annual feast which was to be observed throughout their generations. God was to spare His children from the awful fate that awaited Egypt. They were to observe the Lord's Passover and remember the night when death passed through the land and they were spared from the last plague God sent among the Egyptians.

In the new land which God would give to the Israelites they were to teach their children the real meaning of the Passover when asked the question, "What do you mean by this service?" Later when God gave the law to Israel through His servant Moses on Mount Sinai the people were to learn His commandments and then to teach the same to their children. In Deuteronomy 6:4-9 we read, "Hear, O Israel: The Lord our God, the Lord is one! "You shall love the Lord your God with all your heart, with all your soul, and with all your strength. "And these words which I command you today shall be in your heart. "You shall teach them diligently to your children, and shall talk of them when you sit in your house, when you walk by the way, when you lie down, and when you rise up." The parents were to be able to answer properly the question raised by their sons, "What is the meaning of the testimonies, the statutes, and the judgments which the Lord our God has commanded you" (Deuteronomy 6:20)?

The responsibility of teaching children the ways of the Lord belongs to the parents. The apostle Paul wrote in Ephesians 6:4, "And you, fathers, do not provoke your children to wrath, but bring them up in the training and admonition of the Lord." The church and Christians schools can assist in this matter; and, the parents should utilize such organizations in the fulfilling of their responsibilities. Fathers, mothers, are you able to answer intelligently and scripturally the questions raised by your sons and daughters regarding the existence of God, the deity of Jesus Christ, the inspiration of the Holy Scriptures, the Lord's Supper, baptism, instrumental music, acceptable worship and the need to keep oneself unspotted from the world when they ask, "What do you mean by this service?" Are you carrying those children to the periods of Bible study on Sunday morning and Wednesday night? Are your children in attendance for all the periods of worship? Do you encourage them to read the Bible, religious periodicals and books written by our brethren that would strengthen their faith in God? If you cannot answer their questions today you should not expect them to be able to answer your grandchildren tomorrow.

Section 5

PERSONALITIES AND PRIVILEGES

A GIRL NAMED SKYLAR

A long time before this beautiful girl named Skylar was born, I visited the church where she and her family worshiped together. It was in 1953 or 1954 I went with a preacher friend and his family one Sunday to worship with this group of Christians. I was a freshman in college at the time. I remember it so well because the brethren at that time used real wine in the communion. I didn't know it was wine and not just grape juice before I drank it but I will guarantee you that I knew it was wine after I swallowed it. Forget worship, I coughed and gagged for the next thirty minutes This small congregation is located just south of a community called Deatsville, Alabama. The building sets a good distance off the highway. There are massive Oak trees practically on every side of the building with large roots protruding from the ground. The steps leading up to the front entrance are steep and many. The setting is serene and pastoral as a rural church building should be. Over the intervening years I have preached in gospel meetings, spoken on special occasions and I have 'filled in' for the regular preacher for this congregation numerous times. During these visits with the Cold Springs church I became acquainted with most of the families that attend the assemblies there. And that brings me to Skylar Norton.

On the Sunday mornings when Virginia and I would arrive at the church building for Sunday School usually Rick Norton and his two children would already be there. Jamie, the wife and mother would arrive later. The father would open the building and he and his two children, Skylar and Tyler, would begin various duties. Usually Tyler would begin sweeping the leaves off the front porch and the steps. Skylar would go to the room where the communion bread and grape juice were located. She then would prepare the communion for use in the worship assemblies. It seems that this was her job. She did it for a long time.

Virginia tried to help her once and she replied kindly, "I can do it myself." Skylar was a beautiful and sweet child. You could see it in her eyes and hear it in her voice. She was always 'lady-like'. She was a Daddy's girl. He would take her hunting with him and give her the opportunity to harvest a deer. She and her younger brother were inseparable.

She was greatly loved by all her family. I knew her grandfather, Tillman, while we were in college. It was on a Friday evening of October 3, 2008, that as a member of the Holtville High School Marching Band she was preparing for the football game that old Death descended like a tornado and struck down this precious thirteen year old child in the presence of her classmates. But Death did not get the victory because God sent His angels quickly to gather the spirit of Skylar and brought that lovely child to rest in a paradise prepared for His children. And there was much rejoicing by the host of angels that such a beautiful child had been brought home.

But on this side of eternity there were the hearts of her father, mother, brother and all her family and friends that were broken. There were uncontrollable emotions being vented through the rivers of tears that were being shed. As frail human beings we began to ask "Why"? It is not that we doubted God but as little children we just did not understand why such a beautiful child like Skylar should have her short life to end so soon on this earth. When all the disasters struck Job, and that included the deaths of his ten children, he still said, "Though He slay me, yet will I trust Him" (KJV, Job 13:15). Perhaps in that better land we will know the answers to our questions about the tragedies we have had to suffer in this life.

GOD'S LENT CHILD

"I'll lend you, for a little while, a child of mine," God said,
"For you to love the while he lives, and mourn for when he's dead.
It may be six or seven years or twenty-two or three;
But will you, 'till I call him back, take care of him for me?
He'll bring his charms to gladden you and, should his stay be brief,
You'll have his lovely memories as a solace for your grief.
I cannot promise he will stay, since all from earth return;
But there are lessons taught below I want this child to learn.
I've looked the whole world over in search for teachers true;
And from the things that crowd life's land I have chosen you.
Now, will you give him all your love nor think the labor vain?
Nor hate me when I come to take this lent child back again?"

— *Author unknown*

A PROMISE FULFILLED

My only sister and sibling remaining out of a family of six children born to Walter and Victoria Elliott, Avanelle Elliott Newman, died on July 14, 2011 at the age of 82. She would have been 83 had she lived until November 12. Avanelle was born in Dekalb County near Elliott's Crossroad which is located about 3 miles south of the small town of Henagar, Alabama in the year 1928. In 1933 my parents and three children moved to Trion, Georgia for work in the Riegel Glove Mill and Cotton Mill.

Before Avanelle died, she learned that her term insurance had expired so there were not sufficient funds for the burial expenses. Individual Christians of the Buckingham Road church of Christ in Garland, Texas where she was a member and some relatives gave the money needed to have her body cremated. Her daughter and only child, her three grandchildren, along with the congregation, had a memorial service for "Ninny" on Sunday, July 24. I shall always remember the compassion and love manifested toward my beloved sister by the members of the Buckingham Road congregation. After several weeks had past, I make arrangements for her remains to be sent to the Kirby Funeral Home in Henagar. On Thursday, October 6, Virginia and I drove up to Henagar and took possession of my sister's remains. A cousin of mine, Wendell Elliott, of Rainsville, Alabama and I prepared a grave site where my sister's remains would be buried. There was a space between the graves of our parents and our younger brother Frank who was killed in an accident at the age of 35 where my sister's remains would eventually rest. Avanelle had always expressed a desire to be buried in the Unity Cemetery next to our parents and I promised her if it was possible, I would fulfill her wish.

Over the 55 years that I have been preaching and speaking at funerals and graveside services, I had never experienced such as this one. On a beautiful autumn Friday morning, October 9, 2011, I spoke in the presence of a few relatives and friends who had gathered in the quietness of the rural surroundings near an old church building. I spoke of Avanelle's struggle to survive after she became a single mother with a teenage daughter to rear. The daughter earned a degree from a university and became a nurse. When our mother died in 1988, Avanelle moved to the greater Dallas, Texas area where Vickie and her family lived. She existed only on a meager income but she survived. She suffered with emphysema for years and finally cancer took her life. When most of the relatives and friends had left, I went to the car and removed the container that held my sister's remains. I still think of the weight of the ashes in my hands that once was my dear sister. I knelt down beside the opening in the earth and with love in my heart and as gentle as I could, I placed the container in the small grave. I then took a shovel and began filling the opening with the dirt previously removed by my cousin and me. Needlessly to say, I had difficulty in controlling my emotions. We all made sure that the sod of grass that I had removed was situated just right and Virginia placed a vase of flowers that she had bought where the marker I ordered for my sister's grave would eventually rest. When we drove away, my emotions were mixed but I felt like I had done what my sister desired and that was to be buried next to mother and dad. I had fulfilled my promise.

BYRON BENSON'S BELOVED

He had just completed his freshman year at Alabama Christian College and she had just completed the eleventh grade in the ACC High School. It did not matter with either one of them that Carolyn was only sixteen years old; they were madly in love with one another. Her parents gave their consent for them to marry but they had to 'sign' for her in order for them to obtain their marriage license. There was a song during the 50s that went something like:

They tried to tell us we're too young
Too young to really be in love
They say that love's a word
A word we've only heard
But can't begin to know the meaning of
And yet we're not too young to know
This love will last though years may go
And then some day they may recall
We were not too young at all
And yet we're not too young to know
This love will last though years may go
And then some day they may recall
We were not too young at all

— *Sylvia Dee, 1951, Wikipedia Free Encylopedia*

And their marriage lasted for over 52 years. Their love had staying power. Byron cared for and provided for his beloved. Carolyn stayed largely in the background. You would likely see her rather than hear her. Byron was just the opposite. You saw and heard him! She was a devoted wife and added to that, she was a preacher's wife which is most demanding in various ways. She could say, as did Ruth, "Where you go, I will go..." She was a talented individual. She was an artist and she created a series of Bible study material for use at the Grady church where they labored for some 36 years. While Carolyn was of a quiet disposition she had convictions. She was a very sweet Christian lady and was a joy to know. She had many friends who loved her dearly. Carolyn was a devoted mother and grandmother. Her sons, Lee and Blaine, and their wives, Layla and Patty, will testify to that truth. She loved to go up to their property on Lake Martin and enjoy the quietness and the beauty of the scenery.

Bryon and Carolyn, Roger and Helen Dill, Virginia and I often ate out together, especially on birthdays and wedding anniversaries. We had been friends for over 50 years. In fact, Virginia and I helped to sing at the wedding of Byron and Carolyn back in August of 1957 in the old West End church building in Montgomery. In the picture of the ACC Chorus you will find Carolyn on the first row, Roger and Byron were standing by one another (yes, they had slender faces) on the back row. I was standing on the second row on the end. Virginia had been in the chorus for two years but was now working and Helen was at home caring for our firstborn son. Incidentally this picture was taken in the Capitol Heights church building where Byron preached for five years.

Byron and Carolyn had been apart for a little over five months. He died on August 24, 2009 and she passed from this life on February 3, 2010. Several artists recorded a love song that was popular many years ago and I think it is suitable for this occasion because we have the blessed assurance that our dear friends are now together in the eternal care of our Heavenly Father.

Together Again
My tears have stopped falling
The long lonely nights
Are now at an end
The key to my heart
You hold in your hand
And nothing else matters
We're together again
Together again
The gray skies are gone
You're back in my arms
Now where you belong
The love that I knew
Is living again
And nothing else matters
We're together again
And nothing else matters
We're together again

— *Buck Owens, 1964, Wikipedia Free Encyclopedia*

"CAST YOUR BREAD UPON THE WATERS"

The Preacher wrote in Ecclesiastes 11:1: "Cast your bread upon the waters, For you will find it after many days." Bible students generally agree that this verse, in the light of the immediate context is speaking of being a benevolent person who sees others in need and displaying a charitable attitude toward them, regardless of their moral status. It may be a gift of money, some food or a word of encouragement. Jesus Christ was the perfect example of this principle while He lived on this earth and He taught His disciples to profess the same attitude as found in the 'sermon on the mount' (Matthew 5-7). The apostle Paul later wrote: "And let us not grow weary while doing good, for in due season we shall reap if we do not lose heart. Therefore, as we have opportunity, let us do good to all, especially to those who are of the household of faith" (Galatians 6:9, 10). Our Lord stressed that when we "do a charitable deed" we should not do such to be seen of men (Matthew 6:2-4); but, our heavenly Father knows when we give and the intent of our heart: "For God is not unjust to forget your work and labor of love which you have shown toward His name, in that you have ministered to the saints, and do minister" (Hebrews 6:10). To help a friend, a fellow Christian or a stranger without a desire and expectation of recognition is indeed rewarding. The joy is in the giving and not in the recognition.

> "Wouldst thou too narrowly inquire
> Whither thy kindness goes!
> Thy cake upon the water cast;
> Whom it may feed who knows?"
>
> — *Johann Wolfgang von Goethe*

But the Preacher further states: "For you will find it after many days." The recipient of your kindness and generosity may, in fact, inform others of your deed. You may even be recognized in a public manner without your fore-knowledge of the happening. This might occur soon or later. You just never know. "The seed sown in the morning of life may bear its harvest at once, or not till the evening of age. The man may reap at one and the same time the fruits of his earlier and later sowing, and may find that both are alike good" (Plumptre).

Please pardon the personal experience but I would like to share with you a blessing I received recently. I was in a large department store when I saw a lady who works where the ladies cosmetics are sold. I approached her and mentioned that I saw her at the funeral service of a mutual friend. She and the friend's daughter had worked together in years past. Before I could say but a few words, she quickly stated that she knew who I was and how much she had appreciated my encouraging words to her when a niece had died many years ago. She mentioned that she thought her departed niece would be so concerned about her three small children, all under the age of seven. I had explained to her that her beloved niece would not be worrying about the care of her precious children and used scripture to explain why I said that. This kind lady informed me of some of the words of comfort I had spoken to her, especially that if this lady was indeed a Christian, she and the children could be united again in eternity. She then looked me squarely in the eyes and asked, "Do you remember this conversation" and I had to be honest and say "I do not". But, she did and my words had brought comfort to her troubled soul. I asked her how old the children were presently. She began to brag on them as to how they were excelling in their studies in various universities. Now, here I am in the "autumn of my life" and the bread that I had cast upon the waters years before had returned to me. As I walked away, tears were beginning to dampen my eyes as I became emotional. I had truly received a blessing. My friends, you may never know in this life how much good you do when you cast your bread upon the waters; but, on the judgment day, the Judge of all of mankind will remind you that "you did it to Me" (Matthew 25:34-40).

"FOR CONSCIENCE' SAKE" – MY VOTE

I am almost apolitical. I was 35 years old before I cast my vote for individuals seeking elective offices in my state and that was due to the encouragement of one of my best friends. And when I did vote, I 'killed' his vote for the person running for the office of governor. Since that time, I have voted more for the man rather than for the party. I am conservative by nature and usually I have voted as a Republican but not always when I had to make a choice on an individual basis for a certain office. I have never made voting for one's choice a test of Christian fellowship. I have been disappointed in some of my choices of candidates after learning of their lack of moral fortitude and unwise decisions.

I have tried to obey the laws of the land as taught in God's Word; yet, as an imperfect human, I have often failed in my efforts. Also, I pray for those who are in authority on every level of our government (local, county, state and national). The Lord God, the Creator of the heavens and the earth, ordained the civil government but that does not mean He is always pleased with rulers who are evil. (See Romans 13:1-8; I Timothy 2:1-4; 1 Peter 2:13-15). I fervently believe that God still rules in the affairs/governments of men as taught in the book of Daniel 4:25; 5:21.

When it comes to foreign and economical affairs, I am a layman. I do possess certain convictions regarding these matters that might be different when compared with the convictions of some of my fellow citizens. But my vote for the highest office in our country this time will be based primarily on my convictions regarding some moral issues, namely, abortion and same sex marriage.

The present President endorses and encourages both. As a Christian and a gospel preacher, I cannot vote for a person, regardless of the office he seeks, who would support either of these issues. I believe that life begins at conception and it is not within the realm of mortal man to go counter to what God has taught in His Holy Word in taking the life of the unborn child. God made man and woman to be joined in marriage (See Genesis, chapter 2). Jesus Christ gave credence to this account as found in Matthew 19:4-6. The apostle Paul wrote by the inspiration of the Holy Spirit in Romans 1:18-32, that sexual relationship, women with women and men with men was both shameful and unnatural. Sodomy is condemned both in the Old and New Testaments (See Leviticus 20:13; 1 Corinthians 6:9-11; 1 Timothy 1:9-11; 2 Peter 2:4-9; Jude 7).

I am not a prophet nor the son of a prophet (my father was a mill worker), but the time is coming, unless there is a drastic change in the moral condition of our nation, that preachers of the Word of God will be accused of 'hate crimes' when we teach what the Bible says on these subjects. It has happened in other countries and it is probably being considered among some officials in our nation.

I now quote in part the words of the great reformer, Martin Luther, when he was being tried at the Diet of Worms, Germany in 1521:

"Unless I am convinced by the testimony of the scriptures or by clear reason... I am bound by the Scriptures I have quoted and my conscience is captive to the Word of God. I cannot and will not recant anything, since it is neither safe nor right to go against conscience. May God help me. Amen."

Wikipedia Free Encyclopedia

FRANCES STRANGE COCHRAN
"A VIRTUOUS WIFE"

May 1, 1919 – July 3, 2012

I had the privilege and honor of speaking at the funeral service for sister Frances Cochran on Friday, July 6, 2012 in the South Commerce church of Christ building in Summerville, Georgia, my home congregation. Sister Cochran was 93 years old at her passing on Tuesday, July 3. Her husband, Charles, died some 36 years earlier. They had one daughter, Martha Cochran (Ken) Parker. They were dear friends of my family. Sister Cochran had known me for some 70 years.

In December of 1941, my family moved from the community of Welcome Hill (which was located a few miles northwest of Trion) to Summerville, the county seat of Chattooga County, Georgia. There was a small group of Christians meeting in a rented hall downtown and near the courthouse. It was a short time later that the Cochran and Elliott families met. In 1945, a new building was constructed on South Commerce Street and the church began meeting there. There were several Christian men and women who influenced me as a young boy but none more than Charles and Frances Cochran and Julius and Thelma Sprayberry. I am sure that the Bible class material used in those early years would have consisted of the small cards published by the Gospel Advocate Company and later the quarterlies that were published by the same company.

Charles and Frances were servants in the truest sense of the word. They carried people to their respective doctors; provided transportation for members to the various assemblies of the church; delivered meals to those in need and helped others in ways too numerous to mention. Sister Frances continued to minister to members and friends after the death of her beloved husband. Even when she was physically unable to aid others, she telephoned to check on various ones.

The strength of a church is made of up of individual Christians who are committed to live righteously, serve others and to worship God. This, sister Cochran did all of her life in Christ. Everyone who knew her would testify to this truth. She was 'proud' of the young men who became preachers from the South Commerce Street congregation. Men like Lawrence Garmon (deceased), James Watkins, Tommy Broome and yours truly. She always would tell me when she read an article of mine that had been published in the Gospel Advocate or other brotherhood publications. She desired that I come by to see her when I was in the area. She always was cheerful even in spite of her ailments and would inquire as to how Virginia, the children and grandchildren were doing. I would often visit with her via the telephone.

I believe what John wrote in Revelation 14:13 would summarize her life and death: "Then I heard a voice from heaven saying to me, "Write: 'Blessed are the dead who die in the Lord from now on.'" "Yes," says the Spirit, "that they may rest from their labors, and their works follow them." She, like Paul could say: "I have fought the good fight, I have finished the race, I have kept the faith. Finally, there is laid up for me the crown of righteousness, which the Lord, the righteous judge will give to me on that Day, and not to me only but also to all who have loved His appearing" (2 Timothy 4:7, 8). I am so grateful to God that this faithful Christian lady and her husband exerted so much influence on me during my youth. I longed for the day when we can be together again in eternity with God and the redeemed of all the ages.

GIFTS YOU CAN GIVE DURING THE ENTIRE YEAR

Of course, it is the time of giving. It is Christmas time! People love to give gifts at this season of the year to their loved ones and friends. There is nothing wrong with giving gifts anytime of the year. The spirit of kindness, thoughtfulness and cheerfulness are certainly welcomed during this festive period of the year. It would be wonderful if such expressions were to be found among people the rest of the year. Some gifts that are being given during the Christmas season are very expensive and the number of gifts is too plentiful at times. There are numerous families who get into financial difficulties simply because they go into debt in buying gifts for their family and others. However, there are several gifts that are free that can be and should be given at all times of the year. Here are special gifts you can give to your loved ones, your brothers and sisters in Christ and your friends and neighbors.

1. *The Gift of Praise*. Mark Twain said he could live for two months on one compliment. Critics destroy while encouragers build us up. We need to make it a point to express sincere compliments when we can. The apostle Paul wrote to the church in Corinth these words: "Now I praise you, brethren, that you remember me in all things and keep the traditions just as I delivered them to you" (1 Corinthians 11:2).

2. *The Gift of Understanding*. We all desire to be understood and we should have the same desire to be understanding of others, especially during the times of difficulties, trials and failures. Solomon requested of God that He give him "an understanding heart" (1 Kings 3:9, 12).

3. *The Gift of Kindness*. You can't help but to notice how kind people are to one another during this season of the year. Someone opens a door for a complete stranger. You speak to people you do not even know. Christians need to be kind toward others all the time. One of the true characteristics of a child of God is "brotherly kindness" (2 Peter 1:7). Paul exhorts us to "Be kindly affectionate to one another with brotherly love, in honor giving preference to one another" (Romans 12:10). In Ephesians 4:32, he writes, "And be kind to one another, tenderhearted, forgiving one an-

other, even as God in Christ forgave you." Please notice the word "kind" in this verse. If you remove the "d" from the word "kind" you have 'kin'. You see, we are all "children of God by faith in Christ Jesus" (Galatians 3:26); therefore, we are 'kin' and we should be "kind to one another".

4. *The Gift of Personal Presence.* There is no substitute for a visit to see someone in the hospital, the nursing home or persons confined to their own homes. Of course wisdom must be used in deciding whether or not a visit is wise in certain situations. But, "Pure and undefiled religion before God the Father is this: to visit orphans and widows in their trouble..." (James 1:27). On the judgment day, the faithful who will be saved eternally will be Christians who gave and visited (Matthew 25:34-40).

5. *The Gift of Gratitude.* Someone has written that "Gratitude is the mother virtue of all virtues." The apostle Paul encourages us that "in everything give thanks; for this is the will of God in Christ Jesus for you" (1 Thessalonians 5:18). In Romans chapter 1, Paul describes the unbelieving Gentle world as being sinful and idolatrous in their corrupt manner of life. One of the specific sins he mentioned was that they "did not glorify Him as God, nor were thankful" (vs.21). In Luke 17:11-19 we read of Jesus healing the ten lepers. When they were instructed to show themselves to the priests, only one of the ten lepers returned and with a "loud voice glorified God, and he fell down on his face at His feet, giving Him thanks. And He was a Samaritan". So Jesus answered and said, "Were there not ten cleansed? But where are the nine?" Probably the percentage is about the same today; only 1 out of 10 will pause and give God the thanks for all the blessings of life which He gives to us from His bountiful hand of grace.

6. *The Gift of our Prayers.* Christians are taught in the Scriptures to "pray without ceasing" (1 Thessalonians 5:17). The writer James instructs us to "Confess your faults one to another, and pray one for another, that ye may be healed. The effectual fervent prayer of a righteous man availeth much" (KJV). A hymn that we have sung in our worship assemblies over the years is "For You I Am Praying" and we should practice what we sing!

7. *The Gift of our Forgiveness.* In the prayer Jesus gave to the disciples as a pattern for their prayers He mentioned that we should forgive those who sin against us. The only comment the Lord made following the prayer can be found in these words: "For if you forgive men their trespasses, your heavenly Father will also forgive you. "But if you do not forgive men their trespasses, neither will your Father forgive your trespasses" (Matthew 6:9-15). Jesus never asked His disciples to do anything but that he was

willing to do in His life. When He was on Calvary's cross one of the seven sayings he uttered was "Father, forgive them, for they do know not what they do" (Luke 23:34). We learn in the teachings of Jesus Christ that we are to forgive our brother as often as he is penitent of his sins (See Matthew 18:21, 22). I read the true story about a teenager who was killed in automobile wreck when a drunken driver hit his car. The dead teenager's parents, filled with sorrow in the loss of their precious son later visited the person who was responsible for the accident and became his friends. In time they taught him about Jesus Christ and he was immersed into Christ for the remission of his sins. They forgave him as our Heavenly Father forgives us (Ephesians 4:32).

8. *The Gift of our Christian Example.* Jesus taught that we are to be the "salt of the earth" and the "light of the world" (Matthew 5:13-16). The apostle Paul instructs us to be "blameless and harmless, children of God without fault in the midst of a crooked and perverse generation, among whom you shine as lights in the world" (Philippians 2:15). We may be the only 'Bible' that our neighbors and friends may see. "I'd rather see a sermon than to hear one any day..." is the consensus of millions of our fellowmen.

9. *The Gift of our Love.* This is the greatest gift ever given and it was given by God the Father when He gave His Son Jesus Christ to die for our sins (John 3:16). Jesus taught His disciples to love one another: "A new commandment I give to you, that you love one another; as I have loved you, that you also love one another. "By this all will know that you are My disciples, if you have love for one another" (John 13:34, 35). "And now abide faith, hope, love, these three; but the greatest of these is love" (1 Corinthians 13:13). "Greater love has no one than this, than to lay down one's life for his friend" (John 15:13) "But God demonstrates His own love toward us, in that while we were still sinners, Christ died for us" (Romans 5:8). Our love for everyone should be manifested in our desire that all people come to believe in and obey the Lord Jesus Christ.

"It is more blessed to give than to receive" (Acts 20:35). Our giving should not be limited to special occasions but we should give these gifts throughout the year. Furthermore, if we have not done so, we need to give our lives to Jesus Christ because He gave His life for us that through the shedding of His precious blood we could have the remission of our sins (Matthew 26:28; Ephesians 1:7). The apostle Peter on the Day of Pentecost told the believers to "Repent, and be baptized every one of you in the name of Jesus Christ unto the remission of your sins; and ye shall receive the gift of the Holy Spirit" (ASV, Acts 2:36-38). Have you given your life to Christ?

I CAN SEE MUCH CLEARER NOW

Recently I had cataract surgery on both eyes. The doctor removed the cataract from my right eye first. There was a week interval before he removed the cataract on my left eye. During this time I began to observe that things like the wall paper in the bathroom was not as dark as I thought previously. One day I received a flyer announcing a gospel meeting. The vision in my right eye showed me that the paper was blue; however according to the vision in my left eye the flyer was a dirty looking light green. Or you might say a coffee stained shade of green. It was then that I asked my wife what color was the paper and she replied that it was indeed blue. It was then that I realized that over a period of time my vision had been discolored without my realizing that I was not seeing things as they really were.

Another example of how that I was not seeing things as they really were was when I looked at the address of some friends and saw the opposite of their true address. Ironically, I thought their address was on Summer Street when actually my friends lived on Winter Place. You see, I had already made up my mind that these Christian friends lived on Summer Street so when I looked up their address in the church directory I read Summer Street instead of Winter Place. I don't usually do that but this time I really had a preconceived idea as to where this family lived. Of course I was wrong. When I realized that they did not live where I was looking I went to another friend's home who lived in the area and obtained the proper address of the family I wanted to visit.

To some degree all of us have had preconceived ideas about various matters. I suppose that it could be said to deny this would be evidence that we have already made up our minds that we have never been prejudiced concerning anyone or anything. It is especially difficult to be intellectually honest in dealing the Word of God. A person can be one of integrity regarding his/her financial obligations, fidelity in marriage relationship, in work ethics, etc. and yet not have an open and receptive mind when it comes to the study of the Holy Scriptures. If we are not careful, most of us have gone to the Bible to prove what we believe instead of going to the Bible to learn what God desires for us to know and to do. Perhaps the discoloration has been there so long that we see things that are shaded rather than viewing them with clear vision.

It is a real challenge for a person to study the Bible through glasses that are clear rather than being tinted blue, green or red. The discoloration of our vision may have been influenced by our parents, our Bible class teachers, preachers or our friends. The books and periodicals that we read, the television programs we watch and other medias influence us in biblical matters whether we realize it or not. Of course, not all the influence exerted upon our thinking is to be construed as being negative regarding biblical subjects. But prejudice has prevented many people from understanding and accepting God's eternal truths. Webster defines prejudice as "a judgment or opinion formed before the facts are known; preconceived idea, favorable or, more usually, unfavorable 2.a) a judgment or opinion held in disregard of facts that contradict it; unreasonable bias ..." Nathanael had formed a prejudicial opinion of Jesus before he met Him. He asked, "Can anything good come out of Nazareth" (John 1:46)? Someone had influenced him to be biased toward people who lived in Nazareth. Aren't we happy that Jesus performed 'surgery' on his eyes that he could see more clearly that Jesus was indeed "the Son of God" and the "King of Israel" (John 1:51).

A preacher friend of mine related to me in recent times his conversation with a gentleman regarding how Jesus saves people today. The discussion involved the purpose and action of water baptism. My friend referred the man to I Peter 3:21 and had him to read aloud this verse. He read it as follows from the King James Version, "The like figure whereunto even baptism doth not save us..." He requested the individual to read the verse again. And he did, "The like figure whereunto baptism doth not save us..." My friend knew at this time he had a real problem. He thought for awhile as what to do and then he asked the man to read the verse one word at a time. The gentleman responded by complying with the request of my friend. When he got to where he had inserted the word 'not' he saw that the passage read "...baptism doth also save us..." He stopped and became embarrassed. Prejudice had prevented him from seeing clearly what the verse truly taught. This isn't to necessarily indict the person as being dishonest; rather, it is most likely that his vision had been shaded over the years by the influence of those who do not accept the scriptural teaching on the subject of baptism.

I am reminded of the time when a fellow gospel preacher and I were studying with a family in their home during a campaign that was being conducted in

213

another state. This group believed in immersion but for the wrong reason. So it came down to why a person should be baptized. The gentleman said that he could quote a verse that explained how to be saved and that was Acts 2:38. I was surprised by his statement and asked to him to quote the verse. He began, "And Peter told them to repent and believe..." I knew then he had his mind made up as to what this passage taught so I turned to the verse and read it.

There have been in every generation individuals who have fulfilled the prophecy of Isaiah 6:9, "Hearing you will hear and shall not understand, And seeing you will see and not perceive; For the hearts of this people have grown dull. Their ears are hard of hearing, And their eyes they have closed, Let they should see with their eyes and hear with their ears, Lest they should understand with their hearts and turn, So that I should heal them" (Matthew 13:14, 15). Prejudice is not peculiar to any particular people; rather, such an attitude has even permeated the body of Christ. We often permit our opinions to shade our understanding of the teaching of the Bible.

None of us possess all the truth. How wonderful that we can continue to learn and have a greater understanding of the Word of God. After all we are exhorted to "grow in the grace and knowledge of our Lord and Savior Jesus Christ" (II Peter 3:18). It is not a disgrace to change when we learn better. This is not a reflection on objective truths found in the Scriptures but rather upon our obtaining a greater understanding of the same. It is doubtful that any of us achieved a complete knowledge of the teaching of God while we were "newborn babes" in Christ. The apostle Peter exhorts us "to desire the pure milk of the word, that you may grow thereby" (I Peter 2:2). Whenever the Hebrew writer mentioned that "solid food belongs to those who are of full age, that is, those who by reason of use have their senses exercised to discern both good and evil" (Hebrews 5:12-14), he necessarily inferred that babes in Christ do not know nor comprehend as much as the members who are more mature in Jesus Christ.

For a person to assert that he/she has never changed his/her mind on any issue may in fact denote a biased attitude toward learning new and/or additional truths. It is truly difficult to keep an open mind while discussing religious issues.

Someone has said, "My mind is made up; don't confuse me with the facts." We should all stand firmly upon the foundation of truth which is the Word of God. However, we should never permit a discoloration of our eyes to prejudice us against learning the way of the Lord more perfectly where there is a need to do so. Remember the prayer to God by the prophet Isaiah when he prayed that the eyes of his servant might be opened to see what he otherwise had not be able to see with his natural eyes (Isaiah 6:17). It would be good if we all ask God to help us to understand more fully His will for us to know and do. The Bereans who "received the word with all readiness of mind, and searched the Scriptures daily, whether those things were so" (Acts 17:11) are worthy of our emulation.

"I DIED LAST NIGHT"

The story is related about a businessman who went to his banker once each year and inquired, "I died last night. Please tell me what happened to my family, my business and my estate." This was probably a sound practice. Too many people manifest little or no interest for the right use of their wealth that they leave behind after their death. However, if this man had died the night before, it is certain that he would not have been interested in his business affairs. Now, let us suppose that we died last night. What would our concerns be? Or, suppose that we stand, like Stephen (Acts 7), between two worlds. Only a moment of time stands between this world and eternity. Here are some pertinent questions that would fill our minds.

Did I Obey The Gospel of Christ?
This question is placed first because when men are dying, it is of utmost importance. One must believe in his heart that Jesus is the Son of God (John 8:24; Acts 8:37). The facts of the gospel that are to be believed are that Jesus Christ died for our sins on Calvary's cross and was resurrected from the dead on the third day (I Corinthians 15:1-3). The commands to be obeyed are repentance of sins and baptism in the name of Jesus Christ in order to receive the blessing of salvation (Mark 16:15, 16; Acts 2:37, 38). Had you died last night, were you obedient to the gospel? One might reply that he intended to obey but as the expression goes, "The road to hell is paved with good intentions."

Was I Faithful To My Lord?
If you have ever thought you were dying, you know this question is of grave concern. Faithfulness in Christian living is necessary to receive a crown of life (Revelation 2:10). A good beginning is not enough. It is important how one finishes the race (Hebrews 12:1, 2). Diligence should be given that we do not fall from grace (I Corinthians 10:12). Many members of the church return to the beggarly elements of the world, making their latter state worse than the first (II Peter 2:20-22). One may plan to return to the Lord but often dies before doing so. The main objective is to watch, that is, being ready when death overtakes us (Mark 13:33-37).

What Kind of Influence Did I Exert On My Family?

This is a very important point to ponder inasmuch that each person does have some amount of influence on family members. This influence can be for good or bad. And, children often learn more by example than they do by what they are taught orally. There is the example given by the Lord as recorded in Luke 16:19- 31 of an individual who left the wrong kind of example for his loved ones to follow. The rich man who had left God out of his life died without the Lord. In Hades, he lifted up his eyes, being tormented by the flames. Among the various requests that he made to Abraham was that he desired for Lazarus to return to the land of the living so he could inform his five brothers not to come to "this place of torment." But, it was too late. Surely, we do not want our loved ones to be lost eternally. We need to live presently in such a manner that is worthy of imitation by others. We need to influence our family members to live for the Lord. Now is the time to set the proper example for our friends and family. After death, it will be eternally too late. What if you had died last night? It is a sobering thought. Where would you be in vast eternity?

I SAW A MAN KILL HIMSELF

It was a beautiful afternoon several years ago when I was about to enter a local bank for my weekly business transaction. Suddenly, I heard three rounds of rapid gunshots. Automatically, I turned toward the direction of the sounds and saw a man across the street with a pistol in his hand. In a moment of time, he placed the gun to his temple and pulled the trigger. I heard the sickening sound of another shot and then the man slumped to the ground. The bizarre events were over in a very short time. I, along with others, had become unwilling witnesses to a terrible tragedy. The man had tried to murder a person in a parked car and then he killed himself. To say the least, it was a very unnerving experience.

I am not a novice regarding death. It has been a part of most of my life. I was only ten years old when my oldest brother was killed in World War II. Several members of my family and my wife's family have died. As a preacher and friend, I have been associated with death in many ways. I have in been in a hospital room when the spirit of a Christian lady took flight, relieving her of the intense pain caused by cancer. I have entered a hospital room just seconds after a small boy gave up the struggle with death and his precious soul went to be with the Lord. I vividly recall the Sunday evening, as I was about to get into my car to go to worship when my neighbor cried for help. Her husband was dying with a heart attack. I tried in vain to get assistance but my friend died while his wife and I stood helplessly by, praying and hoping that the rescue squad would arrive in time. And, I have lost track of the occasions when I have been with grieving families when death came to claim their loved ones but I had never seen a person take his own life. You just don't forget such a horrible scene.

Life is so precious. Man was made in the likeness of his Creator. Cain was sorely punished for taking the life of his brother Abel (Genesis 4:9-15). God prescribed punishment for those wicked people who had no respect for human life (Genesis 9:5, 6). "You shall not murder" was a part of the law of God given to Israel (Exodus 20:13). Jesus even restricts our intimate thoughts regarding our feelings for others (Matthew 5:21, 22). The civil government is commissioned to render punishment to violators who take the life of their fellowman (Romans 13).

Self-destruction gives the offender no opportunity of repentance, reform and forgiveness. Only God knows the state of mind of the individual committing suicide. Mental disorders sometimes motivate the deed. Some, however, have no regard for human life, even their own. How sad for the spirit of a man to be hurled into eternity without God and without hope. Eternal destruction and despair await that person.

As children of light in a world of darkness, we should endeavor to inform others of God's love, the value of man and his soul, the salvation in Christ and the assurances and hope for the Christian. We should teach them that life can be beautiful and meaningful; and, there are no problems so great but that we can find help from God and His people. Fatalism is the fruit of living in a world apart from God who is loving and caring. Our present society is trying to solve problems without His divine guidance. It can never be done, individually or collectively. Christ is still the hope of mankind. It is the privilege of the Christian to teach the message of redemption and hope to a world seemingly determined to destroy itself.

IN MEMORY OF BYRON L. BENSON

If you called him at his home it would indeed be a rarity to reach him. You would get his answering machine and hear him say, "You have reached the BENson residence..." I really don't know when he slept. He was always on the go somewhere. He was consistently doing something for his family or visiting the hospitals or training his grandchildren to eat catfish downtown at the Farmers Market Café. He was a connoisseur of good country cooking. Since he spent so much of his time in the lower part of Montgomery County and in Crenshaw County, the people at Chic's in Highland Home or the Chicken Shack in Luverne would have known him by name. I have never known any gospel preacher who attended more gospel meetings than Byron. Oh, how he loved to sing. Regardless of the weather or the distance, you could count on Byron being present for these occasions. He served on the Board of Regents of Amridge University (I encouraged him to do so). He was on the planning committee for the Capitol City Prayer Breakfast and he would call 40-50 people to attend this bi-monthly service. No one worked more diligently for this good work. He and I alternated in being the Master of Ceremony for this event. Often we would take a jab at one another in fun.

Byron loved to preach. He was zealous for the congregation where he labored part time (a misnomer in his case). He seldom missed preaching on Sundays while he was with the Grady church of Christ for some 36 years. His last work was with the Capitol Heights church in Montgomery (5 years). He loved to do his radio program live. Brethren knew they could depend on him for brotherhood news regarding singings, gospel meetings, lectureships, etc. It seems that he knew everyone and everything that was going on among the congregations in central and south Alabama. He preached for some 37 years on a radio station in Montgomery, Alabama.

Byron was my friend. Virginia and I helped to sing for the wedding of Byron and Carolyn which was conducted in the West End church building some 52 years ago. Byron, Carolyn, Roger and Helen Dill and Virginia and I would often eat together on special occasions such as birthday and wedding anniversaries as well as other times. On one occasion, the total number of years of marriage between the three couples was 150 years. Our server couldn't believe it. Once, while we were enjoying a meal together, I found a rather large insect in my glass of tea after I had taken a couple of drinks. In a very short time the manager was at my side apologizing for the incident and gave me my dinner free of charge. From that time on Byron and Roger would ask me if I brought my insect with me when we would be eating together.

Christian friendship is one of God's richest blessings. I shall miss the many telephone calls from Byron as we talked about Sunday's assemblies and many other subjects. He retired from AT&T several years ago. He believed in communicating via the telephone. But he didn't have much confidence in emailing others or in taking the time to read the ones sent to him. It was in April of one year when he called me and said that he had just read my Christmas card I had sent him the previous December. We enjoyed a good laugh together. When I would call him on his cell phone I would usually ask him, "Byron where are you?" He would be somewhere doing something for someone. If I could call him now and ask, "Byron, where are you?" He would say something like "For to me, to live is Christ, and to die is gain", or, "to depart and be with Christ, which is far better" (Philippians 1:21, 23). This is the blessed assurance that we have in our Lord Jesus Christ. My good friend, you may now rest from your labors of love but your works and influence will continue for generations to come (Revelation 14:13).

'LONG TERM CARE'

It was over the Christmas holidays that our oldest son approached me about what arrangements his mother and I had made in case one of us needed 'long term care' due to a stroke or some other sickness that possibly could cripple us. Now that question caused some serious thinking on my part. It is something that you really don't like to consider since we are still in relatively good health. But our age is showing. After all, my wife and I will be seventy-eight years old our next birthday anniversary. I think sometimes I am a twenty-five year old man locked in this seventy-seven year old body. I don't feel this old but I am. Aging parents can really be a major problem for caring children. And 'long term care' is so expensive. People have lost their homes, property and savings when in need of 'long time care'. I knew of this Christian couple who was in the same nursing home and a relative of theirs stated the cost was $12,000 per month!!! I couldn't believe what I was hearing. Oh, I know that Medicare will pay some but you still have to give up practically all your earthly possessions in the process of covering the expenses for 'long term care'.

There are 'long term care' policies that can be purchased from various insurance companies for a price and if you can afford it, that can be a wise choice. While my wife and I do not have one of those policies, we do have another 'long term care' policy that we have had for most of our lives. While in our youth we confessed our faith in Jesus Christ as being the son of God and were baptized. The cost for our salvation and 'lone time care' was paid by our Savior who shed His blood on Calvary. We could not afford the cost ourselves so He paid it for us. And we know for a fact that the Owner of this policy has cared for us over the years, including fifty-seven years of marriage. Oh, the road has not been an easy one to travel but it was during the times of trials, burdens and difficulties that His policy really 'kicked in'.

I am speaking of the care of our Heavenly Father that has seen us through the valleys of this life. The apostle Peter wrote in I Peter 5:6, 7: "Therefore humble yourselves under the mighty hand of God, that He may exalt you in due time, casting all your care upon Him, for He cares for you." The providential care of God is greatly emphasized by Jesus Christ in the Sermon on the Mount as recorded in Matthew chapter 6, verses 25-34. He provides for "the birds of the air" and He clothes "the lilies of the field". He then asked his disciples "Are you not of more value than they?" Regarding the material blessings of life the Lord said if we "seek first the kingdom of God and His righteous" He promised that "all these things shall be added to you." God has also given His children this promise as found in Hebrews 13:5, 6: "I will never leave you nor forsake you." So we may boldly say: "The Lord is my helper; I will not fear: What can man do to me?" I have often quoted Psalm 37:25 to express my trust in the providential care of our Heaven Father: "I have been young and now I am old; Yet I have not seen the righteous forsaken, Nor His descendants begging bread."

Civilla D Martin wrote the lyrics to this beautiful song that mentions the promise that "God Will Take Care of You." (Wikipedia Free Encyclopedia)

"Be not dismayed whate'er betide, God will take care of you; Beneath His wings of love abide, God will take care of you. Thro' days of toil when heart doth fail God will take of you; When dangers fierce your path assail, God will take care of you. No matter what may be the test, God will take care of you. God will take care of you, Thro' every day, O'er all the way; He will take care of you, God will take care of you."

But the care of God does not end when this life is over for His children. His 'long term care' policy is extended into eternity. Our bodies are daily growing older. The days of our lives are numbered "For the living know that they will die" (Psalm 90:10; Ecclesiastes 9:5). The fear of death does not overwhelm the faithful followers of Jesus Christ, knowing that they will be in the care of their Heavenly Father (Psalm 23:4). In fact, the apostle Paul wrote in Philippians 1:23 that to die and be with the Lord "is far better". John was instructed to write in Revelation 14:13 the following: "Blessed are the dead who die in the Lord from now on.'" "Yes," says the Spirit, "that they may rest from their labors, and their works follow them." Isaiah, a prophet of God penned these words of encouragement: "Good people pass away; the godly often die before their time. But no one seems to care or wonder why. No one seems to understand that God is protecting them from the evil to come. For those who follow godly paths will rest in peace when they die" (Isaiah 57:1, 2; NIV). Eternity cannot be comprehended by our finite minds but we have the promise that God will take care of us. The sentiments expressed in the following song fills the believer's heart with full assurance of that great truth:

"Safe in the arms of Jesus, safe on His gentle breast,
There by His love o'er shaded, sweetly my soul shall rest.
Hark! Tis the voice of angels, borne in a song to me,
Over the fields of glory, over the jasper sea.
Safe in the arms of Jesus, safe from corroding care,
Safe from the world's temptations, sin cannot harm me there.
Free from the blight of sorrow, free from my doubts and fears;
Only a few more trials, only a few more tears.
Jesus, my heart's dear refuge, Jesus has died for me,
Firm on the Rock of Ages, ever my trust shall be.
Here let me wait with patience, wait till the night is o'er;
Wait till I see the morning break on the golden shore:
Safe in the arms of Jesus, safe on His gentle breast,
There by His love o'er shaded, sweetly my soul shall rest."

– Fanny Crosby, 1864: William H. Doane, Music, 1870,
Christian Biography Resources
Copied by Stephen Ross for WholesomeWords.org
from Bright Talks on Favourite Hymns...
by J.M.K. London: The Religious Tract Society;
Chicago: John C. Winston Co., [1916?].

MY MEMORIES OF MARTIN

My brother's name was actually Walter Martin Elliott, named after our father, Walter Matthew. He was the first child of six born to Walter and Victoria Elliott. Martin was born on March 31, 1926 in the Elliott's Crossroads community in Dekalb County, Alabama. He, along with two siblings, moved with my parents to Trion, Georgia, where they found work in the textile mills in early 1933. Later in 1941 the family made their home in Summerville, Georgia, where Martin grew into his teenage years. He was well known and liked by those who knew him. He worked in a local grocery store in downtown Summerville. I remember him having an automobile with a 'rumble seat' in the back of the car. Martin was over six feet tall and very handsome. He fell in love with a beautiful young lady from Fort Payne, Alabama, Catherine King. They eloped when he was eighteen years old and were married in the small community of Rising Fawn near Trenton, Georgia. Martin was soon drafted into the military and began serving in the U.S. Army in 1944. It was during the time when men were greatly needed in the war with Germany and Japan. The young men did not receive extensive training for combat duty. I remember that he took his basic training at Fort Blanding near Jacksonville, Florida for about three months and was soon shipped off to Europe.

Martin was a Private First Class and served in the 178 INFANTRY 95 DIVISION and was with a machine gun squadron. It was during the winter of 1944-45 that the American military forces were making advances into the northwestern part of Germany. During an intense battle near the town of Hamn, Germany, Martin was wounded and died soon afterward. He was at the age when young men and women were enrolling in colleges and/or going into the work force but our country needed our youth in combat to fight against the forces of the Nazi Regime. Martin celebrated his 19th birthday anniversary on March 31, 1945 and was killed six days later on April 5, approximately two months before Germany surrendered to the Allied Forces.

My father was at work at the cotton mill which was located in the southern part of the town of Summerville when he received the telegram that contained the dreaded news that his oldest son had been killed in action. He then walked the long distance to the house where we lived on West Washington Street to bring that news to us. That part of the road was unpaved and our rental house was located on the top of a ridge. I was standing on the front porch when I saw him coming up the hill and he shouted out the words I have never forgotten, "Martin has been killed." I was almost 10 years old at the time and I remember well the over-whelming sorrow and grief my family experienced upon learning that terrible news, especially my parents. We had not received any 'air mail' letters from Martin for sometime and my parents were greatly concerned about his safety. Following the news of his death we received packages back that my mother had sent to him, some containing food items and I well remember that mother would not permit my younger brother and me to eat the sweets.

Martin's wife had the choice of having his body brought back to the states for burial or to be buried in a military cemetery in Europe and she chose the latter and this decision nearly killed my parents, especially mother who suffered emotionally for several years as they never had any 'closure' relating to the death of their precious first born child. I remember how I believed that he had not been killed but perhaps captured or wounded and that one day he would come home. Martin was buried in the Netherlands American Cemetery in the village of Margraten, 6 miles east of Maastricht. Though I have never seen his grave site, I have a niece who visited his grave; and a friend who attended worship at the Prattville church several years ago who was a native of Holland and while visiting relatives in Rotterdam she made a special trip to the cemetery where Martin is buried. She brought me the flag that was on his grave and here is a picture that she gave me.

I found a letter that was written to my parents from a fellow soldier and friend of my brother Martin but over time the name of that individual had been torn from the bottom of the page and so the writer's identity remains unknown. This individual spoke highly of my brother's bravery during combat and he also expressed his high regard for the character of my brother. Following the death of our mother in 1988, the Purple Heart awarded to Martin was left in my possession. It is a constant reminder of the supreme sacrifices that were made during WWII, thousands of whom were mere teenagers.

REMEMBERING THE FALLEN

I watched the movie 'My Boy Jack' (PBS) on Sunday night. Jack was the son of Rudyard Kipling and his wife. At the insistence of and the help of his father Jack was finally able to enlist in the British Army and became an officer. It was during World War I (1915) when England was fighting against Germany in France. After only three weeks Jack was killed in battle at the young age of eighteen. The Kiplings had already suffered the lost of a daughter years before this tragedy occurred. Their grief was overwhelming. In 1916 Kipling's Sea Warfare was published and contained therein was an emotional poem about his son Jack. Personally I was moved by this story of one of my favorite poets, especially in the death of his son Jack. I could not help but to think of another young man whose life was taken while fighting against the Germans in World War II. And before I present this poem I want to relate the following.

Our oldest son Tim informed us by email that he would be in Washington D.C. this coming weekend. He also mentioned the monument that was finally erected in that city and honors the men and women who died during World War II. I was able to pull up on the internet information about the names listed of the ones who gave the ultimate sacrifice for their country and I found the name of my oldest brother Walter M. Elliott. It only stated that he was from Georgia and that he was buried in a cemetery in a foreign country. Martin, as he was called by his parents and siblings, was only eighteen years old when he was sent by our government to England and eventually to Belgium and Germany where he and thousands of other teenagers became engaged in actual combat. Martin celebrated his nineteenth birthday anniversary in March of 1945. He was killed on April 5 of that year in northwest Germany. The war ended in May of 1945. Many have been the times that I have thought, if only.... I was ten years old when he died. I still remember so well when my father came walking up the hill to our home and announced through his tears that Martin had been killed. I remember also the overwhelming sorrow that filled our hearts for many years. But I am sure that my mother and father suffered the most. The cost of war is not found in the amount of money spent; rather it is in the cost of human lives that are sacrificed for a cause. The following poem could be dedicated to all who have suffered the lost of a loved one in any war.

My Boy Jack is a 1915 poem by Rudyard Kipling. Although Kipling wrote it after his beloved son John (called Jack) an 18 year old Lieutenant in the 2nd Battalion, Irish Guards went missing in September 1915 during the Battle of Loos, during World War I (Wikipedia Free Encyclopedia):

"Have you news of my boy Jack?"
Not this tide.
"When d'you think that he'll come back?"
Not with this wind blowing, and this tide.
"Has any one else had word of him?"
Not this tide.
For what is sunk will hardly swim,
Not with this wind blowing, and this tide.
"Oh, dear, what comfort can I find?"
None this tide,
Nor any tide,
Except he did not shame his kind —
Not even with that wind blowing, and that tide.
Then hold your head up all the more,
This tide,
And every tide;
Because he was the son you bore,
And gave to that wind blowing and that tide!

SIX MINUS FOUR EQUALS TWO
1981

This article could also be entitled, "We Are Back Where Started", or, "The House Is Now Too Big And Too Quiet". My wife and I are now experiencing what countless other parents have experienced and that is the time in our lives when all of our children have left home. In our case, our four exited via the various colleges and universities. We have just recently enrolled our youngest child in college. What has occurred in our lives is being repeated by many of our friends and neighbors. Perhaps the thoughts in this article should be dedicated to all those parents who find for the first time that they are staring at one another across the kitchen table during a meal without a child being present.

This is the first time that a child of ours has not attended a local school system since way back when the first one started in the first grade and his mother cried because she thought she had lost a son for sure... Remember those mornings when we had to wait in line at the bathroom when the kids were rushing around and trying to get ready for school... Remember racing to three different schools and depositing children at each one ... Remember having to wait up until two o'clock in the morning for the band to come in from a trip ... What about their mother having to wash all those clothes, especially those things pertaining to a football player. Oh, and the noise!...We even put the electric guitar players in the garage and closed the door ... But, to no avail ... I still couldn't take a nap for the sound went throughout the neighborhood .. The sound of the radio, tape deck, and record players actually vibrated the walls ... And those dirty rooms (boys) ... I don't see how they could stay in the mess ... They didn't seem to mind and brought their company right in there with an embarrassed mother apologizing every step of the way ... I must mention the times when the children learned how to drive ... I wonder what the life expectancy is for a drivers education teacher... How about all the food the kids could consume...It was a survival of the fittest ... I still possess fork marks on my hands... Teenage years mean a lack of sleep for parents... Listening for them to come home after a date ... Worrying about their safety when they were out at night... Mothers trying their best to help a daughter to fix her hair just right... Fathers worrying where all the money was coming from ... That problem still exist ... I don't like empty rooms ... There is plenty of hot water for a bath ... The mileage on the family car does not add up so rapidly anymore ... The house is too clean and too quiet ... The house is more than adequate for just two people...It will be good to have the children home for the holidays... Laughter and noise will once again fill the well-worn house.

Children are from the Lord (Psalms 127:3). God has loaned them to us. We are stewards of the most prized possession a person could ever have – our children. Parents are required to love them and bring them up in the way of the Lord (Proverbs 22:6; Ephesians 6:4). The time to accomplish this goal is so brief. How blessed are parents whose sons and daughters are Christians. This is a consoling and comforting thought when children leave home. Young parents act swiftly. It is but a short time before you will stand where we are now in these challenging, changing years of our lives. Love, lead, guide and protect those precious children. Prepare them for a life and not just a living.

Please pardon me while I finish cutting this stubborn apron string.

THE 'TIE' THAT BINDS

Perhaps the first thoughts that come to your mind will be the beautiful hymn, "Blest Be The Tie" but the title of this article is not taken from the song. It might seem odd but the 'tie' that I have reference to is the one that I wear around my neck on occasions. You see, the person who taught me how to tie a 'half- Windsor knot' was an older brother in Christ who influenced me greatly when I was but a lad and a member of my home congregation in Summerville, Georgia. Brother Julius Sprayberry was our song leader and he also often taught a Bible class on Sunday morning and/or Wednesday night. It was Christian men like him and brother Charles Cochran, along with several Christian men and women who influenced my life for Jesus Christ. The widows of brethren Sprayberry and Cochran (Thelma & Frances, respectively) still attend the South Commerce congregation in my hometown.

When I was a boy growing up in this small church there was no 'youth minister' as such but the love and influence exerted upon us young people by the adult members guided us in the way of the Lord and gave us a real sense of belonging and security. We did not have a 'full-time' preacher for many years but the men of the congregation would lead us in our worship assemblies. In fact, brother Roland Hemphill baptized me when I was a lad of thirteen. These brothers and sisters in Christ were 'just regular' members. Professionalism was generally unknown among our congregations sixty years ago. We now live in a mobile society and families seemingly are always on the move from one location to another one and often there is not a real sense of having a 'home congregation' by many families today. It is a beautiful thing to witness members of a congregation fulfilling the thoughts found in Ephesians 4:15, 16: "But, speaking the truth in love, may grow up in all things into Him who is the heard— Christ—from whom the whole body, joined and knit together by what every joint supplies, according to the effective working by which every part does its share, causes growth of the body for the edifying of itself in love."

Over fifty years have past since I left my home congregation for college. But I retain precious memories of the time we met in the American Legion Hall in downtown Summerville before the brick building was constructed on South Commerce Street. I have a warm feeling in my heart and often tears will feel my eyes when I think of so many of those members who have gone to be with the Lord. I possess a deep sense of gratitude and debt to those godly men and women who loved me and encouraged me to live for Jesus and to preach the gospel. There was a time when Virginia and I lived in a small trailer on the campus of Alabama Christian College when the church back home learn of our lack of money and they sent us a check in the amount of fifty dollars. It could as well have been a thousand dollars for it provided food for us to eat. It was the love and compassion that motivated the gift that has always endeared the members in my heart. I have a real feeling of loyalty to my home congregation. I have returned for gospel meetings and it was always a joy to see 'old friends' and to reminisce of years past. I would love for all of our children and young people to have such fond memories of a 'home congregation' and to know of their roots in spiritual matters. We owe a great deal to the members of the church who live faithfully and carry on the work of our Lord.

I seldom tie my 'tie' without thinking of brother Sprayberry who taught me how to tie the knot and who influenced me to live for Jesus Christ. And when I think of him I also remember fondly my home congregation. I firmly believe that God, by His infinite grace will supply unto us the entrance "into the everlasting kingdom of our Lord and Savior Jesus Christ" (2 Peter 1:11) where there will never be a separation from those of His children we have known and loved in this life. Here are a couple of stanzas from the beloved hymn that we often sing and that expresses my inward feelings.

BLESS BE THE TIE

"Blest be the tie that binds
Our hearts in Christian love;
The fellowship of kindred minds
Is like to that above.
When we asunder part,
It give us inward pain;
But we shall still be joined in heart,
And hope to meet again."

— John Fawcett, Wikipedia Free Encyclopedia, Public Domain

WAR HEROES

Recently I read The Pacific, a book written by Hugh Ambrose, the son of the late Stephen E. Ambrose who was the author of Band of Brothers. His latest novel chronicled the lives of five men and their comrades who were in the U. S. Marine Corps and the Navy during World War II. The battles on the sea and on the land were fought in the Pacific Ocean and the enemy, of course, was the Empire of Japan. The loss of lives on both sides of the war was extremely high. There were battles on some islands that would be unknown to many of our people like Cape Gloucester and Peleliu. The more familiar ones were Iwo Jima, Guadalcanal and Okinawa. During the latter part of the war the Japanese realized that they were on the losing side so they began to use drastic measures to destroy the American aircraft carriers, destroyers and other ships. The Kamikaze were suicide attacks by military aviators from the Empire of Japan against Allied naval vessels in the closing stages of the Pacific campaign of World War II, designed to destroy as many warships as possible (Wikipedia Free Encyclopedia). Thousands of lives were lost and scores of ships were damaged or destroyed.

While visiting with our son in Texas, we drove over to San Antonio to visit the Alamo and other places of interest. We were privileged to spend the night in the historic Menger Hotel which is located just across the street from the Alamo. My wife and I, along with our daughter-in-law, were sitting in the beautiful lobby of the hotel and I was listening to a couple of older men exchanging stories of their experiences while serving on a particular ship in the Pacific Ocean during World War II. Both of them wore a cap with the name of the ship on it. The more I listened to these men talk, the more I realized that the book The Pacific was coming to life. I got up and moved over to the couch where one gentleman was sitting so I could hear what they were saying more clearly. They were relating how their ship was being hit by bombers and not fighter planes. One gentleman said that he was the only one who survived in his immediate group while serving in a lower compartment of the ship. The other gentleman related that he was the only survivor of his company at a gun turret when another bomber hit the ship. Their ship sank but they were rescued.

They were staying in the hotel where their annual reunion was being held by the surviving members of their ship that sank. One gentleman stated that only six members were still living. The men were in their mid eighties. I introduced myself to them, shook their hands and thanked them for their service to our country during WW II. These men would not consider themselves as 'heroes' but they were. They simply would say that 'they were just doing their job'.

There is another book that I have been reading for years. It is called The Bible. It is actually the Holy Scriptures that came from God Himself who is the Divine Author (2 Timothy 3:16, 17). Since the Garden of Eden there has been a different kind of warfare being fought in the heart of every accountable being who has lived on this earth. It is being waged in the hearts of men and women even today. Jesus Christ the Savior and His army are opposing Satan and his forces of darkness. Jesus Christ is the "Captain" of our salvation and He leads His army in this ongoing conflict (Hebrews 2:10). The apostle Paul describes this type of warfare in 2 Corinthians 10:3-6: "For though we walk in the flesh, we do not war according to the flesh. For the weapons of our warfare are not carnal but mighty in God for pulling down strongholds, casting down arguments and every high thing that exalts itself against the knowledge of God, bringing every thought into captivity to the obedience of Christ..." Again in Ephesians 6:10-16: "Finally, my brethren, be strong in the Lord and in the power of His might. Put on the whole armor of God, that you may be able to stand against the wiles of the devil. For we do not wrestle against flesh and blood, but against principalities, against powers, against the rulers of the darkness of this age, against spiritual hosts of wickedness in the heavenly places." Paul then describes the Christian soldier's armor: "Therefore take up the whole armor of God, that you may be able to withstand in the evil day, and having done all, to stand. Stand therefore, having girded your waist with truth, having put on the breastplate of righteousness, and having shod your feet with the preparation of the gospel of peace; above all, taking the shield of faith with which you will be able to quench all the fiery darts of the wicked one. And take the helmet of salvation, and the sword of the Spirit, which is the word of God..."

There is a 'wall of faith' mentioned in Hebrews chapter eleven that list the names of many of the heroes who died while fighting the forces of evil beginning with Abel and including Enoch, Noah, Abraham, Sarah, Isaac, Jacob, Joseph, Moses, and many others. In the second section of the Book of God you find names like John who was called the Baptist, Matthew and the apostles including Paul and Peter. There was Stephen who died in the thick of the battle. There were saints who became martyrs for Christ and righteousness as mentioned in Revelation 6:9-11. Undoubtedly under the oppression of the Roman Empire literally thousands of believers suffered horrible deaths because they would not deny their Lord. Their names, along with scores of believers in Christ over the centuries, have their names recorded in the "Lamb's Book of Life" (Revelation 21:27). This is the highest award, 'The Medal of Honor', which the Christian could ever receive.

There have been other faithful men and women in whom The Book of God has come alive, a vast number of those saints have gone on to be with the Lord (Philippians 1:23). There were the pioneer preachers who blazed the trail of Christianity across our nation and their devoted wives who stayed home, reared their children and kept the home fires burning. We have known elders who have committed their lives to the care of the members of a local congregation; deacons who have fulfilled their obligations by serving faithfully in their various roles as servants of the church and Bible teachers who have devoted hours of preparation in order to teach effectively adults and young people the Word of God There are saints who have endured hardships and discouragement over the years yet they have remained faithful to the Lord. And consider the missionaries and their families who often serve the Lord under adverse conditions and do not enjoy the same luxuries of life as other Christians while they live in foreign countries.

There are Christian educators who sacrifice much in order to provide an education that includes the teaching of the Bible and opportunities for spiritual growth and Christian fellowship. There are members of the body of Christ who are "steadfast, immovable, always abounding in the work of the Lord... (I Corinthians 15:58). Christ truly lives in them (Philippians 1:21). They can say with Paul: "I have been crucified with Christ: it is no longer I who live, but Christ lives in me; and the life which I now live in the flesh I live by faith in the Son of God, who loved me and gave Himself for me" (Galatians 2:20). And when they come to the end of their journey here on this earth they will also declare: "I have fought the good fight, I have finished the race, I have kept the faith. Finally, there is laid up for me the crown of righteousness, which the Lord, the righteous Judge, will give to me on that Day, and not to me only but also to all who have loved His appearing" (2 Timothy 4:6-8). Heroes, not really, just devoted soldiers of the cross, 'doing their job', and carrying the blood stained banner of their King, the Lord Jesus Christ.

WHAT A DIFFERENCE
SIXTY-SIX YEARS MAKE

I was only ten years old when the atomic bombs were dropped on Hiroshima and Nagasaki, Japan on the dates of August 6 and August 9, 1945, respectively. Later when I viewed the pictures of that awful looking mushroom cloud caused by an atomic bomb explosion, my young heart was filled with fear when I thought of the destructive power such a weapon possessed. It was during the years of 1941-1945 the American populace was informed just how horrible the 'Japs' were in the many atrocities they committed during WW II, beginning with Pearl Harbor. Even the movie industry used propaganda in their movies to cause us to hate every person who was born in the country of Japan. Our government even incarcerated Japanese who were American citizens. I feel sure that the people in Japan were influenced to believe that all Americans were evil. History has proven over the years that not all the citizens of Japan desired to engage the United States in warfare. As often is the case, those in authority, along with the military leadership pushed for the surprise attack on Pearl Harbor and thus to become engaged in warfare with United States.

One of the sweetest and dearest Christian friends that Virginia and I have had in our lives was a gentle Japanese lady by the name of Kim Ellis who was a member of the church in Wetumpka, Alabama. She stated that her father did not want to go to war but he was forced to enter the military service. I recalled how Kim related to us that they were notified the Americans were going to firebomb her city and how she was led to safety by a family friend. Following the bombing of her city, she never saw her loved ones again. She told us that she and others were starving to death until the American soldiers gave them food to eat.

Doug Andrews, who is married to Ann, my wife's sister, had an aunt, Sarah Sheppard Andrews, who spent her adult life (1916-1961) as a missionary in the country of Japan. She lived there during WW II and was treated kindly by those who knew her and her many good works, along with her teaching the Bible to them. This Christian lady saw the other side, the good side, of the people in that country. She influenced many to give their lives to Jesus Christ. Her life as a child of God and her labors of love among the Japanese people are recorded in the book, Virtuous Servant (Providence House Publishers, Franklin, TN, Fiona Soltes, Author).

Presently the nation of Japan is suffering because of the earthquakes, tsunami and of all things, the fear of radiation from their nuclear plants. And it is the United States of American that has sent our military personnel to aid the citizens of this country. With all the moral decadence and ills found in our country, the United States remains the most benevolent nation on earth, in my opinion. Those who were once our enemies are now treated with compassion and kindness.

YOUNG HEARTS AT 201 YEARS OLD

Now before you jump to any conclusion, I am speaking about two lovely Christian ladies who have served the Lord Jesus Christ faithfully for many, many years. I was associated with these beautiful ladies for some 29 years while serving as the preacher for the two congregations where they are members.

I speak, first of all, of sister Gertrude Jones who i   ɲʰ   ꜟ the church in the city of Opp, Alabama. I met sister Jones when uɪc ... .y and I moved to that city in 1971. This sweet lady endeared herself to my family because of her kindness and gentleness. We ate in her home during gospel meetings with the visiting preacher and on many other occasions. She loves our children very much. Even now she will ask about them. Sister Jones informed me of her sister who was bedridden and asked me to visit her which I did regularly until her death. This act contributed to our closeness because she was so thankful for my doing so. Sister Jones was always busy visiting and helping her neighbors and brothers and sisters in Christ. She was indeed concerned with the needs of others.

We moved from Opp in 1983 to Prattville. Over the years Virginia and I have visited with sister Gertrude. I remember one visit when she was in her early 90s. She said to me that it was difficult to get someone to go visiting with her because most of her friends had died that were in her age group. But she informed me that she still cooked food and carried it to the 'elderly' people. Now that really impressed me and caused me to smile. "Gert", as her close friends call her now resides in a nursing home. She celebrated her 100th birthday anniversary with family and friends in July of this year. A couple of months ago Virginia and I visited with her. She was in bed and she looked frail in body but her reception was as cheerful as ever. She welcomed us in deep emotions with her usual greeting, "You are just like family to me." And that feeling is mutual.

The second Christian lady of whom I speak is sister Dessie Snell, a member of the Prattville church of Christ. She might be affectionately called the 'card lady'. For nearly seventeen years she would often call me on Monday morn-

238

ings to inquire about someone's address that had been mentioned as sick or of someone who had been visiting with us during the Sunday assemblies. I can still hear her as she began speaking in her sweet voice, "Hello Brother Elliott...." I knew immediately why she was calling me. It was in February of 1983 that we moved to work with the Prattville congregation. In May, 1983, we were invited to attend her birthday party. She was only 75 years old. This year she celebrated her 101st birthday anniversary with family and friends! Over the years she has sent approximately five thousand cards to the sick, sorrowing, visitors, new members, and for special occasions like birthdays and anniversaries. Just recently we received a sweet card from her. She is apologetic that she just can't do as much as she once did. While in good health and even when she didn't feel well you would always see her sitting up near the front during the worship assemblies. If her health would permit her she would be in attendance even now. She informed me that she is presently trying to meet the challenge of reading the Bible through in forty days. She loves to have company. You always feel blessed by being in her presence. I thank God for her wonderful Christian example.

I have endeavored over the years to ask God in my daily prayers to bless our aged saints. So many like sister Jones and sister Snell have strengthened and encouraged me by their kind words and holy and dedicated lives in Jesus Christ. I have learned more from them than I have ever taught them in my preaching. I think the following poem best describes these saintly ladies.

THE AGED CHRISTIAN WOMAN
Titus 2:3

You tell me I am getting old;
I tell you that's not so!
The "house" I live in is worn out,
And that, of course, I know.

It's been in use a long, long while;
It's weathered many a gale.
I'm really not surprised you think
It's getting somewhat frail.

The color's changing on the roof;
The window's getting dim,
The walls a bit transparent
And looking rather thin.

The foundation's not so steady
As once it used to be.
My house is getting shaky,
But my "house" isn't me!

My few short years can't make me old;
I feel I'm in my youth.
Eternity lies just ahead,
A life of joy and truth.

I'm going to live forever there.
Life will go on – it's grand!
You tell me I am getting old?
You just don't understand!

The dweller in my little "house"
Is young and bright and gay,
Just starting on a life to last
Throughout eternal day.

You only see the outside,
Which is all that most folks see.
You tell me I am getting old?
You have mixed my "house" with me!

— Dora Johnson, Christian Woman

240

Section 6

SCENES FROM MY
OFFICE WINDOW

MY PLACE FOR STUDY, MEDITATION, AND WRITING

This is where I sit for long periods of time as I read and write articles. I read the Bible and other books. I work on my computer and write articles to be sent to others and to various Christian publications. I pray as I kneel by the window in my office here in the early morning hours. I am surrounded by my books and material to be found in the filing cabinet nearby. I feel right at home in this particular section of our house. I can shut out the rest of the world at times. But not completely for you see, I observe many things from the only window in this small room I call 'my study'. For example, there is a beautiful tree across in the yard of a neighbor. It is radiant with its leaves in red and golden colors. Further back I see Hickory trees, Oak trees and various other kinds of trees with foliage ablaze in full color. The Bradford Pear trees nearby are so beautiful but the Japanese maple stands out among them all with the red leaves shining in the sunlight. Much to my surprise we have experienced one of the most beautiful autumns ever in central and south Alabama! There is a certain melancholy about the fall of the year and I suppose it is in knowing that winter will soon follow when these same trees will have lost all their leaves. But our autumn has been gorgeous!

You know life is compared to the various seasons of the years. Many of us are presently in the 'autumn' of our lives but it is not a time to be depressed knowing that God is good. It is a time of reflection. There have been many disappointments but the good memories outweigh the bad. You are as young as you feel. How you think of life greatly affects how you feel in the 'fall' of your life. I love the mountains. I feel closer to God when I view His creation from a lofty height. Someone has suggested that youth is compared to the valley while adulthood is the mountainside. The view becomes better as we climb higher to the top of the mountain.

"As ripe fruit is sweeter than green fruit,
So is age sweeter than youth, provided the youth
Were grafted into Christ.
As harvest time is brighter time than seed time,
So age is Brighter than youth;
That is, if youth were a seed time for good;
As the completion of a Work is more glorious than the beginning,
So is age more glorious than youth;
That is if The foundation of the works of God was laid in youth.
As sailing into port is a happier Thing than the voyage
So is age happier than youth;
That is, when the voyage from youth
Is made with Christ at the helm."

— *J. Pulsford, New cyclopaedia of prose illustrations:*
Adapted to Christian ..., Volume 1
By Elon Foster

A HERITAGE FROM THE LORD

We who are older remember well the Beatles. One of the popular songs they sang over forty years ago was Yellow Submarine. Well this article is not about a yellow submarine but a big yellow school bus, in fact, a couple of yellow school buses that come into our neighborhood every school morning. I see our neighborhood children congregating together waiting for the bus to come pick them up. In the afternoon those same buses come again into our subdivision to deposit those precious children at various spots along the way. How wonderful that the children have opportunity to be educated so that they can contribute to our society in various ways.

There was a time in my parent's generation that many boys and girls did not have the opportunity to obtain a high school education. The farm children were often kept out of school to work in order to provide food for the family. In contrast to the school days when the buses run through our neighborhood it is quite a different sight on Sundays. I see very few automobile coming by the house with families on their way to Bible classes anywhere. I wonder what percentage of the school children attends Bible classes on Sunday at any religious organization. It probably would be discouraging to learn that most children are not taken by their parents to Sunday school. You see many parents are too involved in the cares of this life to provide an education in the Word of God in the home and/or in Bible classes. The Psalmist declared, "Behold, children are a heritage from the Lord, The fruit of the womb is a reward. Like arrows in the hand of a warrior, So are the children of one's youth. Happy is the man who has his quiver full of them..." (Psalms 27:3-5). Children are not ours to do with as we so please. They actually belong to God and He has loaned them to us for a time. It is the responsibility of the parents to provide an education in the most important book known to mankind and that is the Word of God. The apostle Paul placed the responsibility of rearing children in the way of the Lord on the head of the family when he wrote in Ephesians 6:4, And you, fathers, do not provoke your children to wrath, but bring them up in the training and admonition of the Lord." True and complete education should prepare children not only for a living but rather for a life presently and in the world eternal life.

FROM GOD WITH LOVE

"Children are a blessing sent from God above
For us to care and nurtured and most of all to love.
God calls us to be parents and gives us all the tools
And when we feel like giving up, our strength He will renew.
Children are a gift from God that He so freely lends
To make it through the childhood years, on Him we must depend.
We have shared the Word of God, we've taught them right from wrong
Now it's time to let them go and let them write their song.
The faith instilled, the examples lived, and the lesson taught
All gifts that we've given our child, which will never be forgotten.
There are many paths a child can take, right or wrong will remain unknown
But rest assured that in the end, they all lead back to home."

— *Author Unknown*

A LOVE THAT LASTS

One day the door bell rang so I opened the door and a lady who is a neighbor of ours pushed a small girl into the foyer and asked if she could stay here for a few minutes. It wasn't long until the door bell rang again and this time it was a young man standing at the front door and instructing his daughter to come out to him. I really did not know at the time what was going on but here I was right in the middle of things I soon detected as being a real family problem. The neighbor who brought the child to our house was only trying to help but the father was wanting his daughter so I had no alternative in the matter but to have the child leave our house. I watched the activities across the street at the house where the girl and her mother were staying with the child's grandparents. A few days later the grandfather came to visit me and explained that his daughter and her husband were in the process of getting a divorce and things had gotten out of hand. His daughter and the child's mother obtained a legal document that prevented her husband from coming near her and the daughter.

It was only a short time that I began to see a man visiting this lady who was divorcing her husband. Soon she moved out of her parent's house and left with this man. However, the little girl (I would say about eight years old) has remained for the most part with her grandparents. Undoubtedly her mother and this man now live in a different school district from where her daughter has been attending school so in order for the child to remain in her school she has to live temporarily with her grandparents.

Just this morning I saw her leave with her grandfather on her way to school. Now I know that some of this is my own surmising but I think I am correct on most of this story. To my right and across a different street live a vey nice couple and friends of mine. Their situation is this. He has a son and she has two sons by a previous marriage. They were married last summer and now she is expecting their child. You heard it before, "his, hers and theirs." Sadly to say this has become common place in our society today. I feel sorry for people in homes where there has been a divorce. Children suffer so deeply when their parents do not stay together. Without passing judgment I may say that there are no good divorces. Someone has sinned and souls may be in danger of being lost. Children are being separated from one parent and can only see him or her on occasions. Longevity in marriage is fast becoming obsolete. It 'blows their minds' when I tell young people that my wife and I have been married for fifty-two years. "Until death do us part" may already be an antiquated statement that is no longer being used in marriage ceremonies for many couples.

Love seems the swiftest, but it is the slowest of all growths. No man or woman really knows what perfect love is until they have been married a quarter of a century.

— Mark Twain's Notebook
www.twainquotes.com

A successful marriage requires falling in love many times, always with the same person.

— Mignon McLaughlin
www.BrainyQuote.com

"Have you not read that He who made them at the beginning 'made them male and female,'? "and said, 'For this reason a man shall leave his father and mother and be joined to his wife, and the two shall become one flesh'? "So then, they are no longer two but one flesh. Therefore what God has joined together, let not man separate" (Matthew 19:4-6).

— *Jesus Christ*

AN ILL WIND THAT BLOWS NOTHING GOOD

On Sunday, February 17, 2008, I was watching the progress of a dangerous cell containing a tornado that was heading for Prattville when the power went off at 3:15 p.m. I immediately turned on my battery operated radio and learned that the tornado had touched down in our city. The power was restored in about fifteen minutes and the television station began broadcasting details about the location where the tornado had hit. It was in the neighborhood where we first lived when we moved to Prattville, Alabama in 1983. The tornado was later classified as EF 3 with winds about 150 mph. The devastation was great with some 800 homes damaged and at least 30 homes completely destroyed. Some 50 businesses were damaged. Scores of people were injured but there were no fatalities. That within itself is amazing when you consider the damage done to the various homes and buildings.

On Tuesday I began working in one house that would be declared a total loss. This modest house was the home of a saintly Christian lady who had died in December of 2007. Her daughter was living in the house when the tornado hit. Fortunately, she was at the home of a Christian friend having lunch. I especially wanted to work in this house that once was the home of a dear Christian friend of ours, sister Lois Gipson. She was one of sweetest persons I have ever known. She was known and greatly loved for her kind and gentle ways and for her thinking of others with gifts she had made with her hands. As I worked with other Christians, I found many personal items that had been tossed about by the strong winds. As I would find an item she had made or pictures of the family I would give them to her daughter Martha. These were items that insurance could not replace. The roof had been torn off of about half of the house but we were able to save much of the furniture, clothing, personal items, etc. It was an emotional thing to pick up something that was very personal and think that this was something that was greatly cherished by this Christian lady. While I, along with others, was helping her son and daughter to remove everything that was not ruined by the wind and rain, I thought within myself that there were so many families all around the area who were going through their possessions and trying to save what they could. I saw a family looking through the debris in the house back of us doing this very thing. I expressed my concern to them and simply said that "I am so sorry and that I was praying for them." They in turn expressed their gratitude that others cared and were praying for them. The destruction I saw was just overwhelming.

It is indeed heartwarming when you see so many people working feverishly to do what they can to aid the victims of the tornado's destructive power. It is in times like these that the best in people is manifested. I want to applaud members of the church locally and from other areas who were/are doing what they can to alleviate the suffering of so many. Doors of opportunity will be opened for brethren to encourage individuals to know more of Jesus Christ and His kingdom. Prejudice will be lessened as brethren manifest their love by their kind and thoughtful deeds. How wonderful to live in a community of caring people.

One of the last things I saw before leaving this house that was demolished was a small mirror on a bathroom door with this inscription underneath it: "This person is not to be taken too seriously." This brought a smile to my face because I knew of the humor of the lady who had lived in this house. In spite of the difficulties in life we should always remember to "Smile because God loves you."

BUYING AND SELLING

My neighbors across the street and two houses removed from our house have a very familiar sign in their front yard that reads 'For Sale'. The house has been bought and sold several times over the years, so I am told. You see, we are a mobile society. Each year in the spring our community is affected by several military families moving to different locations throughout the world. It seems that this is a bad time to have a house on the market. Buying and selling products and services is an integrated and important way of life in our country. However, there is a commodity of which I presently speak that should only be purchased and never to be sold at any cost.

In Proverbs 23:23 an important exhortation is given by the writer: "Buy the truth, and do not sell it, Also wisdom and instruction and understanding." Notice first of all this commodity is called "truth". It was Pilate who asked Jesus, "What is truth" (John 18:38)? Jesus in His prayer to God had already answered this question when He said, "Sanctify them by Your truth, Your word is truth" (John 17:17). Jesus himself is the "truth" (John 14:6). The "truth came through Jesus Christ" (John 1:17). In this last passage, the Law of Moses was used in contrast to "the truth". In this sense, the truth revealed through Jesus Christ is the gospel with its facts to be believed, its commands to be obeyed and the promises to be enjoyed (I Corinthians 15:1-3; Acts 2:38; Mark 16:15, 16). Why should we purchase (obtain) the truth (gospel)? The apostle Paul declared that the gospel "... is the power of God to salvation for everyone who believes, for the Jew first and also for the Greek" (Romans 1:16).

Second, we should buy only the truth. Not everything is as good as it is said to be. There are some products that we may purchase that may be inferior to the standard that it claims. Even in religious matter not every teaching presented is the truth. We must examine such in the light of the Word of God. Paul taught in I Thessalonians 5:21 to "test all things; hold fast what is good." The apostle John later wrote: "Beloved, do not believe every spirit, but test the spirits, whether they are of God; because many false prophets have gone out into the world" (I John 4:1). We must discriminate between truth and error. The counterfeit is very difficult to detect because it so like the real thing.

Third, we are to buy all the truth. It is a critical mistake to fail to buy all the truth. When we purchase a product we desire and expect to receive all of that which pertains to the product. However there are those who will not buy all the truth. The rich young ruler who came to Jesus and inquired, "Good Teacher, what good thing shall I do that I may have eternal life?" (Matthew 19:16-22) was not willing to buy all the teachings of the Lord. Because when he was instructed to sell his riches and give to the poor, he was unwilling to buy into all that Jesus told him to do. There are many religionists who will accept only partial truth. They refuse, however, to follow all the teachings of Jesus Christ regarding the plan of salvation and how to worship God acceptably. May we all possess a deep desire to learn all the truth that we can and have the faith and fortitude to obey the same.

Fourth, the sincere seeker of truth will purchase this precious commodity regardless of the price. In parables presented by Jesus He emphasized this very thing. "Again, the kingdom of heaven is like treasure hidden in a field, which a man found and hid; and for joy over it he goes and sells all that has and buys that field. "Again, the kingdom of heaven is like a merchant seeking beautiful pearls, "who, when he had found one pearl of great price, went and sold all that he had and bought it' (Matthew 13:44, 45, 46). Whether we speak in regards to the truth or the kingdom of Christ, the principle is the same; one must make every effort and exert every ounce of energy to obtain the truth.

Fifth, it is not enough to merely hear and know the Word of God; we must accept and obey the truth. Jesus said, "Not everyone who says to Me, 'Lord, Lord,' shall enter the kingdom of heaven, but he who does the will of My Father in heaven" (Matthew 7:21). The person who only hears the words of the Lord and does not do them is like the man who built his house on the sand. However, the disciple who hears the words of Jesus Christ and obeys them is like the man who built his house upon the rock which stood the ravages of nature (Matthew 7:24- 27).

Sixth, we should buy the truth while we have the time and opportunity. Procrastination is a work of Satan. Many are the souls who planned to obey the gospel but delayed such a decision and died without Christ. We should never assume that additional opportunities will be afforded us to give our lives to Jesus. The wise man wrote in Proverbs 27:1, "Do not boast about tomorrow, For you do not know what a day may bring forth." Also James gives this advice in James 4:13-17, "Come now, you who say, "Today or tomorrow we will go to such and such a city, spend a year there, buy and sell, and make a profit"; whereas you do not know what will happen tomorrow. For what is your life? It is even a vapor that appears for a little time and then vanishes away. Instead you ought to say, 'If the Lord wills, we shall live and do this or that.' But now you boast in your arrogance. All such boasting is evil. Therefore, to him who knows to do good and does not do it, to him it is sin."

Seventh, the passage in Proverbs 23:23 which exhorts us to "Buy the truth" also informs us to "sell it not." The purchase of the truth is a permanent investment and we should never depart from it. We should never exchange the truth for fame, popularity, wealth, position, power or pleasure. These are solemn words of our Savior as found in Matthew 16:26, "For what profit is it to a man if he gains the whole world, and loses his own soul? Or what will a man give in exchange for his soul?"

Each person should study the Holy Scriptures in order to learn the truth. It said of the inhabitants of Berea that "These were more fair-minded than those in Thessalonica, in that they received the word with all readiness, and searched the Scriptures daily to find out whether these things were so" (Acts 17:11). In the Sermon on the Mount Jesus gave this promise, "Blessed are those who hunger and thirst for righteousness, For they shall be filled" (Matthew 5:6). Again our Lord assured seekers of truth that they would be able to find it as explained in this passage in Matthew 7:7, 8, "Ask, and it will be given to you; seek, and you will find; knock, and it will be opened to you. "For everyone who asks receives, and he who seeks finds, and to him who knocks it will be opened."

One may ask can a person know the truth? The answer is found in John 8:31, 32: Then Jesus said to those Jews who believed Him, "If you abide in My word, you are My disciples indeed. And you shall know the truth, and the truth shall make you free." In verse 36, we read, "Therefore if the Son makes you free, you shall be free indeed." As dedicated disciples of the Word of God, we can be assured we can know the truth and that the Son will set us free from the bondage of sin and death. And that is why we should make every effort to "Buy the truth" and never permit it to be taken from us.

EXERCISE THAT IS PROFITABLE
FOR ETERNITY

There is this nice gentleman who often walks his beautiful dog right by my house where I can see him from my window. Also there are two ladies who live in our small subdivision who walk together regularly where I can see them from my office. And from time to time there are others who either walk or jog through our community. This is good exercise for one's body and mind. After all, God formed our bodies in the beginning of time and He expects us to care for it. The problem area lies not in the exercise itself but in the amount of time consumed, when it takes place and how much we spend on it. For example we often see individuals jogging on Sunday morning while on our way to the worship assembly. But that would also be true of people who go to some place of recreation like the lakes and coastal area on the weekends where they can ride in their boats and/or go in swimming. Great emphasis is being placed in our modern society as to what we should eat and the amount of exercise that we should engage in on a regular basis. Untold millions of dollars are spent on exercise equipment, vitamins and other products that would make us feel and look better. No problem unless we speak of extremes and exclusions.

I can walk in my garage on a treadmill for thirty minutes and not move but a short distance. I can ride on a used exercise bike for thirty minutes and remain in the same spot where I began. However we must understand that that which is perfectly harmless and even useful and healthful can be wrong if that which is more important is excluded. I mean by that, the man or woman who is riding a bicycle or jogging on the Lord's Day and not attending the worship assembly of the Lord's church is doing wrong. A person who is careful and zealous for eating the healthiest foods may in fact be neglecting eating the Lord's Supper on the first day of the week. There is the matter of priority. What is more important, the care only for the body or the care for one's spiritual needs?

Jesus said, "It is written, 'Man shall not live by bread alone, but by every word that proceeds from the mouth of God'" (Matthew 4:4). The Preacher wrote in Ecclesiastes 12:13 to "Fear God and keep His commandments, For this is man's all." And the wise man wrote in Proverbs 3:7, 8, "Do not be wise in your own eyes; Fear the Lord and depart from evil. It will be health to your flesh, and strength to you bones." In his speech to the elders of the church of Ephesus, Paul said, "So, brethren I commend you to God and to the word of His grace, which is able to build you up and give you an inheritance among all those who are sanctified" (Acts 20:32).

That which will strengthen the inner man is found in the words of Paul concerning brethren who had been "nourished in the word of faith and of the good doctrine which you have carefully followed (I Timothy 4:6). "Therefore we do not lose heart. Even though our outward man is perishing, yet the inward man is being renewed day by day" (2 Corinthians 4:16). But we must also exercise ourselves in order to have a proper balance in spiritual matters. The apostle Paul wrote in I Timothy 4:7, 8, "But reject profane and old wives' fables, and exercise yourself toward godliness. For bodily exercise profits a little, but godliness is profitable for all things, having promise of the life that now is and of that which is to come." We are to "walk humbly with your God" and "run with endurance the race that is set before us..." We are to "finish the race" "and a crown of righteousness" will be given to us (Micah 6:8; Hebrews 12:1; 2 Timothy 4:7, 8).

GOD OF THE MOUNTAINS AND VALLEYS

I heard the siren and I knew that the rescue squad vehicle was near. I opened the blinds at the window here in my office and sure enough there it was and it stopped across the street from my house. I knew the elderly lady and her son who lived down the street so I hurriedly dressed and went over to see how she was doing. She is ninety-seven years old and was not doing well at all. She was taken to the hospital by the rescue squad. Her son was emotional in expressing his concern for his beloved mother and I can understand why he would feel that way.

I have mixed feelings when I hear the sound of a siren. In this case it was the rescue squad coming to the aid of someone in distress. First of all I am thankful that such help is available. One of the reasons we live where we do is because of the availability of medical assistance. It is encouraging to know that when you need help in a hurry it is there. On the other hand when I hear the sirens of such vehicles I know that someone is in need of medical care or even it might be indicative that someone has died.

Life is like that. Each day we involve ourselves in our work and our family affairs. The sun is shinning and life goes on. Though we might have some aches and pains we go about our business. There is no need of emergency type of medical help. The children are doing well in school and parents are proud and healthy. Sounds of happiness can be heard as the family gathers around the table for an evening meal together. Then someone is injured or a heart attack occurs. The mountain top experiences come crashing down. In the dark valley of life someone becomes incapacitated or even death occurs. Life has turned upside down. To the Christian there is the blessed assurance that God is always there. The writer of Hebrews in chapter thirteen and in verses five and six exclaims, "...For He Himself has said, "I will never leave you nor forsake you." So we may boldly say: "The Lord is my helper; I will not fear. What can man do to me?"

In I Kings 20 we have record of Ben-Hadad and the Syrians fighting against Israel and the Israelites fought valiantly and the Syrians fled. A servant of the king of Syria surmised that they lost the battle because "Their gods are gods of the hills. Therefore they were stronger than we; but if we fight against them in the plain, surely we will be stronger than they" (verse 23). Wrong. "then the man of God came and spoke to the king of Israel, and said, 'Thus says the Lord: Because the Syrians have said, 'The Lord is God of the hills, but He is not God of the Valleys,' therefore I will deliver all this great multitude into your hand, and you shall know I am the Lord" (verse 28). Needless to say, the Israelites again won the battle against the Syrians. You see, God was and is the God of the valley as well as the hills. And we must understand that in life He will be with us in the good times but He will also be with us in the bad times. Thanks to the Lord God for His infinite grace, love and mercy.

HOLIDAYS AND FAMILIES

As I look to my left and across the street I see the lights in my neighbor's front yard. He has really worked hard this year to put up the 'Christmas lights' and decorations. It is the same as you drive through our small community and our entire city. It is indeed a festive time of the year. In fact I really like this season of the year. Why? Because it is when most families can be together. The young father across the street is especially happy this year because his wife gave birth recently to baby boy. Now the older son will have someone to play with — in time.

I have so many fond memories when our four children were all at home during this season of the year. There were occasions when the older boys and I would go to some friend's farm and cut a 'Christmas tree'. Virginia and I would really enjoy seeing the children opening presents on Christmas morning. Virginia would have a delicious meal prepared which would be consumed by our brood. Those were precious years when the children were young and were at home. How fortunate you are if you have sweet memories of family gatherings.

Now we look forward to the children returning home with their families. It is something else when our tribe assembles in one place. It seems that we 'wear the house' because the space is so restricted. What a wonderful sight to see grandchildren opening presents on Christmas morning. What a mess to clean up afterward! How much food is required for so many hungry mouths waiting to consume grandmother's delicious meats, vegetables, salads, pies and cakes? Well, it doesn't matter. Her love reveals itself in the joy she experiences when she cooks for those who are so close to her heart. After all, what are grandmothers for? We want our grandchildren to have pleasant memories of Papa and Ma's home during the holidays.

The Christmas – New Year holidays provide a break from the everyday and sometime mundane affairs. People tend to be kinder and friendlier. Friends get together and enjoy festive occasions. Parents attend seasonal musical programs at school. Old friends are remembered as well as new friends with Christmas cards. And everyone needs a new tie, socks and underwear to wear. Ah, life is good. So enjoy this festive time of the year with your friends and loved ones. Yes, remember those family members who have gone before but don't permit those memories to rob you of the blessedness and happiness of the present.

A New Year's wish for you: "Beloved, I pray that you may prosper in all things and be in health, just as your soul prospers" (3 John 2).

SHOWERS OF BLESSINGS

What I am presently seeing from my office is rain, beautiful rain. When I think of rain I begin to hum, "Rain Drops Falling on My Head". I think of the big rain that occurred during the days of Noah (Genesis 6, 7, 8). Of the time when Elijah prayed that it not rain and it didn't for three and one half years. And then he prayed that it would rain and the Lord God sent the rain upon the land (I Kings 17:1; 18:1, 2: James 5:17, 18). Because of the lack of rain there was a severe drought in the land and I am sure that it was a delight to the eyes and strengthening to the heart of man when the rains finally came. Then there is the statement made by our Lord Jesus Christ as recorded in Matthew 5:45, "...For He makes His sun rise on the evil and on the good, and sends rain on the just and on the unjust." It was in Lystra when Paul had healed a crippled man that the people wanted to worship him and Barnabas as gods that Paul said, among other things, it was God who "gave us rain from heaven and fruitful seasons, filling our hearts with food and gladness (Acts 14:27).

Both saints and sinners enjoy the manifold physical blessings from the bountiful hand of grace of our Heavenly Father, the creator and sustainer of life. In this section of our great country we have experienced a real drought and we have seen what can occur when there is a lack of moisture in the earth. The farmers and cattlemen suffer loss because there are no crops and the cattle have no food. Cities of various sizes have faced a critical shortage of the precious commodity called water because their supplies have dwindled down so drastically. The absence of one of God's greatest blessings should cause thoughtful people to consider what it would be like if He continued to withhold rain from the earth. Mankind should realize that we do not have full control over matters in this life and on this earth, the footstool of God Almighty. Rather thoughtful people will be thankful people who give God the honor and praise for all the blessings of life, physical and spiritual. It was the writer James that declared in chapter one and in verse seventeen, "Every good gift and every perfect gift is from above, and comes down from the Father of lights, with whom there is no variation or shadow or turning.

THERE SHALL BE SHOWERS

"There shall be showers of blessing:" This is the promise of love;
There shall be seasons refreshing, Sent from the Savior above.
"There shall be showers of blessing:" Precious reviving again;
Over the hills and valleys, Sound of abundance of rain.
"There shall be showers of blessing;" Send them upon us, O Lord!
Grant to us now a refreshing; Come, and now honor Thy word.
"There shall be showers of blessing:" O that today they might fall,
Now as to God we're confessing, Now as on Jesus we call!
"There shall be showers of blessing," If we but trust and obey;
There shall be seasons refreshing, When we let Him have His way.
Showers of blessing, Showers of blessing we need;
Mercy drops round us are falling, But for the showers we plead.

— *Lyrics by Daniel Webster Whittle, Wikipedia Free Encyclopedia,*
Copyright, 2003
Broadman Press (Admin. by music services, Inc.)

THE GIFT THAT IS GREAT
BECAUSE OF THE GIVER

Trash and garbage bags everywhere! I know because I carried a dozen bags out from our collection. You see there were grandchildren in the house on December 25th. It was a joyous occasion but I am happy that it is now 'Christmas past'. No it was not a white Christmas but it was a wet one. I mentioned to my wife that the rain that God sent was truly one of the best presents we could have received on a dry and parched land. Other gifts were great because they were from friends and family who love us. The giver is more important than the gift. It is good to be remembered and appreciated. Life would indeed be difficult if it were not for those we love so much. Pity the poor person who is alone and without anyone caring. The Psalmist certainly felt alone when he wrote, "Look on my right hand and see, For there is no one who acknowledges me; Refuge has failed me; No one cares for my soul" (Psalm 142:4).

As we are now in the last days of this year it is good that we dispose of some our 'garbage' if such we have in our hearts and lives. The apostle Paul stated it in this fashion: "Therefore put to death your members which are on the earth: fornication, uncleanness, passion, evil desire, and covetousness, which is idolatry. Because of these things the wrath of God is coming upon the sons of disobedience, in which you yourselves once walked when you lived in them. But now you yourselves are to put off all these: anger, wrath malice, blasphemy, filthy language out of your mouth. Do not lie to one another, since you have put off the old man with his deeds, and have put on the new man who is renewed in knowledge according to the image of Him who created him..." (Colossians 3:5-10). In other words we all need to take an inventory of our lives and make sure that we discontinue those habits and sins that hinder our running "the race that is set before us" (Hebrews 12:1, 2).

In the case of the gift and the giver, both are most important in spiritual matters. We are informed in John 3:16 that the Lord God gave the greatest gift ever – His Son to die for our sins on the cross of Calvary. The apostle Paul wrote in Romans 5:6-8, "For when we were still without strength, in due time

Christ died for the ungodly. For scarcely for a righteous man will one die; yet perhaps for a good man someone would even dare to die. But God demonstrates His own love toward us, in that while we were still sinners, Christ died for us." Just ponder for awhile what is said here. We were not friends of God when He gave the greatest gift, His Son; rather, it was when by our own sins we were alienated from God (Isaiah 59:1, 2). Not only that, the Gift (Jesus Christ) also gave Himself for our salvation (John 15:13). The motive was pure love of the Father and the Son.

The inspired writer in Hebrews 12:12 gave this exhortation, "Therefore strengthen the hands which hang down, and the feeble knees..." Being alone does not always imply loneliness. The children of God have this precious promise, "Let your conduct be without covetousness; be content with such things as you have. For he Himself has said, "I will never leave you nor forsake you." So we may boldly say: "The Lord is my helper, I will not fear, What can man do to me?"

Because we have been the recipients of salvation, "the gift of God", (Ephesians 2:8), we should give ourselves in the service of our Lord Jesus Christ. There are teeming millions of lost souls who need to hear the good news of our Savior Jesus Christ (I Corinthians 15:1-3) which "is the power of God to salvation for everyone who believes" (Romans 1:16). There are lonely souls who need our attention and affection. "Pure and undefiled religion before God and the Father is this: "to visit orphans and widows in their trouble..." (James 1:27). To be like Christ we should understand that one of the purposes in this life is to serve others (Matthew 20:26-28).

THE RESURRECTION OF LIFE

As I look out the window and across the street I see a beautiful Bradford pear tree in full bloom and a Redbud tree also in full bloom. God, the Creator of the universe, is causing the vegetative kingdom which has been dormant to come alive! The display of such beauty that we presently see and will be seeing for weeks to come as the trees bloom and the flowers and shrubbery break forth their radiant colors should cause the believer's heart to praise and glorify the name of the Almighty God. The Psalmist wrote in Psalm 19:1-4: "The heavens declare the glory of God; And the firmament shows His handiwork, Day unto day utters speech, And night unto night reveals knowledge. There is no speech nor language Where their voice is not heard. Their line has gone out through all the earth, And their words to the end of the world."

Someone has said that there are two books, nature and the Bible that declare there is a Supreme Being. The heavens and the earth in their splendor and magnificence should cause every person to have faith in God but that is not the case. The apostle Paul in writing about the depravity of the Gentile world in his day mentions this very thing in Romans 1:18-21: "For the wrath of God is revealed from heaven against all ungodliness and unrighteousness of men, who suppress the truth in unrighteousness, because what may be known of God is manifest in them, for God has shown it to them, For since the creation of the world His invisible attributes are clearly seen, being understood by the things that are made, even His eternal power and Godhead, so that they are without excuse, because, although they knew God, they did not glorify Him as God, nor were thankful, but became futile in their thoughts, and their foolish hearts were darkened." Some people have eyes that will not see and hearts that will not accept the truth that God, by the power of His word, brought the universe into existence.

With the renewal of life in the vegetative kingdom at this time of the year our hearts are made to think of the resurrection of Jesus Christ from the tomb. This is one of the cardinal doctrines of the New Testament. A part of the good news of Christ is the teaching regarding His resurrection from the dead. Had Jesus not risen from the dead early that first day of the week, His death on Calvary would be meaningless. We would still be in our sins, our faith would be in vain and we certainly would be miserable (See I Corinthians 15). The apostle taught in chapter fifteen that because our Lord arose from the grave we have the promise that we shall also rise from the dead at His second coming. Jesus Himself said as recorded in John 5:28: "Do not marvel at this; for the hour is coming in which all who are in the graves will hear His voice and come forth— those who have done good, to the resurrection of life, and those who have done evil, to the resurrection of condemnation." When I witness the beauties of spring with its shows of new life I cannot help but think of the words of my Lord Jesus Christ:

"Jesus said to her, "I am the resurrection and the life,
He who believes in Me, though he may die, he shall live.
And whoever lives and believes in Me shall never die,
Do you believe this?"

— *John 11:25, 26*

WOULD YOU BELIEVE SNOW?
January 18, 2008

Would you believe I am looking at snow falling to the ground? This is indeed a rarity here in the Deep South. I also see children cross the street playing in the snow. This is such a beautiful sight! I have fond memories of my childhood when we would receive snow in my hometown of Summerville which is located in the northwestern section of the state of Georgia. As boys we would eventually get into a 'snow fight', build a snowman and where we lived on a ridge, we were able to make a sled and slide down a hillside. Once we were out of school for a week because of the ice and snow. Often we would drive up to the top of Lookout Mountain and enjoy looking at the beautiful snow covered valleys below. I believe that most children (and adults) would like to see snow at least once in their lifetime.

In Psalm 148:7, 8 we learn that snow is the handiwork of God: "Praise the Lord from the earth, You great sea creatures and all the depths; Fire and hail, snow and clouds; Stormy wind, fulfilling His word." Snow is mentioned 20 times in the Bible. It is found 5 times in the book of Job. In Job 37:8 we read the following: "For He says to the snow, 'Fall on the earth'; Likewise to the gentle rain and heavy rain of His strength."

Snow is even mentioned figuratively regarding man's inability to cleanse himself of his sinfulness as is found in Job 9:30: "If I wash myself with snow water, and cleanse my hands with soap, Yet You will plunge me into the pit, and my own clothes will abhor me." King David made this passionate plea as recorded in Psalm 51:2, 7: "Wash me thoroughly from my iniquity, and cleanse me from sin", and, "Purge me with hyssop, and I shall be clean; wash me, and I shall be whiter than snow."

God, in His tender mercy pled for Israel to turn from their sins and come to Him for forgiveness as is found in Isaiah 1:18: "Come now, and let us reason together," says the Lord, "Though your sins are like scarlet, they shall be as white as snow; though they are red like crimson, they shall be as wool." Of course we know that it is by God's grace and the blood of Jesus that our sins are washed away. The apostle John wrote in Revelation 1:5: "...To Him who loved us and washed us from our sins in His own blood." Again in Revelation 7:13, 14, we read: "Then one of the elders answered saying to me, "Who are these arrayed in white robes, and where did they come from?" And I said to him, "Sir, you know." So he said to me, "These are the ones who come out of the great tribulation, and washed their robes and made them white in the blood of the Lamb." In the chorus of the beautiful hymn written by Wm.G. Fischer, 'Whiter Than Snow', we have these beautiful words, "Whiter than snow, Yes, Whiter than snow, Now wash me and I shall be whiter than snow."